Thinking In School and Society

Philosophy of Education Research Library

Edited by
Dr Vernon Howard and Dr Israel Scheffler
Harvard Graduate School of Education

Recent decades have witnessed the decline of distinctively philosophical thinking about education. Practitioners and the public alike have increasingly turned rather to psychology, the social sciences and to technology in search of basic knowledge and direction. However, philosophical problems continue to surface at the center of educational concerns, confronting educators and citizens as well with inescapable questions of value, meaning, purpose, and justification.

PERL will publish works addressed to teachers, school administrators and researchers in every branch of education, as well as to philosophers and the reflective public. The series will illuminate the philosophical and historical bases of educational practice, and assess new educational trends as they emerge.

Thinking in School and Society

Francis Schrag

University of Wisconsin, Madison

ROUTLEDGE
NEW YORK AND LONDON

First published in 1988 by
Routledge
11 New Fetter Lane, London EC4P 4EE

Published in the USA by
Routledge, in association with
Routledge, Chapman & Hall Inc.
29 West 35th Street, New York, NY 10001

Set in 10/11 Times
by Butler & Tanner Ltd,
and printed in Great Britain
by Butler & Tanner Ltd

Library of Congress Cataloging in Publication Data

Schrag, Francis.
    Thinking in school and society.
    (Philosophy of education research library ;)
    Bibliography: p.
    Includes index.
    1. Thought and thinking—Study and teaching.
2. Cognition in children.   I. Title.   II. Series.
LB1590.3.S36   1988   370.15′2   87–28518

British Library CIP Data also available
ISBN 0–415–00174–9

Contents

Acknowledgments

In a work as wide-ranging as this one, an author needs guidance and feedback from experts in a variety of fields. I am grateful to the many friends and colleagues who suggested sources, gave me helpful advice, and provided constructive feedback on one or more chapters. I expected no less from my friends, but that doesn't lessen my gratitude. But I am equally pleased that a number of scholars with whom I have no personal relationship took the time and trouble to provide detailed criticisms of early drafts of chapters. Thanks to them I avoided some serious misstatements; I'm only sorry that I couldn't do justice to all their criticisms.

Acknowledgments
Acknowledgments

Those whom I'd like to recognize include: Michael Apple, Jonathan Baron, Carl Bereiter, Gary Borisy, Berent Enc, Lee Hansen, Carl Kaestle, Richard Lehrer, Alan Lesgold, Daniel Liston, Jim McClellan, Richard Merelman, Mary Metz, Fred Newmann, Joseph Onosko, Daniel Pekarsky, Harvey Siegel, Elliott Sober, Stephanie Stone, Howard Temin, Ian Westbury, Erik Wright, and Steven Yussen. I'm also grateful to the editors, Vernon Howard and Israel Scheffler, for their helpful suggestions.

I received generous institutional support which I would also like to acknowledge from: The Center for John Dewey Studies, the University of Wisconsin Graduate School, and the National Center on Effective Secondary Schools. Needless to say, the views expressed in this volume do not represent those of any of these institutions.

My daughters, Naomi and Stephanie, supported me (psychologically, of course) and tried valiantly, though without success, to come up with a jazzier title. Stephanie went through the entire manuscript to check my references, for which I am grateful. Teri Frailey did a fine job typing up the Bibliography. I'm fortunate to be married to a talented editor, who not only suggested innumerable improvements along the way but was gracious enough to let me use the word processor even when she needed it for herself. And most important, she had confidence in my ability to write this book although my own doubts loomed large.

Introduction

"'Critical thinking' displaces rote and drill" according to a headline in a recent *Newsweek* (27 January 1986, p. 59). The story takes note of distressing evidence concerning the reasoning abilities of American students and documents the spread to twenty-seven states of "critical-thinking-programs" designed to remedy the alleged deficiency. The fact that such a feature appeared in a national news magazine suggests that the movement to teach thinking in schools has gathered considerable momentum. As with any educational reform movement, there are some who say that this is just what schools have *always* done, and others who say that it is *impossible*. Still others herald significant developments which they claim will make possible the heretofore impossible. The National Educational Association's monthly newspaper, in a recent lead article, alludes to "exciting breakthroughs in cognitive research" which are paving the way for new approaches to the teaching of thinking (November 1986, p. 4). At the same time, many would agree with Mortimer Adler, educational reformer and philosopher, who labels the entire movement an ill-conceived "voguish panacea" (1986, p. 2).

The concern with thinking is hardly a new one. The alleged demise of humdrum routines in school has been in progress for at least a century. Already in 1885, Herbert Spencer announced that the "once universal practice of learning by rote, is daily falling more into discredit" (p. 103). Even the anticipation of new approaches to teaching thinking based on the discoveries of psychologists is old hat. In 1967, a leader in the educational research community made a strikingly similar announcement:

> Recently studies of thinking have been undertaken which promise to revolutionize the concept of thinking as well as the way of teaching thinking (Taba, 1967, p. 27).

We would be mistaken in supposing that the hope of altering classroom practices to emphasize the development of the ability to think effectively was limited to school reformers of the progressive or pragmatist persuasion. Consider, for example, the following statement by W. T. Harris, generally regarded as an educational conservative by historians of education:

> It is believed that the arrested development of the higher mental and moral faculties is caused in many cases by the school. The habit of teaching with too much thoroughness and too-long continued drill, the semi-mechanical branches of study, such as arithmetic, spelling, ... and even the distinctions of formal grammar, often leaves the pupil fixed in lower stages of growth and unable to exercise the higher functions of thought (1898, p. 7; cited in Mann, 1979, p. 349).

Once we realize that this particular criticism of schooling is at least a century old, the fact that we are presently no better at responding to it than we were, suggests that the issue is perhaps more complex than most educational researchers or practitioners have been ready to believe.

The more seriously I considered the problem of teaching thinking, the more it began to seem that the perspectives of the principal participants in the discussion were severely limited by the narrow perspectives of their academic disciplines. I was upset by the tendency of philosophers and psychologists to travel on paths which scarcely ever intersected. Reading the reports of educational psychologists, I was especially troubled by the absence of an awareness of the social realities of classrooms—to say nothing of the wider social context beyond the classroom. Even otherwise exemplary books like David Perkins's *Knowledge as Design* (1986) virtually ignore the social context within which learning takes place.

What I have tried to do here is to write a book which integrates the perspectives of a number of disciplines, each of which, I believe, has something to contribute to a better understanding of the extent to which the schools might help the next generation of adults become better thinkers. Let me sketch out the argument: if we are to discuss the teaching of thinking, we must have a clearer understanding of what thinking is. This is my task in the first chapter. The conception I develop is one specifically tailored to the needs of educators although it is at variance with the way in which most of those involved in the "critical thinking movement" talk about it. I argue, in fact, that the dominant way of referring to thinking as a set of skills is not only not apt but potentially pernicious. The second chapter focusses on experimental investigations of thinking with a view to understanding what research in cognitive psychology over the last decade has to tell us about the nature of thinking and its relationship to learning. The significant educational implications of that research are then carefully examined. In chapter 3, I focus on the school, more specifically on the conventional classroom as a context for thinking. The limitations of that context are identified and accounted for, and suggestions for creating "thoughtful" contexts are adumbrated. Chapter 4 goes beyond the school to discuss the extent to which three contexts elicit and reward thinking: the economy, the polity, and television. I also discuss the relationship of these contexts to the school. Finally, in my conclusion, I propose some changes both in the educational sphere and in the broader society which have the potential to improve the quality of thinking in future generations.

Before beginning, I need to say something about the nature of the inquiry, especially for those who might be expecting a more conventional philosophical treatment. I do not deny that philosophical works of a more usual kind are necessary and important. Yet I share some of the misgivings about the conventional approaches which Foster McMurray (1981) has articulated. Even the best writers in philosophy of education rarely have anything novel or compelling to say about the practical task of education, and although they are well informed in contemporary philosophy, they tend to appropriate rather than to develop the ground covered by their colleagues in philosophy departments.

Many disciplines attempt to illuminate educational situations, but rarely is there an effort to see an issue steadily and see it whole, to borrow a phrase from Matthew Arnold. This is an important job, and one which philosophers (though not only philosophers) are equipped to perform. Philosophers of education do have two handicaps to overcome here. One is the dogma I "grew up" with that philosophers deal with conceptual matters rather than matters of fact, which are best left to "empirical" researchers. But many among the best academic philosophers have come to see this neat dichotomy as more of a limitation than an opportunity. In education, at any rate, I believe it is silly to suppose that any worthwhile directions can be charted if one has not ascertained relevant facts about schools, human learning and social requirements. Of course, the selecting of facts as relevant is connected to notions of educational and social purpose that are at root philosophical. I see no vicious circularity here.

A second handicap *I* needed to overcome was the belief that the philosopher's role is to analyze, not to propose. But if a sound analysis leads naturally to the formulation of certain proposals, is there good reason to stop short of making them? Is not our traditional reticence here one reason why those who are trying to decide what to *do* have stopped reading us? I am not suggesting, I should make it clear, that philosophers ought to stop the other things they are doing. There are many styles of philosophizing in education, and most are fruitful when done well. I only say that here is an equally worthy enterprise.

A word about my own philosophical debt. Many of the ideas found here have already been presented by John Dewey, but this is not necessarily because I first read Dewey and then formulated my own position. Often, having developed my own point of view, I later found that Dewey had beaten me to it. Seeing that Dewey had already said some of the things I wished to say dulled my sense of originality but it did not discourage me for there is ample reason to be suspicious of "new" or "radical" ideas in education. In human affairs and especially in education, new or radical ideas are almost always either restatements of worthwhile ideas advanced by earlier thinkers or they are plain silly. Each generation responds to another idiom than did its predecessor, so that a convincing restatement is hardly superfluous

Finally, just a word to prospective readers. This is not an easy book to read but it is not addressed only to professors, certainly not just to professors of philosophy of education. I hope that any serious student of education, regardless of political or disciplinary allegiance, will be able to read it and come away with something worthwhile. For those whose frame of reality is the world of actual classrooms, I'd suggest starting with chapter 3 and then working either forward or backward.

CHAPTER 1

What is thinking?

What I wish to say about education for thinking presupposes a particular view of the nature of thinking. Accordingly, my principal task in this initial chapter is to formulate and defend that view. The chapter is organized as follows: section 1 offers a guiding metaphor which informs the entire volume. In the second section I delineate the distinction between virtues and skills before going on in section 3 to discuss whether thinking is a skill. In section 4 I ask whether thinking comprises operations that are domain specific or that generalize across domains. Section 5 examines attempts to identify different modes of thinking. A brief discussion of the value of thinking concludes the chapter.

1 Thinking as exploration

I begin with the formulations of three eminent students of thinking, John Dewey, Frederic Bartlett, and Gilbert Ryle. I cite them in the order in which they were written.

(a) reflective thinking, in distinction from other operations to which we apply the name of thought, involves (1) a state of doubt, hesitation, perplexity, mental difficulty, in which thinking originates, and (2) an act of searching, hunting, inquiring to find material that will resolve the doubt, settle and dispose of the perplexity (Dewey, 1933, p. 12).

(b) The broad objectives of thinking remain very nearly the same, in whatever field the thinker operates, and with whatever kind of evidence he is concerned. Always he must try to use the information that is available to him so as to reach a terminus, based upon that information, but not identical with it, and he must so set out, or be prepared to try to set out, the stages through which he passes, that he can reasonably hope that where, for the time being, he comes to rest, everybody else who is not mentally defective or mentally ill, or abnormally prejudiced, must come to rest also. In some instances ... the thinker's hope is that others will approve of, rather than be compelled to reach, the result which he eventually attains, and at which he stops (Bartlett, 1958, p. 97).

(c) Thinking is trying to better one's instructions; it is trying out promising tracks which will exist, if they ever do exist, only after one has stumbled exploringly over ground where they are not (Ryle, 1979, p. 78).

There are differences in the formulations, but I wish to call attention to two common threads, one of content and one of form. Each quote contains the notion of thinking as necessitated by an insufficiency of information;[1] certainty renders thinking superfluous. Each author makes either explicit or implicit use of the metaphor of physical search and exploration.

I propose that we liken thinking to an activity which is the cognitive equivalent of territorial exploration. I mention here a few of the ideas whose analogues will be developed below. Successful explorers do not begin an expedition without extensive preparation and planning. They know their tools. They find out as much about the terrain beforehand as they can, and if possible, practice on similar terrain. Yet no matter how rigorous their preparation, they are bound to meet the unexpected, to be tested by challenges they could not precisely anticipate. Character, as well as natural endowment account for their success. There are skills involved in rock-climbing or white-water canoeing but no skills of exploration *per se*. Later travellers, benefiting from better equipment and well-marked trails, may pass with ease over what was once inaccessible to all but the strongest and most intrepid.

The kind of exploration I am describing seems to be purposeful, deliberate. Cannot thinking be random and capricious? Isn't daydreaming also thinking? This raises a problem: Is my conception of thinking normative or descriptive? Suppose a student confronts the following problem for homework: $\frac{1}{2} + \frac{1}{3}$. The student writes down $\frac{2}{3}$. Was the student's thinking defective or non-existent? How can we tell? We ask the student: why did you put down $\frac{2}{3}$, and he says, "$\frac{1}{2}$ of $\frac{2}{3}$ is $\frac{1}{3}$, so if I add $\frac{1}{2}$ to $\frac{1}{3}$, that would be two thirds." The student was certainly thinking even though he came up with the wrong answer. Now suppose he says, "I wanted to have something down so the teacher would know I did my homework. But I was in a hurry, so I figured since I don't really remember how to do it, I'd better put something down, and $\frac{2}{3}$ seemed like it might be about right." That may be reprehensible thinking but it is thinking about the problem. Now how about this: "I was thinking about the punchball game yesterday and I just wrote down the first fraction that came into my head." Here we have thinking but not about the arithmetic problem at all. Finally, "I just wrote down any numbers that came into my head." We could say that this reveals the absence of any thinking, yet why put a number down at all? Doesn't that indicate some kind of mental processing? The answer to my question about what to count as thinking appears somewhat arbitrary but not inconsequential. If we define thinking by way of a certain normative model, say Dewey's (1933) complete act of thought, then our conception seems one-sided, since thinking we might label intuitive would fail to be included. On the other hand, if we label as thinking just any mental process, such as daydreaming, how can we focus on the kind of mental activity schools ought to foster?

Could neuroscience eventually determine whether the student was thinking? Suppose we had electrodes attached to the brain of our student as he did his homework and let's suppose that we have some theory which says that a certain pattern of recorded waves indicates information processing in the brain. Let's hypothesize that some pattern present in the first three was absent in the last case. Would that be decisive? Wouldn't we need to know what the thinking was about before we could say whether we'd want to count it as relevant to the task at hand? Maybe there is a "number" center in the brain but how do we know the numbers refer to the addition problem rather than the number of runs in the punchball game. I don't think that advances in neuroscience will solve our problem.

Let me *stipulate*, therefore, that we call mental activity *purposeful* thinking, only if it is experienced as *directed* to a problem or task one has set oneself. By this stipulation, the third and fourth answers of the student reflect no purposeful thinking about arithmetic. This, admittedly normative, conception is meant to include cases in which we may suddenly see a solution without any awareness of "wrestling" with a problem. But notice that even in such cases, an idea does not appear as a *solution* unless it is experienced in relation to some difficulty one has been worrying about.

Am I equating thinking with problem solving? Is all thinking directed to the solution of problems? Not much hinges on this so far as I can see. "Problem" is not a concept with clearly defined boundaries. Visual artists as well as scientists are often comfortable describing their activity as problem solving. As our quotes suggest, thinking is evoked in situations where one is not quite sure how to go on. I am calling such situations problems.

Some readers are likely to be dissatisfied for two reasons: the boundaries of my conception are very vague. And I have tried to say what thinking is like but not what it *is*. The two concerns are related. If we knew exactly what thinking was, perhaps the boundaries would be clearer. What is the dissatisfied reader seeking? The neuroscientific identification of thinking with some particular brain processes? No such identification has been made? It may be that there is no single process or set of processes which corresponds to our notion of problem solving just as there may be no single process which corresponds to our ordinary notion of learning. But should we not have some rigorous definition of thinking, expounding the necessary and sufficient conditions for application of the term? It is not at all clear that such a formulation would advance our inquiry. On the contrary, it would merely focus attention on the adequacy of the definition. We can say many true and important things about exploration without a precise formulation. One of them is that it is difficult to identify a rigid boundary where familiar terrain ends and exploration begins. I take this to be one respect in which the metaphor is apt.

2 Skills and virtues

In saying of someone that he or she is a good thinker we may mean one of two things: that the person is *intelligent* or that the person is *thoughtful*. A person may be clever without being thoughtful and vice-versa. In the first sense, we commend something skill-like. In the second we commend something more like a virtue or trait of character. *The educator's focus, I shall argue in this book, ought to be on the development of the virtue or character trait of thoughtfulness.*

Before going further, a few words about the notions of skill and virtue may prove helpful. One way of thinking about this is to distinguish three kinds of impediments to effective action. When a person (or animal) lacks a fundamental *capacity* for some task, we imply that training will not remedy the deficit; it is built into the organism, so to speak. (Of course some capacities can be trained, but these must rest on fundamental capacities which cannot be.) Both skills and virtues, on the other hand are acquired, though they depend, of course, on innate capacities. But lack of *skill* and lack of *virtue* may be distinguished because the impediments they overcome are different. A person may be unable to perform some activity because of a lack of skill. J. Wallace considers such an inability to be due to "technical" difficulty:

> the difficulty is inherent in the doing of the action itself. In some cases, the technical difficulty is due to the complexity of the action itself, as in cooking or theorizing. There is much one must know in order to do these things. In other cases, however, such as hitting a baseball or performing eye surgery, the action is hard because of the co-ordination required. Still other actions are hard because their performance requires a complex set of reflexes, as in riding a bicycle or typing rapidly and accurately (1974, p. 187).

Virtues are needed because of a different kind of impediment:[2]

> Virtues, however, are not masteries of techniques; technique has
> very little to do with being brave, generous, or honest, nor do
> these necessarily involve being proficient at anything. Some
> virtues involve being able to do difficult things, but the difficulties
> involved are due to contrary inclinations, not to technical
> difficulties in the actions themselves (ibid., p. 187).

Consider a related point: skills and virtues have different scopes. A
skilled person is skilled at performing some rather well-defined
activity be it playing the piano, driving a car, climbing rocks, or
diagnosing mental illness (Von Wright, 1963, p. 33). How are we to
individuate skills? Is shifting gears a different skill from driving an
automobile or is it part of that skill? Is playing piano with the right
hand a different skill from playing with the left? "Skill" is not a
technical term; there are no precise criteria for demarcating different
skills. As our interest is in the acquisition of skill, it makes sense to
take transferability as a way of demarcating skills. *Let us say that if
a skill learned in setting A is not transferable to setting B, then B
requires a different skill. If mastery of skill A is necessary but not
sufficient for skill B, then we will say that it is a sub-skill of B.*

Virtues, since they are antidotes to contrary *inclinations* are not
tied to well-defined activities at all. A person can show courage in
each of the following activities, e.g. a pianist filling in for a famous
artist at short notice, a psychiatrist interviewing a psychopath, but
in each case he will be doing very different things which "need not
have any 'outward' feature in common" (Von Wright, p. 141). It's
true, though, that were he to give in to his fear he might be disposed
to similar actions such as running away in each case. The main point
is that virtues are traits of character which may be exhibited in many
different ways in different contexts.

There is, finally, one more distinguishing feature of a virtue as a
trait of character which needs to be introduced. In distinguishing
virtue from habit or temperament, I borrow from L. Hunt (1978).
Hunt notes that a character trait involves a *judgment* of what is
important or worthwhile in a way that habit or temperament do not.
Neither the thoughtful person nor the phlegmatic person normally
rushes into action. How can we distinguish them? The difference
resides in the thoughtful person's understanding and appreciation of
the need to think things over before acting. He or she does not
respond blindly or mechanically. The difference between the thoughtful and the lethargic person may manifest itself in behavior from
time to time, for the thoughtful person can and does rush into action
when time is of the essence whereas the phlegmatic person does not.

The thoughful person's character is animated by an awareness that thinking is worthwhile. Although Hunt doesn't mention this, the thoughtful person's appreciation of the value of thinking has an emotional component as well. The thoughtful person not only believes that thinking is worthwhile but he has a modicum of confidence in his ability to "figure things out" for him or herself.

The distinctions between skills and virtues which I have drawn are not beyond challenge (see Roberts, 1984). I do not think we need to confront all the subtleties. My reason for drawing the distinction is the bearing it has on the way the *pedagogical* task is conceived. How are skills acquired?

> What is learned ... is a technique, and instruction in a technique may take the form of verbal instructions, demonstrations, diagrams, and leading the trainee through the action (Wallace, 1974, p. 187).

These means are not excluded from the inculcation of virtue but they are not sufficient. Character traits are not formed simply by acquiring some know-how. Technique can be acquired almost anywhere and from almost anyone who has himself a mastery of the technique. *Once the educational focus is on the development of a character trait though, concern necessarily extends to the environment in which it develops.* Our fundamental attitudes and dispositions are influenced by all those with whom we come in contact, whether directly or vicariously through various media. We learn to value what they value and to steer clear of what they shun. An educator whose prime interest lies in the development of character needs to be sensitive to the total physical and, more importantly, the social environment in which any specific training takes place. (Of course a skill teacher cannot overlook the environment entirely, for a technique cannot be developed effectively in conditions very different from those in which it will be exercised.) I don't think any of the philosophers who have discussed the contrast between skills and virtues would deny the point that where virtues and dispositions are concerned, the educational influence resides in the total *milieu* in which the student finds him or herself. Every wise educator since Plato has agreed on this. Here is Dewey's recognition of it:

> The development within the young of the attitudes and dispositions necessary to the continuous and progressive life of a society cannot take place by direct conveyance of belief, emotions, and knowledge. It takes place through the intermediary of the environment. The environment consists of the sum total of

conditions which are concerned in the execution of the activity characteristic of a living being (Dewey, 1916, p. 26).

3 Is thinking a skill?

Thinking is an activity. I have already intimated though that it cannot be reduced to skill, but why not? The study from which Bartlett's quotation is taken is indeed based on the notion that it is useful to study thinking by conceiving of it as analogous to a bodily skill. Bartlett does not go so far as to claim that thinking is a skill, but that claim is explicitly made by P. N. Johnson-Laird (1983), an eminent contemporary investigator, and is implicit in R. Sternberg's influential "componential" theory of intelligence (Sternberg, 1980; 1983; 1985).

Clearly, thinking has some of the characteristics of skills like woodworking, driving, typing, playing tennis etc. (People improve as they practice, they often benefit from tutelage, their performance is subject to breakdown under conditions of stress, some are naturally more adept than others, and so on.) Isn't conceiving of thinking as skill useful, *especially* for educators? I think not; let us see why. One of the hallmarks of a skill, such as driving, is that it can be analyzed into a number of sub-skills which are both sequentially and hierarchically organized (Elliott and Connolly, 1974). The skilled differ from the unskilled in their ability to integrate a number of sub-routines into a smooth, efficient flow. As the novice driver gains experience, for example, she begins to coordinate the movement of the clutch, accelerator and gearshift lever in such a way that shifting from first to second becomes a single operation rather than a series of separate maneuvers. And her shifting becomes increasingly responsive to appropriate signals from the environment which includes her own vehicle. Bartlett saw directionality, sequencing and timing as central to both thinking and bodily skills.

One reason the skill model of thinking is so attractive to the educational community is that our considerable effectiveness in imparting skills is based, at least in part, on our ability to "break them down" into sub-routines which may be demonstrated, practiced, and corrected independently. If we could identify the separate components of thinking, then learning to think could be made much more efficient. Thinking could be gradually "built up" out of components, missing or weak components could be identified, practiced in isolation, and so on (see e.g. Beyer, 1985 a,b; Pellegrino, 1985). What might the sub-skills of thinking be?

Dewey identified five phases or stages in what he called a complete act of thought (Dewey, 1933, chap. 7). More recently, Bransford and

Stein (1984) have come up with a very similar list of what they call parts or components in the problem solving process: "Identify the problem.... Define and represent the problem.... Explore possible strategies.... Act on the strategies.... Look back and evaluate the effects of your activities" (p. 12).

Each problem solver, whether auto-mechanic called on to diagnose a car which won't start, mathematician struggling to derive a theorem, cook planning a festive meal for a large family, painter deciding on the color of a background in a portrait, needs to "define and represent the problem" but it makes little sense to identify these as a *single sub-skill* on a par with shifting gears in driving, sawing wood in carpentry or serving in tennis. For surely the consummate cook may not have the slightest ability to define and represent the problem facing an auto mechanic or vice-versa (see McPeck, 1981).

Moreover, it is not clear that any of these sub-skills can be practiced independently of the others. How, for example, does one practice "define and represent the problem" by itself? Suppose one were given these instructions: "Define and represent each of the following problems" followed by a list of problems from different fields. To follow those instructions successfully would one not have to go through *each* of the five phases?

Consider whether the "information processing" components which Sternberg (1980; 1983; 1985) has identified might provide us with a set of sub-skills of thinking. Sternberg's project is an attempt to *analyze* intelligent performance into its elementary components. He assumes that when people perform intellectual tasks, such as the analogies problems which are found on scholastic aptitude tests, they are engaged in the processing of information. Working with analogical reasoning as well as other test-type tasks capable of being manipulated and studied in the laboratory, Sternberg has identified a number of different species and different specific individual component processes according to their function in the completion of the task. Consider "inference" and "mapping" as illustrative.

In inference, a person detects one or more relations between two objects, both of which may be either concrete or abstract. In the analogy (Lawyer is to Client as Doctor is to (a) Patient (b) Medicine), the person detects relations between Lawyer and Client such as that a lawyer provides professional services to a client.

In mapping, a person relates aspects of a previous situation to aspects of a present one. In an analogy, the person seeks the higher order relationship between the first half of the analogy (the previous situation) and the second half of the analogy (the present situation) (Sternberg, 1980, p. 577).

How did Sternberg discover these elementary processes? In fact, the elementary processes were not so much discovered as postulated by introspection of what is involved in solving a particular kind of problem. The problems were then "broken down" into a series of sub-problems so that subjects could perform each problem in its entirety or as a series of sub-problems of increasing magnitude. In this way the time needed for each "step" could be measured. Sternberg is probably right that what may appear to the subject as a single, instantaneous performance is actually comprised of several separate operations. What he fails to supply, however, is general criteria for identifying elementary processes across tasks. His model embraces intellectual tasks which appear to me to be strikingly similar rather than different (Sternberg, 1985, Appendix). So far as I can see, armchair analysis provides the only way of telling whether "inference" is a component common to two different types of problems, a test of analogical reasoning and planning a dinner party, for example, or whether a specific "step" is identified as "inference" or "mapping". Strangely enough, as U. Neisser (1983) points out in a trenchant criticism of Sternberg's work, not only have Sternberg's elementary processes proliferated as he has extended his studies to different laboratory tasks, but there is hardly any overlap in the processes required by different tasks. This lack of generality is hardly consistent with his goal of providing an analysis of the elementary components of intelligence or thinking.

Be that as it may, let us admit that the ability to see relations between current and previous situations does seem to be essential to good thinking. But is this "component" an isolable *skill*? Consider an analogy: All explorers must be prepared to traverse difficult and inhospitable terrain. But there is not a single skill or even a single set of skills which will suffice for every kind of terrain; Amazonian jungles, Andean peaks and African deserts require very different skills.

It seems to me that the same situation prevails in the case of Sternberg's components. Many thinking tasks involve detecting relationships between objects. The mechanic, mathematician, cook, and painter mentioned earlier certainly need to do this in solving the problems they are working on. But there is no reason to suppose that there is a *single skill* involved such that a person carefully trained to detect relationships between words in analogy tests would be developing a skill readily transferable to the garage, the blackboard or the kitchen. Such a person may well be developing skill in solving analogy problems, but there is no good reason to suppose that he is mastering one of the "component" skills of *thinking*. (For empirical evidence on this issue, see Baron, 1985b.)

Still it may seem that even if Sternberg has not isolated these elementary sub-skills, they must surely exist. Each of us solves a prodigious number of problems every day, many never previously encountered, at least by us. Surely, as in the case of the locomotor system, such flexible performance relies on our ability to combine some possibly large but still finite number of elementary operations. All bodily skills, for example, can be analyzed into combinations of muscle contractions of 501 voluntary muscles (Vannini and Pogliani, 1980). But note that the contractions of individual muscles are *not* the sub-skills of, say, rock-climbing or canoeing, soccer or carpentry; it is almost impossible for people to move single muscles independently, and even if they could, canoeing or climbing a cliff is not experienced as an initial contraction of this muscle, then that one, and so on. We do not and probably could not learn a skill by mastering a programed sequence for the contraction and relaxation of individual muscles. (On the other hand, programing a human-like robot to maneuver a canoe or climb a cliff, would probably call for precisely such an analysis.)

The contrast just made between what might be called the *experiential* and the *physiological* levels of analysis is an important one. At the physiological level of analysis, there may be elementary processes of thinking. It is conceivable that neuroscientists will discover what these are. But there is no basis for the assumption that these processes will map neatly on to the steps, stages, phases, or elementary processes revealed through introspection, even when these are supported by experiments in the psychology laboratory (see Norris, 1985). It may even turn out that the same fundamental processes are involved at each stage. Take a nutritional analogy: from the digestive point of view, potato and sugar are quite similar, yet they do not taste at all alike. Sugar and aspartame (an artificial sweetener) on the other hand, are almost indistinguishable to the taste buds but are broken down by different enzymes in the digestive process.

In contrast to the view that thinking comprises a set of general skills, I propose that we consider the character trait of thoughtfulness to be the hallmark of the good thinker. What contrary inclinations must the thoughtful person grapple with? There are two: impulsiveness and rigidity. The good thinker avoids precipitous action and avoids getting "stuck" in a stereotyped response. He or she is deliberate as well as flexible.

In fact, not all contemporary psychological theories of thinking depend on the skill model. J. Baron (1981) is a psychologist who bases his work in part on Dewey and whose conception of thinking is congenial to my own, although he does not use the terminology of character traits or virtues. In *Rationality and Intelligence* (1985a), he develops a theory of good or rational thinking according to which thinking is elicited when some decision (to act or believe) is in doubt. Thinking comprises distinct phases or functions, each of which may be thought of as a search process. There is a search for possibilities, for evidence, and for goals. The evidence is used to strengthen or weaken the possibilities in light of the goals. One of the aims of the theory is to identify and account for some of the deviations from rationality which people are prone to. Baron reviews and systematizes evidence showing that people "overweigh the immediate costs of thinking relative to the long-term benefits", and that they "gather and interpret evidence in a way that does not challenge possibilities about to be adopted" (ibid., p. 85). If we consider these biases, it is certainly arguable that what accounts for them is more adequately characterized as "inclination" rather than absence of "technique" or ignorance. Inasmuch as thinking is usually effortful and often frustrating, it is easy to see why its long range benefits would not loom large. Finding non-confirmatory evidence may require us to rethink conclusions or decisions already taken and to look at a situation from other perspectives than our own. This is frequently a painful process in its own right, and moreover often leads to loss of face. It is "natural" to look only for good news.

These biases do not depend on mental capacity or information available. Though pervasive, they are, according to Baron, remediable through education, but not through skill training (see also Perkins, 1986b). Baron appears to be unique among contemporary psychologists in contending that, "Although thinking is often referred to as a skill, it is probably unproductive to teach it in this way" (Baron, 1985a, p. 252). In chapter 7 of his book, he does identify some promising pedagogical interventions, but more important is an acknowledgment he makes in the final pages. He notes that good thinking develops in social groups which cherish specific goals and beliefs about its importance.

It is such sources of beliefs and goals that might turn out to be more important, in the long run, than any special courses or tinkering with educational methods (ibid., p. 279).

I shall return to an investigation of these sources in chapter 4.

4 Is thinking unitary?

Are there general thinking skills, that is cognitive skills which are invariant across domains? Some psychologists, such as Sternberg (1980; 1983; 1985) and Pellegrino (1985) would argue that there are domain invariant skills; others such as Perkins (1985) argue against the notion. The previous discussion suggested that only the concept of thoughtfulness as a character trait permits one to grasp a unity in all good thinking, but given the popularity of the notion of general thinking or cognitive skills we must take a closer look at the issue. I have agreed with Sternberg that, say, the ability to detect relationships between objects is needed for thinking in every domain. The suggestion is certainly plausible that expertise in a field is dependent on a store of information in that field *together* with mastery of a small set of cognitive skills like Sternberg's "inference". An objector might claim that my apparent dismissal of this possibility was based on the assumption that the acquisition of such skills was *sufficient* for thinking in any domain, which it obviously is not. But suppose, the objection goes, we begin by assuming that problem solving requires two ingredients, a set of well-developed cognitive skills and sufficient information about the field to exercise those effectively. Failure of transfer may now be attributed to a deficiency in the information component rather than the skill component.

Consider the bird-watcher and the art historian, each of whom must be able to detect subtle similarities and differences between the objects in their respective domains. Of course each must know as much as possible about his or her field: the one about birds, their sizes, shapes, markings and colors, the other about artistic styles, the history of art, etc. We would not expect the birder to correctly identify a painting by Titian nor the art historian to identify a snowy egret, but that does not show that they possess different cognitive-perceptual skills. The skills are the same; only the information needed to apply them in different contexts is different, so the objection would go.

But how, I would reply, is the necessary information acquired? Would memorizing a text (minus illustrations) describing the salient characteristics of paintings by different artists be sufficient for the birder to transfer his capabilities from the woods to the museum? Could he on the basis of the information acquired from texts together with his general perceptual-cognitive strategies acquired in identifying birds distinguish Titian's *Venus* from Giorgione's, or discern the difference between an authentic and a fake Titian? Surely not. Would he not have to study an enormous number of paintings under the tutelage of experts, before he could make such determinations? A connoisseur, be it of birds or paintings, knows where to look and what to look for: there is no shortcut to acquiring that capability except through careful study of the observations of experts in a particular field as they call attention to the sometimes exceedingly subtle clues upon which their judgments are based. (Of course, illustrated books serve as a vehicle for developing such expertise.)

But would not the birder have an advantage in a basic art appreciation course? Perhaps; this is, of course an empirical question. But it is equally likely that the birder would be handicapped because what one needs to look for in order to appreciate a painting is very different from what one needs to look for in order to identify a bird. The birder, we may say, needs to learn not just about painters and paintings: he needs to learn *how to look* at them. But, the objector will now reply, is this not a matter of compiling detailed information about paintings? One may construe it that way, but could such information be acquired with one's eyes blindfolded? I hardly think so. And why do the eyes play such an important role in the learning if the birder has *already* mastered the "skill" of "detecting relations between objects"? Of course, I am here talking about the experiential level. It may be that a closer study of the eye movements, brain waves, or other physiological indicators of brain activity will reveal common neural patterns across fields. Such findings could be very significant, but do nothing to support the claim that there are general, introspectively available cognitive-perceptual skills.

There are two further bases for arguing that from the pedagogic point of view, one ought to view all thinking in a unitary way. One derives from psychometric studies of intelligence which reveal a general factor (g) underlying competent performance across domains. Another is based on the existence of courses and programs which claim to enhance people's capacity to think in a very general way. On the other side, there are philosophical arguments designed to show that thinking *cannot* be unitary. I shall consider each position in turn.

Spearman was the first to postulate the construct (g) to account for the positive correlation among tests of mental ability (see Vernon, 1983). Without wishing to get embroiled in the controversy about IQ, let us assume that this general factor can be legitimately inferred. What is its source? Summarizing his own work, and that of A. Jensen, Vernon maintains:

> there is a growing body of evidence supporting the hypothesis
> that a significant amount of the variance in general intelligence
> can be explained in terms of a number of RT (reaction time)
> variables, representing the speed of execution of cognitive
> processes. It is important to point out that in many of the studies
> described, and most particularly in Jensen's simple and choice

RT research, the measures of RT involve virtually no prior learning (or what is ordinarily thought of as mental ability) or else tap highly overlearned knowledge such as the letters of the alphabet or digits (ibid., p. 395).

Suppose the hypothesis is correct and suppose that the criterion measures of IQ do indeed reflect "highly complex tests of reasoning and intelligence" (ibid., p. 395) across different domains. Would this suggest that thinking is a unitary set of mental operations? Not necessarily. Consider the analogous question: Suppose level of performance in tennis, basketball and hockey were found to depend on a common factor (C) which correlated highly with a simple test of muscle coordination. In what way would that make the three sports unitary activities? It would certainly suggest that a person who performed very well in one sport had the potential to reach high levels in the others, and this could well be because a common capacity underlies each activity. But the presence of a common factor underlying performance in the three sports would not give one the slightest reason for thinking that a person mastering one was *thereby* also mastering the others. Indeed, trained tennis players might have a harder time mastering hockey than a non-tennis player with the same "CQ". Analogously, controversy surrounding the existence or non-existence of a common factor underlying intelligence may be relevant to determining whether a person who learns to solve algebra problems quickly could also learn to repair automobiles quickly; it may, in other words, explain differences in people's undeveloped *capacities* to solve problems in diverse domains. It is not relevant to determining whether a person with a high degree of competence in algebra is, in fact, able to repair my fuel pump.

If thinking is not unitary, how can one explain the existence of courses of study designed to help people become better thinkers (*simpliciter*)? One such course is traditional, logic. Other programs are newer. E. de Bono (1970) and Reuven Feuerstein (Feuerstein et al., 1980) are among the most prominent designers of curricula for teaching thinking directly.

In what way is a course in logic, a course in learning how to think? Logic is concerned with the evaluation of arguments which are composed of statements usually designated as premises leading to a conclusion. The focus in logic is not on the truth of the individual premises but on the relationship between them and the conclusion. A succinct definition of the scope of logic is that of B. Skyrms (1975):

Logic is the study of the strength of the evidential link between the premises and conclusions of arguments (p. 4).

Logic is not coextensive with thinking. The mechanic working on the car and the cook preparing her meal may properly be said to be drawing conclusions from evidence, but not all evidence is in the form of statements. The mechanic, for example, has learned to draw inferences from the sounds of the engines, the cook from the aromas of cooking food. I do not deny that the mechanic's or the cook's or even the painter's thinking could be *re*formulated as an argument to be assessed by someone schooled in logic: my point is that none of these thinkers is *reaching* decisions (conclusions) about what to do on the basis of a series of statements of the kind found in logic textbooks.

I do not deny that an understanding of the forms valid arguments may take and a skill in detecting fallacies can be extremely useful both in the formulation and the criticism of *arguments*. Logic does supply standards by which to judge the cogency of arguments, but it does not provide one with rules for thinking, for there are no such rules. Ryle (1949) showed that positing the existence of such rules leads to an infinite regress, for rules would be needed for applying the rules, etc.

Exercises in logic, like exercises in any other subject require an understanding of the terminology and concepts of that subject and they require thinking which is never the mechanical application of rules, not even rules of logic. Here is a sample problem from Skyrms's introductory textbook in logic:

> Using presence tables, find out which of the following properties are universal, which are null, and which are contingent:
> a. $\sim FvGvF$ b ... (p. 85).

Here is a sample problem from an introductory text in informal logic:

> Determine which fallacies (if any) are committed by the following, and explain why you think so:
> Joan: Most men who have never been married are obsessed with sex.
> Eugene: Oh? I don't know.
> Joan: Well, I do, because I know all bachelors are.
> (Kahane, 1976, p. 68)

As with textbook problems in physics or economics, answering these questions requires thinking, which is to say it requires the student to go beyond the information given, to go through each of the stages of problem solving we mentioned previously, such as defining, and representing the problem, exploring possible suggestions and so on.

Defining and representing problems is no easier in logic than in any other subject and there is no *a priori* reason to think that acquiring adeptness in such representation mysteriously transfers to other fields such as automobile repair. Curiously enough according to its author, the correct answer to the fallacy detection question is that Joan does commit the fallacy of "begging the question" since bachelors are never married men (ibid., p. 239) so if you did not identify any fallacy (as I did not when I read the problem) that must be because your representation of the problem was not the one the author intended.

Does the study of logic then, make no distinctive contribution to the development of good thinking? It may, though little evidence on the question is available (see, however, Hudgins, 1977, pp. 180–202). If the study of logic does improve thinking in other domains, it does so, I would suppose, by reinforcing the flexibility and deliberateness which constitute thoughtfulness, not by imparting concepts or rules which are then merely applied to other domains.

I should maintain the same thing for E. de Bono's program or for R. Feuerstein's or for any of the other programs available today. Let's look briefly at these two. De Bono has written a large number of books about teaching thinking, but he is probably best known for his *Lateral Thinking* (1970).

Here is de Bono's definition of the distinction between lateral and vertical thinking:

> Vertical thinking is concerned with proving or developing concept patterns. Lateral thinking is concerned with restructuring such patterns (insight) and provoking new ones (creativity) (ibid., p. 14).

De Bono sometimes speaks of lateral thinking as a skill but he recognizes that what he is after is really best thought of as an attitude:

> Like logical thinking, lateral thinking is a general attitude of mind which may make use of certain techniques on occasion.... There is nothing special about the techniques. It is the attitude behind them that counts. But mere exhortation and goodwill are not enough (ibid., p. 16, 17).

One of the difficulties a thinker confronting a problem may encounter is "to get going, to get some movement, start a train of thought" (ibid., p. 167). A technique to stimulate a train of thought is the invention of analogies.

The analogy is a provocative device which is used to force a new way of looking at the situation (ibid., pp. 169, 170).

In one exercise, students are asked to develop different analogies for the same problem. For example finding the way in fog could be likened to a shortsighted person finding his way around, a traveller in a strange country trying to find the railway station, looking for something that has been lost in the house, or doing a crossword puzzle (ibid., p. 173).

Many of the exercises make use of simple geometric shapes. For example, de Bono asks students to describe a geometric figure consisting of two squares which overlap at one corner. He offers several descriptions:

Two overlapping squares.
Three squares.
Two L shapes embracing a square gap.
A rectangle divided into half with the two pieces pushed out of line (ibid., p. 70).

De Bono's comment reveals his concern to counteract our inclination to perceive phenomena in stereotyped ways:

The "two overlapping squares" seems so obvious a description that any other seems perverse. This illustrates how strong is the domination by obvious patterns .... it may be felt that "two squares overlapping" is the same as "three squares" since the latter is implied by the former. This is a tendency that must be resisted because often even a minor change in the way a thing is looked at can make a huge difference (ibid., p. 70).

Designed for culturally disadvantaged adolescents, Feuerstein's Instrumental Enrichment program (1980) comprises 15 instruments designed to correct specific deficits in thinking such as "blurred, sweeping perception", "impulsivity and the lack of planning behavior", and to facilitate acquisition of basic concepts and operations, habits and motivation (chap. 8). Feuerstein's materials are rich and ingenious. He also makes extensive use of geometric shapes as in an exercise called Organization of Dots in which geometric figures identical in size and form to those in a model must be found in patterns of dots which at first sight appear random (Feuerstein et al., 1980, p. 130).

Note once again, both de Bono's and Feuerstein's spatial problems require moving through all the stages of the problem-solving process, and require the generation *and* testing of solutions. Yet in their programs as in the examples presented, their emphases are somewhat different. De Bono wants to stimulate flexibility, to counteract stereotyped responses to patterns. Feuerstein, on the other hand, although he by no means overlooks the importance of learning to see familiar things from different points of view, is more interested in fostering habits of planning and systematic analysis, in combating impulsivity. Now how could solving problems with shapes foster more effective thinking? A student working with Feuerstein's dots problems may develop skill in perceiving patterns in the dots. A student of de Bono's may also develop facility in mentally "cutting" shapes in unconventional ways. But surely these are skills of rather limited applicability. Many effective, even brilliant problem solvers in numerous domains might not score very high on tests of this sort. Once again, if these programs do foster effective thinking across domains, it is because they develop those broader attitudes and dispositions which we identify with thoughtfulness.

That the development of thoughtfulness lies at the heart of Feuerstein's program is illustrated in a quotation by a social studies teacher he cites approvingly:

> In *Organization of Dots*, we are given a model. We have trouble in finding a figure and we do it wrong. What do we do? Do we tear up the page? Do we throw it away? Do we yell? Do we sit down and cry? No .... We see if it can be fixed. And, if it can be fixed, how can we fix it? Now let's look at our real-life situation. Is this the kind of government we want? ... Something isn't right. Shall we cry? Shall we throw it away? Or do we see where we made our mistakes? ... Just like in *Organization of Dots*, we saw whether the figure we drew was too big or too small, or crooked; here, too, we have to see. Slowly, in a systematic manner, we can find what isn't right. And we can correct it (ibid., p. 136).

There is neither argument nor evidence to support the notion that thinking is comprised of a single set of rules which are domain invariant and may be developed through specific programs of study. Some philosophers, well-aware of this context-dependency of thinking, have indeed put forward *a priori* arguments to show that there can be no such thing as learning to think or teaching someone to think (*simpliciter*). Though not entirely unsympathetic to their conclusions, I find these arguments specious. J. McPeck (1981, chap. 1), in his investigation of critical thinking, denies that there is any *general* thinking ability on the basis of the claim, found also in Ryle (1979, chap. 4), that there is no *generic* thinking. This inference is hardly convincing. One could as well deny that there is such a thing as reading or playing the piano because one must always read a particular text or play a particular tune. The reason we are prepared to say of someone that he is learning or has learned to read or play the piano (*simpliciter*) is that the skills and dispositions acquired in mastering particular texts or pieces of music are readily transferable to others. If for example, playing Debussy on the piano were sufficiently different from playing Mozart, we would probably not talk about learning to play piano without qualification. On the other hand, we usually do not describe people as learning to perform music (*simpliciter*) presumably because, for example, learning to play the piano is very different from learning to play a string or a wind instrument. We would do well here to recall Dewey's (1938; 1963) notion of continuity:

> the principle of continuity of experience means that every experience both takes up something from those which have gone before and modifies in some way the quality of those which come after ... the principle is of universal application. There is some kind of continuity in every case.... Perhaps the greatest of all pedagogical fallacies is the notion that a person learns only the particular thing he is studying at the time. Collateral learning in the way of formation of enduring attitudes, of likes and dislikes, may be and often is much more important than the spelling lesson or lesson in geography or history that is learned. For these attitudes are fundamentally what count in the future (pp. 35, 48; italics in original).

One ought not to ask whether transfer does or does not take place. The question is always: how and to what extent does the acquisition of a particular attainment facilitate or impede the development of other attainments? Take a simple example. If a person learns to climb rocks, she develops certain skills and propensities which will serve her well when she attempts to climb glaciers. Yet in other respects, her skills may put her at a disadvantage because what have become instinctive responses need to be unlearned. In still other situations (exploring waterways) those responses may be simply irrelevant. There are no general skills of exploring; the skills depend on the terrain, the season, the equipment, and so on. Still it is conceivable that a particular Outward Bound Program may help develop the character traits of self-reliance, courage, determination, judgment, and most important, a love of the wilderness, which will be vital to any explorations of uncharted terrain.

Similarly it is possible that particular programs do make some contribution to fostering effective thinking in a wide variety of domains, at least for some people. The effective thinker, whatever his or her level of intelligence, manifests certain character traits. In the philosophical tradition, following Aristotle, Aquinas and Dewey, these are thought of as virtues or habits. In contemporary psychological research, these dispositions are studied primarily under the rubric of cognitive style (Brodzinsky, 1985; Kogan, 1985).

5 Modes of thinking

Neither psychologists nor educators usually refer to thinking *simpliciter*. They focus instead on divergent or critical or intuitive thinking. Typically such "modes" of thinking are organized in dichotomous categories. But are there really different kinds or modes of thinking? What might a mode of thinking be? Let's see if our analogy offers help. How can we classify modes of exploration? One way would be by terrain and climate. Presumably terrain and climate set up different possibilities and different hazards to the explorer. Exploring mountains is clearly different from exploring deserts. Obtaining water and maintaining a comfortable temperature can be a problem in both settings, but how one satisfies one's needs will vary tremendously. Different terrain requires different tools, different clothing, different provisions. The knowledge required for desert survival and the equipment which will facilitate that survival will be quite different from what is required for survival at high altitudes. But is exploring the Himalayas different from exploring the Andes? The answer is clearly arbitrary to some extent; gross distinctions can be drawn easily, but finer distinctions may also be sustained. If the weather or the rock or glacier formations are sufficiently different in two mountain ranges, then perhaps different precautions, different provisions or different equipment could be called for.

If we drew on the analogy to classify different modes of thinking, we would probably call the thinking done by the auto-mechanic, the painter, the cook and the mathematician different modes of thinking. Each intellectual "terrain" requires distinctive knowledge and equipment. Of course, where one draws the lines between kinds of terrain is also to a large extent relative to one's purposes. In a discussion of the humanities and the sciences, thinking in physics and biology may be conflated. A more fine-grained analysis may reveal significant differences between the two domains of scientific inquiry. But someone might say: neither in the illustration nor in the analogue have you identified different *modes of exploration*. You have simply identified different kinds of terrain to be explored. The challenge is to identify modes of thinking which do *not* depend on what the thinking is about. Can this be done? It is hard to know what modes of exploration might refer to if they are not related to what one is exploring. One might distinguish between small and large expeditions, those that make use of native guides and those that do not, but analogues do not come readily to mind, which may simply mean that the analogy will not serve us here. Students of thinking classify different modes of thinking in innumerable ways, as I mentioned. Among the labels used are: inductive and deductive, theoretical and practical, divergent and convergent, critical and creative, visual and linguistic, conscious and preconscious, analytic and intuitive, and so on. There are also taxonomies based on the kinds of thinking done by children at different stages of development. Of these, Piaget's is no doubt the best known.

Do the various dichotomies just listed really refer to modes of *thinking*? This is far from clear. The relations between the premises and conclusions of deductive and inductive arguments are different but this does not entail that the mental *processes* used in formulating or criticizing the two kinds of arguments differ. As Dewey (1933) noted of logical forms,

> these forms apply not to *reaching* conclusions, not to *arriving* at beliefs and knowledge, but to the most effective way to set forth what has already been concluded, so as to convince others (or oneself if one wishes to recall to mind its grounds) of the soundness of the result (p. 74; italics in original).

Many of the other dichotomies on the list also relate to the results of thinking rather than to the processes. To characterize thinking as divergent or original is to characterize it not in terms of a distinctive process but in terms of how its results compare to those of less creative, more convergent thinkers (see Getzels and Csikszentmihalyi, 1975). To characterize thinking as practical rather than theoretical is to characterize it in terms of the category under which its conclusion may be subsumed but tells us nothing about how the conclusion was actually reached. Why should the reasoning process which leads to, "I believe that the defendant is innocent of the crime he is charged with" necessarily be different from the reasoning which leads to "I vote for acquittal"?[3]

Some of the contrasts do *suggest* authentically different modes of thinking: critical/creative, and analytic/intuitive, and visual/linguistic and the Piagetian. I shall have something to say about the Piagetian stage theory and the contrast between visual and linguistic thinking when I discuss the contribution of cognitive psychology to our understanding of thinking in chapter 2. Here I shall say something about the first two dichotomies.

A Critical thinking

Of all the kinds of thinking which we have identified, none has achieved greater attention from the educational community in recent years than critical thinking (McPeck, 1981; Ennis, 1985, 1986; Paul, 1983). But is critical thinking one kind or mode of thinking? We need to take a look at those who are most closely identified with the concept.

The writers who use the term do not necessarily agree on whether critical thinking is intended as a contrast to some other kind of thinking, possibly to creative thinking, another current focus of interest (see e.g. de Bono, 1970; Perkins, 1981). To McPeck (1981) critical thinking is a subset or dimension of rationality whereas to H. Siegel (1985) and Ennis, it is coextensive with rationality.

Consider Ennis's conception: in contrast to his earlier (1962) work, Ennis claims that his newer conception does not exclude the creative aspects of thinking. Yet a look at Ennis's current taxonomy of thinking abilities still suggests a somewhat restricted focus. Of the over 100 specific abilities identified, more than two thirds of them assume that the task is one of "deciding what to believe or do" (1986, p. 1), *given some set(s) of verbal assertions*. It is revealing that although Ennis recognizes "formulate alternative solutions" (1985, p. 46) as a critical thinking ability, that heading contains no sub-headings, whereas "Employing and reacting to 'fallacy' labels" (ibid.) comprises 22 sub-headings referring to specific fallacies identified by logicians. In comparing his conception with that of others, Ennis notes that " 'informal logic,' the name of a course often taught in philosophy departments ... , seems also to cover the same basic ideas as 'critical thinking'" (1986, p. 6). It is no accident that the illustration Ennis uses in his exposition of the nature of critical thinking is that of a juror in a criminal trial. Here the task is precisely that of *appraising* conflicting argument and evidence in order to come to a reasoned conclusion as to guilt or innocence. Although Ennis's list of thinking abilities may be comprehensive enough for the cook, the mechanic, the painter, and the mathematician to find their own activities subsumed, I think it is fair to say that the list was not formulated with them in mind.

R. Paul (1983), another leader in the critical thinking movement formulates a conception of rational activity which is broader than many, but still embraces a restricted range of tasks. What animates Paul is a keen sense of the gap between the aims and procedures of the academic disciplines and those of Socrates who asserted that the unexamined *life* was not worth living.

To become a reasoner or critical thinker, however, requires skills of concrete synthesis which are as yet not fully developed. We will get little help from the academic world as presently structured with its strict categorical compartmentalizations. We need new skills in the art of totalizing experience rationally, as well as in dialectical questioning of primary categorizations (ibid., p. 20).

Paul rejects the tendency of schools everywhere, including of course universities, to atomize issues and problems in forms amenable to investigation by individual academic disciplines, but I sense that the vision animating his own ideal is still strongly tied to the task of examining something which *already* exists, albeit something as encompassing as a way of life. The same judgment may, I think, be made of Siegel's conception of critical thinking. According to Siegel,

> A critical thinker ... is one who is *appropriately moved by reasons*: she has a propensity or disposition to believe and act in accordance with reasons; and she has the ability to assess the force of reasons in the many contexts in which reasons play a role (1985, p. 11; italics in original).

The two central components of this conception are, "the ability to properly assess reasons" and the "critical attitude or critical spirit" (ibid.) Siegel's formulations may be interpreted more or less restrictively. Are painters, composers and poets and psychiatrists "moved by reasons" when they work? They certainly need a critical attitude, but does that mean that they assess "the force of reasons"? Could a mellifluous tone, a bold contrast, a change in posture be a reason? Possibly, but I think Siegel's exposition suggests that the primary context in which critical thinking operates is that of oral or written discourse.

Most of these formulations do not, in my view, adequately encompass the full range of problems which require thinking. And the authors add the word "critical" to thinking, in a way which might suggest to others that purposeful thinking (*simpliciter*) did not have to be critical. The image from which these conceptions might be derived is that of a person being bombarded by innumerable "messages", many of them contradictory, needing to decide which (if any) to subscribe to. The juror fits this image beautifully.

In contrast, the image which fits de Bono's conception of lateral thinking is that of the city dweller seeking an efficient way to get to the next street, who goes all the way around the block instead of realizing that a back entrance to his own building would put him at his destination in half the time.

Although acknowledging the requirements of logic and the need to be critical, de Bono refers to the logical appraisal of conclusions or what he calls "vertical" thinking with ill-concealed contempt. It is no wonder that philosophers of education identified with the critical thinking movement, however conceived, have little respect for de Bono. It is no wonder that someone who denigrates "vertical" thinking and purveys a bag of tricks to facilitate creative problem solving is, himself, considered something of a trickster. But some of the purveyors of "critical thinking" offer a vision of thinking that is just as restrictive. After all it is de Bono's problems and exercises that often come from the world of practical problems rather than the academic disciplines. De Bono is the one who would recognize that Shakespeare and Leonardo are no less heroic thinkers than Aristotle, that corporate officers as well as professors are professional thinkers. Rigidity, or functional fixedness in the psychologist's jargon is as strong an impediment to effective thinking as inability to identify implicit assumptions and detect logical fallacies (see Mayer, 1977, pp. 75–85).

My main objection to those who employ the term "critical thinking" is that it tends to legitimize a dichotomy between critical and creative thinking which is at best misleading. In fact, *all* thinking, whether the task be the creation of a film or the writing of the review of that film, to take one example, has exploratory phases in which suggestions are generated and developed *and* evaluative phases in which ideas are checked and tested prior to execution. The critical review, if it's worth anything, will contain insights which are original, perhaps more original than the film itself which may have followed a tried and true formula. Of course, the reviewer's contentions will be supported by references to the film. On the other hand, the film's own originality, if it possesses any, is the result of innumerable decisions by the director and her staff, decisions to "go" with or discard ideas which may have simply come into her head. Of the many hours of footage, most will end up on the cutting floor. If they are not capricious, these decisions are made on the basis of "evidence". The decisions *could be* articulated as sets of arguments but this does not carry the implication that the director reaches them by constructing such arguments. Nor would articulating the arguments make for a better film.

Is there any harm in the phrase "critical thinking" and the emphasis it suggests on developing the ability to respond rationally to the myriad attempts to persuade us to do or believe one thing or another? I think there may be. The label presupposes a distinction which leads naturally to the view that certain subjects are inherently creative and others inherently critical, and this is, I believe, a pernicious idea. Courses in drawing and painting, the customary paradigms of creative activity, have as often stifled creativity as fostered it. Some of the most creative intellectual work of the century has occurred in logic, which is almost synonymous with critical thinking, and there is no reason why courses in logic cannot foster inventiveness and even playfulness. Some mathematics educators are beginning to see mathematics in just such a light (see Mason, Burton and Stacey, 1985). If our overall concern is the development of *thoughtfulness*, then I am not so sure that the tasks of identifying fallacies and criticizing documents which form the meat and potatoes of college courses in informal logic are optimally adapted to that goal. Regrettably, some popular approaches to teaching "critical thinking" at the high school level seem every bit as arid (see e.g. Beyer, 1985 a,b). There is no doubt a place for deliberate instruction in such skills as detecting bias in newspaper stories; yet, I suspect that many students find such exercises tedious and uninvolving. If climbing up indoor rope ladders constitutes the main part of their training for future exploration on rugged terrain, many will develop a distaste for the wilderness itself. Such a distaste may encourage the very habits and attitudes that teachers are trying to root out (see Dewey, 1938/1963, p. 49).

B Analytic and intuitive thinking

The distinction between analytic and intuitive or holistic thinking is itself intuitive. Recently it has allegedly been hallowed by "scientific" findings about hemispheric specialization in the brain (see e.g. Grady, 1984). The distinction is not easy to make out, however. In particular it is difficult to separate the intuitive/analytic from the conscious/unconscious and the visual/linguistic distinctions. It is no doubt true that we may suddenly "see" the solution to a problem or that we reach decisions or conclusions on the basis of the way things "feel" without going through a train of reasoning. It is also no doubt true that many perceptual and cognitive processes occur beyond the range of our own awareness. But how exactly are we to differentiate intuitive from analytical thinking?

In a recent work, N. Noddings and P. J. Shore (1984) attempt to clarify the distinction. Although I find much of their discussion of the nature of intuition difficult to follow, some of their formulations are accessible and supported by illustration.

> Intuitive activity involves immediate contact with the objects of knowledge or feeling. Cognitive or conceptual schemes do not intervene or mediate the interaction. When we contact objects analytically or conceptually, we lay structures on them, or we move away from the objects under study to other objects, operations, or principles that we relate conceptually to the

original objects. When we contact objects intuitively, however, we continually return to the objects themselves: We look, listen, touch; we allow ourselves to be moved, appeared to, grasped. If there *is* a structure that we are imposing ... we are unaware of it and have no control over it; indeed, we may be unable to explicate it even upon request (p. 69; italics in original).

To illustrate the difference, Noddings and Shore imagine two individuals asked to list as many uses as they can for a brick.

A subject operating analytically might first associate a brick with building. What can I build with it? he might ask. His list would be constructed from his consideration of the concept "build": Use it to level a short table leg; use it to support a shelf.... A subject operating intuitively would reject the temptation to be diverted by a conceptual line. She might look at it: it's red—hang it on the wall where I'd like a bit of red; it's rectangular and solid— use it to demonstrate a rectangular solid ... it's grainy—use it as an abrasive (ibid., p. 70).

Now notice that if by analytical one implies some sort of mental "taking apart" then the second subject is just as analytical. She is enumerating each of its sensual properties in turn: color, shape, texture, etc. The first subject is the one who is refusing to see the brick as composed of decomposable properties. But the difference Noddings and Shore have in mind is that the first subject is considering the brick under a conceptual category, as a building material, while the second isn't. But is this really true? Is the second subject, in suggesting that it can be hung on the wall, just thinking of it as red or as red *and* hangable on a wall, unlike strawberry jello for example. As just grainy or as grainy *and* holdable in one's hand, unlike a grainy rock formation. I'm suggesting that certain conceptual categories seem to be entering into the responses, categories which are not given by the sensuous qualities alone. In the general formulation they say that even if a person is using conceptual schemes in the intuitive mode, he is unaware of it and has no control over it. But do we know that the first subject's perception is mediated in some way? Is not the association between brick and building as intuitive and immediate from the subject's point of view as any intuition could be? Of course the first has a repertoire of everyday knowledge to guide him but so does the second.

But isn't there a difference between the two subjects? Yes, the suggestions of the second subject are guided primarily by the *sensuous* qualities of the brick rather than by its location within a functional scheme. But does this really capture the distinction between an intuitive and an analytic mode of thinking? I think not. Noddings and Shore claim that "intuition may *look at* and *see clearly* or understand intellectual objects" (ibid., p. 52; italics in original). Indeed, mathematics is a domain where intuitive thinking may profitably be employed. But what does it mean to think intuitively in mathematics? In their discussion of mathematics teaching, Noddings and Shore at times (e.g. ibid., p. 111, 137) appear to equate intuitive thinking with "visual relational thinking" but that seems to me to be collapsing two different distinctions, the analytic/intuitive and the visual/linguistic. It may be extremely useful to represent mathematical ideas visually; a well-chosen diagram may facilitate understanding the Pythagorean theorem much more effectively than a formal proof, but I see no reason to say that the person who makes use of the diagram does not have his perception mediated by concepts. Indeed, the person who saw it simply as a pretty or unusual pattern would not derive any *mathematical* understanding from it.

In a monumental compendium of evidence relating to intuitive thinking, Bastick (1982) identifies various properties which have been thought to characterize it. In contrast to analytical thought, intuitive thought is deemed to be high on emotional involvement, dependent on the past experiences and present situation of the intuiter, preconscious rather than conscious. It is sudden rather than step-by-step, carries a subjective feeling of certainty, and depends on parallel processing of a global field of knowledge rather than on a linear comparing two elements at a time (ibid., p. 51). Let us consider these distinctions. There is no doubt that considerable mental processing occurs below the level of conscious awareness (see, e.g. Neisser, 1967). If we identify these processes with intuition it would follow that when we are consciously working on a problem we are engaged in both processes simultaneously, for whatever we attend to consciously has already been prestructured at the preconscious level. This would entail not attributing one mode to some people and another mode to others; nor could we consciously employ one or the other mode; nor could we strengthen or weaken one or the other. I do not think this captures the distinction most of us, especially educators like Noddings and Shore, are after. The slow/sudden distinction seems to refer not to a mode of thinking but to a moment in time when we see a way out of the impasse which has elicited our thinking. This moment of illumination may arrive after laborious, systematic consideration of every facet of the problem or it may occur upon inspection; of course the more familiar I am with a problem, the more likely I am to just see what needs to be done. I see no reason, however, to identify either the suddenness with which one sees a solution or the subjective feeling of certainty or the emotional arousal present at such a moment with any distinctive mode of thinking which led to the breakthrough (see Perkins, 1981).

Let's look more carefully at the distinction between global and linear processes. Consider an example taken from Wertheimer (1959, p. 130).

$$\frac{274 + 274 + 274 + 274 + 274}{5}$$

One might begin to do this problem by adding each of the numerators in a column and then dividing by five. Upon initial inspection, this is how I thought I would proceed. Such a procedure would seem to be an example of analytic reasoning which is linear, step-by-step, slow. Notice, though, that my readiness to "break the problem up" into two separate parts presupposes some view of the whole as made up of two distinct parts. Before proceeding, I looked again at the problem, convinced that there must be something I hadn't seen. All of a sudden I saw that there were five 274's in the numerator. I of course immediately realized that 274 was being multiplied and divided by the same number, 5, so that the answer was simply 274. I did experience that moment I saw five identical three-digit numbers in the numerator, as one of sudden illumination and delight, for I usually don't do well with such puzzles.

Does that make my thinking here intuitive? Notice that *both* approaches involve inference and an understanding of arithmetical concepts. Notice also that in order to see the solution, I had to see *each* of the elements of the problem, for unless I noticed that each number in the numerator was identical, and that each pair was separated by a " + ", I could not have grasped the solution. Notice, finally, that I would feel just as certain about my solution if I had done the problem the first way.

The global/piecemeal distinction is, I believe, the fundamental one. What led to the illumination was my reorganization of all the elements of the problem in relation to each other. The difficulty was in seeing the numerator as the identical three-digit number repeated the same number of times as the number in the denominator. To avoid taking the problem apart in a more stereotyped way, I did have to "relax the grip" of my initial perception. The immediacy, delight, feeling of certainty were simply the consequences of the reorganization.

Working with any complex pattern of elements, it is natural to try to "break it down" into chunks which can be dealt with separately. Whether the elements are abstract or visual, it is often very difficult to organize them into a different global pattern, especially as much of the structuring is preconscious. I am not quite sure whether one ought to call this "relaxation" required for reorganization a "mode of thinking" or simply a tactic *in* thinking, but in so far as such receptivity can be cultivated, this "mode" must be of interest to the educator. Indeed, de Bono (e.g. 1970, pp. 225-64) believes that some simple techniques can stimulate receptivity, and Noddings and Shore (1984, chap. 5) have some suggestions of their own. I pass no judgment on the efficacy of these suggestions.

I do think the analytic/intuitive distinction, as I have reformulated it, may be an important one for educators. Interestingly enough, an analogous contrast can be found in the physical/territorial domain. I tend to think of exploration as a very assertive, "masculine" activity in which man seeks to dominate unknown terrain. But there is a more passive, equally valuable kind of exploration of the wilderness, in which one tries to blend in with the rest of nature so that it can reveal its secrets. Among its heroes are Thoreau, John Muir and Aldo Leopold rather than Richard Burton and Edmund Hillary.

Within the character trait perspective I've been advancing, the global/piecemeal distinction raises a difficult dilemma for educators. Although I deny that one "mode" uses reason and another emotion, or that one requires detailed knowledge of a subject while the other does not, there is, nevertheless, a tension between the openness and receptivity associated with the global/intuitive approach and the tenacity and precision associated with the piecemeal/analytic approach. Creative thinkers operate in both "modes", though one may be more dominant. The difficulty for the educator lies in drawing the lines between receptivity and laziness and between rigor and rigidity in such a way that the two virtues will be developed rather than the associated vices.

C Well- and ill-structured problems

Another way of classifying kinds of thinking is one that is based on the nature of the problems or tasks which confront the thinker. A fundamental distinction deriving from work in artificial intelligence and cognitive psychology is that between well- and ill-structured problems. The basic notion is that a problem is well-structured if there is "a definite criterion for testing any proposed solution and a mechanizable process for applying the criterion" (Simon, 1977, p. 305). All other problems are considered ill-structured. Most textbook problems, especially in mathematics and science, are well-structured as are puzzles and games such as chess. Most real-world problems, ranging from buying a new car to solving the conflict in the Middle East, are not. Nor is painting a portrait, writing a novel, or writing a philosophical essay about thinking. Our question is whether any distinction between modes of thinking corresponds to these two kinds of problems.

For a problem to be well-structured, it must come with a clearly defined goal, allowable moves, and givens. Moreover, once one has satisfied the criterion through a series of allowable moves, his work is at an end. For an ill-structured problem, on the other hand, a good part of the work of solving the problem derives from the need first to formulate it. Thus Dewey (1938) says,

> It is a familiar and significant saying that a problem well put is half-solved. To find out *what* the problem and problems are which a problematic situation presents to be inquired into, is to be well along in inquiry (p. 108; italics in original).

Since, moreover, in an ill-structured problem there is not an agreed upon set of allowable (and illegitimate) moves, one needs to inquire of any proposed solution whether the costs of achieving it are too great. Proposed solutions to well-structured problems must, of course, also be tested, but the test is straightforward. It should not, however, be inferred from what has been said that well-structured problems are more easily solved. Some well-structured problems in mathematics have resisted solution for centuries despite repeated attempts by the greatest mathematicians. But my point is that an appropriate test of an *ill*-structured problem is, itself, problematic. Ill-structured problems may be said to require stages or phases in their solution which well-structured problems do not. Whether these differences ought to constitute a difference in modes or kinds of thinking is to some extent arbitrary, but the distinction does, I believe, have educational ramifications.

It is no accident that well-structured problems dominate schools, for two distinct reasons. 1 When one is a novice in any domain, one learns best from tasks which eliminate as much irrelevant detail as possible. All the "givens" are relevant to the solution. One also learns to solve problems in a new domain more effectively if one can readily check one's problem-solving effectiveness. Textbooks, therefore, typically avoid problems that are ill-structured because the ill-structuredness would interfere with the need to learn the structure of the field. 2 Well-structured problems, whether in the classroom or as homework, facilitate student accountability and hence support the maintenance of order in the classroom, a point which will be discussed extensively in chapter 3.

We have spoken about modes of thinking, but said nothing so far about different *levels* of thinking. We have an intuitive sense of a hierarchy with "lower" or more basic thinking at the bottom and "higher" or more complex thinking above. The question is whether this kind of intuition can be given any clear meaning. The history of scientific advance provides us with an image of ever-more difficult problems finding solution. But this image can be misleading here. The fact that more difficult problems can be solved does not mean that the *thinking* is more difficult. Thanks to the fruits of previous inquiry, subsequent thinkers have greater resources at their disposal. Individual development presents the same picture. Multiplying 6 × 7 is extremely difficult for an 8 year old, yet presents virtually no problem to most adults. Is that because the adult is a more powerful thinker? Not really, because most adults don't think this out at all; they've simply memorized the multiplication tables. The intuition that there is simpler and more complex thinking is surprisingly difficult to formulate in any satisfactory way.

Let's look at a list of characteristics of "higher order thinking" assembled by Lauren Resnick (1985), a leading applied cognitive psychologist. She identifies eight features; higher order thinking is: 1 non-algorithmic, 2 complex, 3 yields multiple solutions, 4 involves nuanced judgment, 5 involves the application of multiple criteria, 6 involves uncertainty, 7 requires both self-regularization of the thinking process, and 8 imposing meaning (finding structure in apparent disorder) (Resnick, 1985, p. 10). Some of these criteria suggest that higher order thinking can be identified with certain types of tasks or problems. After all it is problems rather than thinking itself which can be characterized as yielding multiple or single solutions, requiring single or multiple criteria. Some of the criteria, especialy 3-6 and 8 seem to fit ill-structured problems much better than well-structured problems. But what reason is there to think such problems require *thinking* of a "higher order"? Why should planning a dinner party, which seems to fit most of the criteria, require higher order thinking than winning a chess match against a formidable opponent? Why should driving a car, which fits all the criteria, require more "higher order" thinking than solving an equation which fits only a few?

One might deny that driving a car, which many of us do virtually without thinking, fits any of the criteria. True for us, but not for a novice. This brings out the point I made earlier, namely that whether a task requires higher order thinking or not depends on the resources of the thinker. Consider whether thinking is algorithmic or not. Is there a recipe which will allow one to solve the problem mechanically? Whether there *is* an algorithm is one question, whether the thinker possesses the algorithm is an entirely different one. We have algorithms for finding square roots and doing long division which our ancestors didn't. Many problems most of us find mundane and routine actually stumped the best and the brightest for centuries.

Identification of level of thinking then, seems inescapably relative to the resources of the thinker.

Consider two ways to try to skirt this conclusion. The first is entirely empirical. We can make an index of the order of difficulty required for solving a problem by seeing how difficult the problem actually is for people to solve. But more difficult for whom? Of course, a problem that offers little to challenge an expert may overwhelm a novice. But that in itself, as we have already seen, does not imply that the *thinking* required of the expert is of a higher order. Perhaps we can arrange problems in order of difficulty in the following way: if, in order to solve problem B, one must first solve problem A, then one can say that B is more challenging than A. If reading comprehension, for example, includes decoding of letters as a necessary component, then reading comprehension is more challenging and requires thinking of a higher order. This is true in some absolute sense. But does it follow from this that a reading comprehension problem will demand a "higher" level of thinking than a decoding problem, *irrespective of degree of expertise*? Assuredly not. Many decoding problems will pose a greater challenge to a novice than many comprehension problems pose to an expert. Notice that this approach provides no way of comparing the demands of problems across domains.

Consider our analogy once again. Within a particular kind of terrain, rocky terrain for example, we do "grade" the degree of difficulty of different routes, *assuming* a climber of average ability and experience. Although a particular route may look very hard or very easy to the untutored, there is a difference between appearance and reality. Consider two routes up a cliff, one graded as slightly more difficult than the other but neither of extreme difficulty, and consider two climbers, a world-class expert and a complete novice. Will the expert be challenged more by the tougher route than the novice by the slightly easier one? Almost certainly not. The second point: although we can rate rock climbs relative to each other, we can't rate them relative to canoe routes or routes through deserts or tropical forests.

Does all this mean that when we go into classrooms we have no way of telling whether or not students are being intellectually challenged? Not in the least. Given that we know something about what students are and are not familiar with, we can ascertain whether the problems they are being asked to solve pose a challenge to them. Given that we know what terrain people are familiar with, we can easily discover if they are being required to explore beyond what they have already mastered. We have no way, however, of "grading" the thinking required by a task until we know the tools and resources the thinker has available for the journey.

6 The value of thinking

I appear committed to the notion that all thinking is creative, and this needs clarification. To call an achievement "creative" implies that it has a certain claim to being admired by society for its originality. Obviously, most thinking is not creative by this standard. There *is*, I claim, some element of novelty in all thinking, but here I am talking about novelty in the context of the *thinker's*—not society's—repertoire. If you already knew how to proceed, thinking would be superfluous. To return to our analogy once more, the toddler learning her way from the kitchen to her own room is exploring unfamiliar terrain, even though her mother can find the way "in her sleep". How challenging a particular mountain trail is will depend on both the objective conditions of the mountain and the expertise of the climber. By the same token, the difficulty a problem presents is a function both of the nature of the problem and the resources which the thinker brings to it. Problems which appear to us to require no thinking at all might be demanding intellectual problems to a young child.

The fact that thinking requires some degree of exploratory behavior does not imply that thinking is always valuable. One might claim just the opposite. In fact in the essay quoted from earlier, Ryle (1979) goes so far as to say, "Thinking is trying to make up for a gap in one's education" (p. 67). What he means by this cryptic comment is that the value of knowing how to proceed saves you from the labor and risk of having to find out. Our ability to *routinize* tasks enables us to direct mental energy to ever more demanding tasks as William James (1923, chap.4) clearly recognized. If people had to expend a great deal of time and energy finding the way out of their own houses, they would never have explored the Andes and the Himalayas.

This fact presents a paradox to the educator who may legitimately argue that people who have learned to think effectively have the only education worth having, for they can extend the knowledge that they do have and what they don't know they can find out for themselves. As James Beattie puts it:

> The aim of education should be to teach us rather how to think than what to think—rather to improve our minds, so as to enable us to think for ourselves, than to load the memory with the thoughts of other men (in A. Kerber, 1968, p. 5).

Now people who have always stuck to the paths and trails forged by others are not well equipped to blaze their own trail, but in settlements without roads, such people are not likely to get very far beyond their own homes. What generates the educational paradox is the assumption that learning or the acquisition of knowledge can be divorced from thinking. Can this be done or does learning, itself, require thinking? I shall defer this important question until the next chapter, for its effective discussion presupposes some understanding of the way these notions are construed in contemporary psychology.

Regardless of the instrumental value of thinking, is it not, itself, an inherently satisfying activity and hence valuable on that account? It is difficult to answer this question in an unqualified way. Our tradition is divided. On the one hand, our capacity to think and reason is what makes us distinctively human. In the tradition that began with Socrates and continues to our own time, human flourishing—which is not the same thing as contentment—depends on the development and exercise of this capacity. J. Rawls (1971) puts himself squarely in this tradition in formulating what he calls the Aristotelian Principle, namely

> Other things being equal, human beings enjoy the exercise of their realized capacities (their innate or trained abilities), and this enjoyment increases the more the capacity is realized, or the greater its complexity (p. 426).

But there is another intuition to be reckoned with. According to Hannah Arendt (1958),

> As early as Aristotle the distinction between quiet and unquiet, between an almost breathless abstention from external physical movement and activity of every kind, is more decisive than the distinction between the political and the theoretical way of life.... It is like the distinction between war and peace: just as war takes place for the sake of peace, thus every kind of activity, even the processes of mere thought, must culminate in the absolute quiet of contemplation (p. 15).

Perhaps these apparently conflicting intuitions are not irreconcilable. Consider some empirical research reported by M. Csikszentmihalyi (1975) who studied people involved in a variety of intrinsically rewarding pursuits ranging from chess to rock climbing to surgery. He calls these "autotelic" activities. Questionnaire responses suggested

> some strong commonalities in the underlying experience.
> Autotelic activities were rated by participants as being most similar to the experiences of "designing or discovering something new", "exploring a strange place", and "solving a mathematical

problem".... Apparently, something that is enjoyable to do gives a feeling of a creative discovery, a challenge overcome, a difficulty resolved (p. 181).

Our common experience tells us that thinking of the kind we have been talking about, far from being a relaxing pastime, is often experienced as burdensome, frustrating, laborious, even futile. Religious leaders have often exploited that insight. But even frustrating work has its satisfying side, especially when it issues in something we can take pride in. I find it noteworthy that Csikszentmihalyi's interviewees from rock climbers to surgeons employed the metaphor of exploration. Whatever the personal rewards of thinking, no one would deny that our life in society is to some extent dependent on the quality of our collective problem solving. I would say, therefore, that the nurture of effective thinkers has ample justification.

CHAPTER 2

The educational significance of cognitive psychology

The main aim of this chapter is to assess the significance of contemporary cognitive psychology for the education of effective thinkers. R. Glaser (1984), one of the leading contemporary educational psychologists claims the knowledge that is accumulating in cognitive psychology concerning the ability of people to reason and solve problems "should have lasting effects on improving and increasing the general use of these abilities" (p. 93). One could properly infer from what I've said in the previous chapter that I do not believe this to be the case, but given the excitement generated in some quarters about the cognitive approach, the matter deserves careful examination.[1] In section 1, I briefly discuss two precursors to the cognitive approach—the gestalt and behaviorist traditions. Section 2 expounds and analyzes the cognitive orientation to the experimental study of thinking. In section 3 I discuss the relationship between thinking and learning as it is understood by cognitive psychology. Section 4 focusses on children's thinking. Finally in sections 5 and 6, I examine the pedagogical implications of cognitive psychology.

1 The Gestalt and behaviorist traditions

The experimental study of complex thinking is far from new in psychology (see Mandler and Mandler, 1964). Pioneering work was done by F. Binet in France, J. Piaget in Switzerland, and F. Bartlett in England. Important early contributions were made in America by E. Tichener and W. James. Before the Second World War, the Gestalt psychologists brought an interest in the empirical investigation of thinking from Germany to America. The focus on complex human mental processes links contemporary cognitive psychologists to the Gestalt school, yet the dominance of behaviorism in American psychology between the 1920s and the 1960s has also left its mark on the means by which such processes are investigated.

Consider a well-known experiment in the Gestalt tradition by Norman F. Maier (1931). In a room filled with various kinds of tools and furniture, two cords were hung from the ceiling to the floor and subjects were asked to tie the ends together. The cords were placed at such a distance that if the subject held the end of one in one hand, he could not quite grasp the other one. Subjects were asked to overcome this obstacle in as many ways as possible using the equipment around them. The most difficult solution involved tying a pair of pliers at the bottom of one cord and then using that as a pendulum to swing it in the vicinity of the second cord. Once subjects had discovered this solution either by themselves or with the help of hints such as the experimenter's swaying the cord, they were asked to describe the reasoning which led them to the solution. Maier was able to show that although many of the subjects availed themselves of the hints, they were not aware of that afterwards. Maier argues that neither "trial and error" nor association by similarity is able to explain the appearance of the solution.

The perception of the solution of a problem is like the perceiving of a hidden figure in a puzzle-picture. In both cases (a) the perception is sudden; (b) there is no conscious intermediate stage; and (c) the relationships of the elements in the final perceptions are different from those which preceded, i.e., changes in meaning are involved (1931, p. 193).

Wertheimer (1959) uses very similar language to describe problem solving in mathematics.

When one grasps a problem situation, its structural features and requirements set up certain strains, stresses, tensions in the thinker. What happens in real thinking is that these strains and stresses are followed up, yield vectors in the direction of improvement of the situation, and change it accordingly. S2 (the situation after the problem is solved) is a state of affairs that is held together by inner forces as a good structure in which there is harmony in the mutual requirements, and in which the parts are determined by the structure of the whole, as the whole is by the parts (p. 239).

Although these experiments and their conclusions challenged the methodology of introspectionist experimenters such as Tichener, the Gestalt psychologists were considered unscientific by the ascendant behaviorist school. No extended discussion of the behaviorist program is necessary at this date, but a brief review of its approach to the study of problem solving is still useful. I shall limit myself to consideration of the views of B. F. Skinner, behaviorism's most eminent contemporary exponent. The goal of a scientific psychology, according to Skinner (1982a), is the prediction and control of human behavior. Such a psychology, hence, should focus on the relation between manipulable environmental variables and observable behavior. Skinner argued that in the case of learning, and any modification of a response which increased the probability of its occurring constituted learning, reference to mental states or events was not necessary for developing scientific laws linking behavior to environmental contingencies. In our prescientific description of human responses to complex environments, we might use terms like "thinking" and "expecting," but they would disappear as scientific knowledge of patterns of reinforcement accumulated. Not only were such ascriptions unnecessary, they were detrimental.

> Theories—whether neural, mental, or conceptual—talk about intervening steps in these relationships. But instead of prompting us to search for and explore relevant variables, they frequently have the opposite effect. When we attribute behavior to a neural or mental event, real or conceptual, we are likely to forget that we still have the task of accounting for the neural or mental event (Skinner, 1982a, p. 44).

Moreover,

> a preoccupation with mental way stations burdens a science of behavior with all the problems raised by the limitations and inaccuracies of self-descriptive repertoires (Skinner, 1982b, p. 129).

Given Skinner's stance, it is little wonder that he did not study the kinds of problem solving which interested the Gestalt psychologists. Since conditioning was the most fundamental process of behavioral change and since the same principles were evident and more easily studied in less complex organisms, much of the experimentation in the behaviorist tradition was on pigeons and rats (see Lachman, Lachman, and Butterfield, 1979, chap. 2). Nevertheless, Skinner did occasionally discuss human problem solving and it is worthwhile to see what he said about it. Here is his (1982d) analysis of taking apart the rings of a puzzle.

> I may learn to solve the puzzle in either of two ways. I may move the rings about until I hit upon a response that separates them. The behavior will be strengthened, and if I do the same thing a number of times, I will eventually be able to take the rings apart very quickly. My behavior has been shaped and maintained by its effect on the rings. I may, on the other hand, simply follow printed directions supplied with the puzzle. The directions describe behavior that separates the rings, and if I have already

learned to follow directions, I can avoid the possibly long process of having my behavior shaped by the contingencies (p. 186).

Now this is a curious passage. Neither alternative appears to be characteristic of most attempts to solve puzzles of this kind. The first is totally mindless trial and error while the second is what most of us would call cheating. We usually adopt either approach only out of desperation. I dare say that the descriptions given by the Gestalt psychologists sound far more plausible to us, but Skinner's methodology forbids such mentalistic description. If his description accurately represents the only options available to him he is truly handicapped. If not, then he is denying his own experience to try to preserve his theory. Ironically, it is virtually impossible to explain either successful puzzle-solving strategy within the framework Skinner prescribes. Consider the second: the idea, presumably, is that when we have followed printed instructions in the past, we have solved such puzzles, so our "following instruction" behavior has been reinforced. But "following instructions" is *not* specifiable behaviorally since instructions can call for virtually any behavior. Skinner would not disagree.

In "An Operant Analysis of Problem Solving" (1984), Skinner contrasts "rule-following" and "contingency-shaped bahavior."

The response which satisfies a complex set of contingencies, and thus solves the problem, may come about as the result of direct shaping by the contingencies ... or it may be evoked by contingency-related stimuli constructed either by the problem solver or by others.... We tend to follow advice because previous behavior in response to similar verbal stimuli has been reinforced (1984, p. 587).

Suppose, then, that we are trying to solve the ring puzzle by following the directions accompanying it. The first instruction reads: "Grasp the top ring with the first two fingers of your left hand." Now Skinner does not pretend that we have ever exhibited this particular behavior before, but what we have done before is follow directions which accompany puzzles. We have done this enough times with enough subsequent reinforcement to attempt the same thing now. But how do we identify the instructions as "similar" in order to activate the relevant rule? How do we know the printed words are instructions for solving *this* puzzle rather than some other or maybe information about securing other puzzles from the same company? It would seem that we must somehow relate the sentences on the paper which we may never have seen before to the metal rings in our hands. If the sentence said, "Place the red disk in the palm of your right hand" we would not even try to follow it and would just throw out the slip of paper. It appears that mental language must be invoked to account for the intelligent following of directions. So even the second rather perverse way of solving the ring puzzle can't be accommodated to the behaviorist account. But the behaviorist account is just as mistaken regarding the first strategy, moving the rings about until a correct response is just hit upon.

If one engages in the manual activity without paying attention to what one is doing, then simply chancing upon the position which will release the rings does nothing to make a future solution more probable. But now, suppose we look carefully at the rings in our hands as we manipulate them. Let's suppose with Skinner that we don't have any particular plan; we just move them around. Now at some moment, they separate and we look carefully at the position they are in. Skinner is right that a future solution will be more probable; it may even be certain. But he is wrong in thinking that what will be reinforced is specific behavior, certain motions of the hands. For once we see how the rings come apart, we not only can do the puzzle ourselves using different motions, holding it with our left hand instead of our right, even with pliers; but we can provide verbal directions to a friend who is holding the puzzle, all novel behaviors let us assume. To account for this kind of immediate transfer without invoking mental states and processes, for example mental imagery, would appear to be impossible.

Most behaviorist research avoids experiments dealing with the kinds of problem solving Maier, Wertheimer and others in the Gestalt tradition were concerned with, in the belief that such "behavior" is built up from more fundamental "atoms" of "learning" which must be understood first before complex processes can be investigated. But the reason the kind of problem situation investigated by Maier is not the subject of research within the behaviorist program is not simply that it is too complex but that the behavior of subjects in such situations is virtually unintelligible within the behaviorist framework.[2] Skinner would no doubt claim that if we knew the reinforcement history of subjects we could predict their problem-solving behavior precisely. Of course, Maier's subjects had no more experience than pigeons with ropes hanging from ceilings, yet their behavior (unlike that of pigeons) involved a systematic (not random) search for ways of bringing the ropes together. Only a psychology that not only countenances but tries to understand what goes on *in the mind* when people think *could* offer a plausible account of the behavior in Maier's laboratory.

2 Cognitive psychology

Contemporary cognitive psychology takes the computer rather than the pigeon for its inspiration:

> Computers take symbolic input, recode it, make decisions about the recoded input, make new expressions from it, store some or all of the input, and give back symbolic output. By analogy, that is most of what cognitive psychology is about. It is about how people take in information, how they recode and remember it, how they make decisions, how they transform their internal knowledge states, and how they translate these states into behavioral outputs (Lachman, Lachman, and Butterfield, 1979, p. 99).

It is important to recognize that although the computer has been one important source of ideas for investigating human cognitive processes, this does not imply that cognitive psychologists presume that computers are minds (or brains) or that either their operations or their capacities are identical with those of humans. Still the choice of the computer is not accidental and is guided by serious considerations (see Haugeland, 1985). What gives the analogy its power is this: first, computers have *some* of the same capacities as mind-brains (e.g. chess-playing programs beat all but the best players); second they are entirely physical and their operations can be described without reference to any mysterious incorporeal substances; third, their capacities and operations can be described at the level of the software which does not refer to the actual materials, circuitry, etc. which constitutes the computer as a machine. By analogy, psychologists have a way of talking about psychological states and processes without either abandoning a materialist outlook or needing to get involved in the anatomy and physiology of the brain.

It's all very well to have a way of thinking about cognitive processes, but what does cognitive psychology wish to understand and how does it go about that task? The range of interests and concepts is extremely large and constantly evolving. One reason is that the cognitive approach discovers *problem solving-like* processes implicated in tasks which we would consider quite *un*problematic such as identifying the President of the United States when asked, obeying a traffic signal, recognizing one's spouse in a crowd, catching a baseball.[3] The fact that we are often unaware of the processes underlying these achievements is not sufficient reason for denying their existence. But if introspection is useless at best and pernicious at worst and if behaviorism is mistaken, how can experimental psychologists study what happens between input and output? The problem is severe and much of the success as well as the limitations of the approach derive from the ingenious methods devised to yield rather precise conclusions about what is necessarily unobservable.

The best way to get a feel for the approach is to consider a few representative studies before drawing any generalizations. I shall consider four exemplars: P. Johnson-Laird's (1983) study of performance on syllogisms, R. Shepard and J. Metzler's (1977) study of mental rotation of three-dimensional objects, A. Tversky and D. Kahneman's (1977) study of probabilistic judgment, and J. Bransford and N. McCarrell's (1977) work on the role of inference in comprehension. My aim here is not to give a detailed description of the studies, much less a comprehensive overview of the field; it is merely to convey an idea of the way in which psychologists' experiments attempt to provide knowledge about the mental mechanisms underlying problem-solving behavior.

A Representative experiments

(1) Johnson-Laird (1983) was interested in finding out what mental processes could account for people's performance in deductive reasoning. In his experiments he gave subjects two premises of a syllogism and asked them to figure out what (if any) valid conclusion could be drawn from them. He recorded the percentages of valid conclusions and the time it took for them to be reached. How could such a simple procedure yield information about the nature of the mental processing the subjects engaged in? The general theory Johnson-Laird was testing was that the way people draw inferences from premises is by "constructing an integrated mental model of them" (p. 177). What does this mean? He uses the following syllogism to illustrate (p. 175):

Some of the scientists are parents.
All of the parents are drivers.

Johnson-Laird suggests one way that subjects might deal with this:

The reasoners' knowledge of language enables them to imagine some arbitrary number of scientists:
scientist
scientist
scientist
and to mentally tag them in some way to indicate that some of them are identical to parents:
scientist = parent

scientist = parent
(scientist) (parent)

The parenthetical items indicate that there may be scientists who are not parents and parents who are not scientists. The information from the second premise, "All the parents are drivers", can then be directly added to this model to yield an integrated representation of both premises:

scientist = parent = driver
scientist = parent = driver
(scientist) (parent = driver)
                 (driver)   (pp. 178–179)

The conclusion, . . . interrelates those items that have not been explicitly related in the premises, i.e. that have not been directly used in setting up the model (p. 178).

In this case most people correctly draw one valid conclusion, namely that some scientists are drivers. Now this way of going about solving deductive syllogisms sounds like a possibility, but how does Johnson-Laird's work go beyond speculation?

There are three terms in any syllogism, pairs of which are related in each of the premises. The structure of any syllogism is conventionally represented by the order in which the terms are presented. Our example illustrates the "figure" A–B, B–C. Johnson-Laird's theory is based on a number of assumptions about how the mind works, of which the most important is that memory operates on a first-in first-out basis. This means that it is easier to recall items in the order in which they are presented. This suggests that a syllogism of the figure A–B, C–B, would be more difficult to represent requiring additional mental operations. An example would be:

Some of the scientists are parents.
All of the drivers are parents.

Now there are relatively straightforward ways of systematically ordering the various "figures" in terms of the number of operations which would be needed to form an integrated model. If we have an experiment in which subjects are asked to solve syllogism problems which include examples of each figure, and if the number of valid conclusions and the time taken to reach a conclusion correlate with the previously determined number of operations needed, then this supports Johnson-Laird's mental model hypothesis. But Johnson-Laird goes further: some syllogisms can yield two or three integrated models of the premises. He provides the following example of a very difficult syllogism:

All of the beekeepers are artists.
None of the chemists are beekeepers (p. 180).

Not only will syllogisms such as this be more difficult, but because subjects may not realize that more than one integrated model is available, it is possible to predict the most likely errors that they would make. They might either draw invalid conclusions or overlook valid conclusions. For example, in the first syllogism, subjects almost never realize that "some drivers are scientists" is also a valid conclusion. Hence, not only the percentage of right and wrong answers but the *pattern* of wrong answers can provide information to test the theory. Finally, Johnson-Laird has written a computer program which simulates the problem-solving processes he proposes and yields the same pattern of correct and incorrect valid deductions as human subjects. All this evidence, he alleges, lends strong support to his "mental models" view.

(2)   Shepard and Metzler (1977) were interested in the role of visual imagery in another kind of thinking. For these experiments subjects were shown pairs of drawings representing three-dimensional objects and were asked to determine as quickly as possible whether the objects were identical. In fact, some of the pairs were identical, but differed in orientation, others were not but were mirror images of each other. These judgments were made in between one and six seconds and were almost always correct. How did the subjects do it? According to their own accounts, they tested the similarity by mentally rotating one of the objects into the identical orientation of the other. Subjects also claimed that they could only perform these mental rotations at a certain speed. If this were so, Shepard and Metzler reasoned, the degree of rotation required to line up the "objects" ought to correspond to the time it took to reach a conclusion. The data from their very carefully designed experiment showed that "reaction time is a strikingly linear function of the angular difference between the two three-dimensional objects portrayed" (p. 536). This tends to show, as Stephen Kosslyn (1985) has also argued, that "the images people experience appear to share many of the properties of pictures, although there is no obvious reason why they should" (p. 24).

(3)   Another common kind of thinking which has been extensively studied is reasoning under uncertainty, that is to say reasoning in situations where we have to make decisions based on beliefs concerning the *likelihood* of uncertain events or states of affairs. In one well-known experiment, Tversky and Kahneman (1977) set subjects a problem in which they had to estimate the likelihood that a large and a small hospital would experience days in which the proportion of male babies born would exceed 60 per cent. A large majority of

the subjects said this would be equally likely at either hospital. They showed, according to the authors, an insensitivity to sample size, a fundamental statistical notion. In another experiment, subjects were given a personality profile of an individual and asked to judge the likelihood that that person was an engineer or a lawyer. One group was told that the profile was taken at random from a group that was 70 per cent lawyers, and the other that the group contained 30 per cent lawyers. Yet there was no difference in their conclusions:

> Apparently, subjects evaluated the likelihood that a particular description belonged to an engineer rather than a lawyer by the degree to which this description was representative of the two stereotypes, with little or no regard for the prior probabilities of the categories (p. 328).

From experiments such as these, Tversky and Kahneman identify certain heuristics or rules of thumb which, though generally reliable, cause identifiable "cognitive biases" which lead to erroneous conclusions on occasion. These "biases" are not merely a matter of ignorance, they claim, for they can be found even among those with training in statistics.

(4) J. Bransford and colleagues (Bransford and McCarrell, 1977) have been interested in discovering the mental operations underlying comprehension of written texts, another lively area in cognitive psychology. Bransford and McCarrell propose that linguistic inputs, whether heard or read, be viewed as "cues or instructions to create meanings" (p. 386). This implies that the semantic descriptions created by a reader or listener might contain more information than is explicitly contained in the communication they receive. Here is one among the many experiments Bransford and his colleagues conducted to test this idea. A group of subjects was read a story which contained the following sentences:

> John was trying to fix the bird house. He was *pounding the nail* when his father came out to watch him and to help him do the work (ibid., p. 388).

A control group listened to this slightly altered version:

> John was trying to fix the bird house. He was *looking for* the nail when his father came out to watch him and to help him do the work (p. 388).

Afterwards both groups listened to the same sentence and had to decide whether they recognized it as one they had heard earlier. The recognition sentence was:

John was using the *hammer* to fix the bird house when his father came out to watch him and to help him do the work (p. 388).

Subjects who had heard the first version were quite sure they had actually heard the recognition sentence (which they had not), while subjects who heard the second were quite sure that they had not. In another experiment (pp. 389–92) subjects listened to paragraphs and were then given comprehension and recall tests. In one group, the subjects were given the title of the passage before hearing it. The paragraphs were written in such a way that if one were not told what the subject was, one would find them quite inscrutable. Branford found that those who knew the title beforehand had a much better subsequent understanding of the paragraph and recalled more about it. From many experiments such as this, Bransford and McCarrell conclude as follows:

Our approach to comprehension focuses on the comprehender's ability to use his general knowledge to create situations that permit the relations specified in input sentences to be realized, ... In short, the ability to create some level of semantic content sufficient to achieve a click of comprehension depends upon the comprehender's ability to think (p. 398).

B Some generalizations

What general lessons can be learned from this brief survey of representative studies? (1) The view of the organism which these studies support is that of a creature who engages in thinking—that is in drawing inferences which go beyond the information given—even in simple tasks such as recall of information. Moreover, the various experiments reinforce our suggestion in the last chapter that all thinking, even deductive reasoning, may be viewed under the general heading of problem solving. The Shepard and Metzler study supports the notion that spatial images form an autonomous medium of thought. This suggests that the processing of verbal and visual information may legitimately be considered distinct modes of thinking.[4]

(2) Some of the mental processes which underlie subjects' performance in the foregoing experiments are not accessible to consciousness whereas others are. Introspective reports, like those given by Shepard and Metzler's subjects may be suggestive but they do

not constitute adequate evidence for the existence of those processes. In Tversky and Kahneman's research, the subjects were aware of drawing inferences, but probably not of the heuristics they were employing. In the case of Branford's research, subjects presumably had no awareness of the inferences they were drawing at all; these inferences would have been quite inaccessible to them, yet their existence is undeniable. Since introspective reports are, therefore, neither necessary nor sufficient, there is no principled reason to identify the domain of cognitive psychology with those situations in which we consciously or effortfully try to solve problems. Since, moreover, performance which is at one time conscious and effortful, such as finding the keys while learning to type, can become so "automatized" that we need not consciously think about individual letters and fingers at all, there is good reason not to restrict our investigations to the former situations. Indeed, since human cognitive development would be impossible without the ability to automatize processes once under conscious control, there is every reason to study the automatic as well as the conscious processes (see Mandler, 1985, pp. 41–5).

(3) All the experimenters are interested in understanding mental processes, but they are equally interested in what cognitive scientists call the problem of mental *representation*. Mandler (1985) claims that "representation and process are the central metatheoretical categories" (p. 31). It would be easy to write an entire volume analyzing the various meanings of this term "representation" as used by cognitive scientists and philosophers. Although the term "mental representation" may not strike as responsive a chord in the untutored reader as "mental process," the idea behind it is not difficult to grasp. Many of us are familiar with the fact that the same number, say five, can be "represented" in a variety of different ways, as V in Roman notation, 5 in decimal notation, and 100 in binary notation. In order to perform tasks such as solving syllogisms, or answering questions about texts or drawings of three-dimensional objects, the mind must have a way of storing and using an immense amount of information; cognitive psychologists want to know what kind of information is stored, the way in which this information is coded, how it is organized, and how the organization is affected by learning and maturation (see Puff, 1979).

Perhaps an analogy will make the idea of mental organization clearer. Recently I read a review of a book which I wanted to read in connection with this chapter. Recalling the name of the author but not the title, I could easily go to the library card catalog to see if the library owned the volume. It did not, so I went to the author volume of *Books in Print* to find out who published it and how much it cost. Several titles were listed under that name and I immediately recognized the one I was looking for. Last year I read a novel I enjoyed very much. Some months later, when I wanted to recommend it to a friend, I found I had forgotten both the author, the title and the publication date. I remembered the theme and the events in the story rather well but that was of little help. It turned out that it was extraordinarily difficult to retrieve the book because neither the library nor any of the fiction bibliographies I found were organized according to subject matter. A visitor from another planet, wishing to investigate the way information about books is "represented" in reference works by studying my behavior could infer that information about works of fiction is organized alphabetically by title and author but not by subject.

Experiments like Shepard and Metzler's support the idea that without employing any propositional representations, we can solve problems by manipulating quasi-pictorial images which "*depict* information in a spatial medium*" (G. Cohen, 1983, p. 44; emphasis in original). Such evidence supports the contention that the manipulation of visual and verbal information may legitimately be considered distinct modes of thinking.[5] Bransford's experiment shows that when we hear about someone pounding a nail we immediately infer that a hammer was used. This suggests that the information we have about building must be organized in such a way that the ideas of nail, pounding, and hammer are very close to each other so that not a lot of "searching" is necessary to go from one to the other as would be the case, say, if our minds were organized alphabetically like dictionaries. Tversky and Kahneman's research shows that although we deal every day with situations where we have to estimate the likelihood of things happening, certain basic concepts of statistical reasoning are not represented at all.

(4) Since the mental processes to be investigated are not, themselves, observable, all of the inferences need to be drawn from the "input" and "output". How can one be sure that the "output" is not a result of processes other than those under investigation, perhaps influenced by dimensions of the experimental setup which are not the focus of the research? How can one be sure that the inferences about mental processes are validly inferred from the experimental data? W. G. Lehnert (1984) distinguishes between "clean" and "messy" experiments. In the former, all variables save the experimental variable are controlled. In the latter, a number of different variables can contribute to the results. Lehnert asserts, correctly that "reputable psychologists tend to steer clear of messy experimental design" (p. 29). The more straightforward the task, the shorter the time the subject has to make a response, the simpler the response (e.g. answering yes or no compared to writing a paragraph), the "cleaner" the experiment. Shepard and Metzler's experiment is a

model of "cleanliness." Although it has been much admired, its conclusions are not beyond debate (see e.g. Carpenter and Just, 1986). Johnson-Laird's is the "messiest" of the experiments and as might be expected, there is enormous controversy regarding the adequacy of the model he proposes (see e.g. Guyote and Sternberg, 1981; Rips, 1986).

Even Johnson-Laird's experiment does not approach the "messiness" of Maier's experiment which we discussed earlier. Here each subject required as much as 20 minutes to solve the problem and the conclusion went considerably beyond the evidence actually available. For example, what evidence showed that the perception of the solution to the string problem is like seeing a hidden figure in a puzzle-picture? It is significant that Johnson-Laird and P. Wason (1977), in an introduction to their anthology on thinking express very guarded praise for the Gestalt psychologists. They write:

> Behaviourism may have been an oversimplification but, at least in its early days, it offered a clear and explicit theory. Gestalt psychology, on the other hand, tended towards obscure formulations in its attempt to define the role of structure. When a member of the school talked, for example, of "grasping the inner relations of a problem", it was natural to wonder quite what he had in mind. (p. 4)

C Comparing cognitive and behavioral approaches

Although behaviorism as a research program appears to be moribund (see Mandler, 1985, chap. 1), the behaviorist emphasis on "clean" laboratory experimentation and stringent criteria in interpreting evidence has been internalized by all psychologists who aspire to wear the mantle of science.[5] Oddly enough, this leaves the cognitive psychologists with some of the same problems as the behaviorists in accounting for complex thinking.

First, consider what one may call the problem of the laboratory as a setting. In the previous chapter I drew the distinction between well- and ill-structured problems. In the case of the former, the goals, constraints, and allowable "moves" are precisely specified. In the case of the latter, none of them may be. Most of the problems we confront, be it in our ordinary or our professional lives, are ill-structured problems, e.g. deciding on a career, maintaining a relationship, planning a vacation, decorating a home, building a budget, writing a book, designing a machine, advising a client about taxes or investments, etc. In such cases, the definition of the problem is itself problematic. Not even the goal is specified in advance. This means that a good deal of time and energy must be devoted to discovering and formulating the nature of the problem (see Hayes, 1978, chap. 11; Johnson, 1984; Yussen, 1985). Ill-structured problems, some of which are engaged in over months and even years, rarely find their way into the psychology laboratory for obvious reasons: "clean" experiments require responses from a number of subjects that can be readily observed, tallied, compared; treatment and control groups that differ by just one variable; a modest length of time to engage subjects who are volunteers or nominally paid.

Another difficulty besets the experimental study of thinking. We may call this the problem of studying extraordinarily complex systems. Any experiment with human subjects involves individuals with varying life histories, motivations, moods, aptitudes, and so on. Cognitive psychologists, unless they are especially interested in the effects of one of these human characteristics on cognitive performance, will do all they can to minimize their impact (see Aanstoos, 1985; Schoenfeld, 1983). This is one reason many of the experiments designed to understand cognitive processes involve tasks which can be performed by any subject virtually instantaneously (see Lachman, Lachman, and Butterfield, 1979, chaps 4, 5). The attempt to isolate and study the cognitive subsystem apart from contaminating influences is not at all reprehensible; indeed, it has its parallels in all laboratory sciences. But this very attempt places a limit on what kinds of thinking psychologists will study. Most of our problem solving is contaminated by our personalities, aptitudes, etc. In wishing to eliminate all such influences, cognitive psychologists are led to eliminate the conditions most of us think under "in the wild."

The ironic consequence of all this is that cognitive psychologists' stance with respect to the study of human thinking is not as different from behaviorists' as one might expect. As behaviorist psychologists eschew experiments on complex human reasoning in natural settings so do a majority of cognitive psychologists. But even when investigators study how authentic experts solve actual problems, those they choose to study are hardly representative of the range of problems humans encounter in their professional lives. A perusal of Greeno and Simon's (in press) review of the entire area of problem solving and reasoning permits ready documentation of this assertion. Of the over two hundred references, only about five deal with problems in which neither goals, nor procedures nor constraints are prespecified. While a section on chess and "Go" contains about ten references, with the exception of a single study of musical composition done in 1965, there are *no* references to problem solving in any of the fine arts or the humanities, to say nothing of the interpersonal domain.

Just as behaviorism assumed that complex behavior is built up of elementary processes, so does cognitive psychology. Only now the elements are given names like "stimulus encoding" and "node activation" rather than "extinction" or "reinforcement." Behaviorists have been criticized for studying artificial tasks in artificial settings with little "ecological validity;" the same charge has been launched at cognitive psychologists, though here at least the subjects are human beings (see Cohen, 1983; Kintsch, Miller, and Polson, 1984; Neisser, 1976). Indeed the responses to these charges have a familiar ring: artificial settings are no bar to the study of fundamental processes; simple tasks must be studied if there is to be any hope of understanding more complex ones; knowledge gained in the laboratory can have enormous practical significance (Simon, 1981; Kintsch, Miller, and Polson, 1984).

To be sure, as I've already indicated, a few researchers have tried to study more complex problem solving "in the wild." Most notable is the work of Herbert Simon and associates (Bhaskar and Simon, 1977; Reitman, 1964; Simon and Simon, 1979). The procedure is to ask people to think out loud as they solve complex or ill-structured problems, and then to record and analyze their verbal protocols. Often an attempt is then made to simulate the reported or inferred cognitive processes in a computer program (Simon, 1981). Sometimes complex cognitive processes are first modelled on the computer and then experimental evidence is sought for the relevance of the model to human subjects. If the pattern of input and output is similar, inferences can be drawn about the similarity of underlying processes and representations (see e.g. Anderson, 1983; Lachman, Lachman, and Butterfield, 1979, chap. 12). The question of the accuracy of subjects' introspective accounts of their own thinking has received ample discussion. The usefulness of computer simulations has also received much attention. G. Cohen (1983, chap. 1) provides a fair-minded survey of the disputes and I will not rehearse them. My purpose here is to acknowledge the ingenuity of the investigators while highlighting the difficulties of achieving a scientific understanding of ecologically valid human thinking—difficulties shared by *both* behaviorist and cognitive research traditions. Despite the current ascendancy of cognitive or information-processing approaches to the investigation of the human mind, many serious questions have been raised about the ultimate fruitfulness of this paradigm (see, e.g. Gardner, 1985, chap. 14; Lachman, Lachman and Butterfield, 1979, chap. 14).

3 Thinking and learning

We have seen that behaviorism eliminated the concept of thinking entirely from its vocabulary. Learning, which is to say the principles of conditioning, could theoretically account for the most complex performance. Until recently, cognitive psychologists outside the child development field have taken comparatively little interest in learning (Lachman, Lachman and Butterfield, 1979, chap. 2). This is due primarily to a focus on the normal functioning of the mature cognitive apparatus rather than on how that apparatus develops, as well as to a belief that learning, at least as conceptualized by the behaviorists, is not central to that development (ibid.). Although cognitive psychologists do not share behaviorists' inclinations to minimize our native endowment, they have come to realize the need for a theory of learning. Such a need derives from their interest in the problem of how knowledge is represented. Long before the ascendancy of the information-processing paradigm, psychologists interested in verbal recall, noticed that such recall reflected subjects' tendency to organize words in particular ways (see Lachman, Lachman, and Butterfield, 1979, chap. 2). Gradually the way in which not only words, but meaning was organized in memory became one of the dominant interests. Although it might seem a natural step to inquire into the evolution of this organization, and the role of learning in that evolution, cognitive psychology's interest in learning has manifested itself only recently (see Mandler, 1985, chap. 4). Of course, there is an enormous literature dealing with just that evolution deriving from Piaget who began studying this question over fifty years ago, but his work began to interest experimental cognitive psychologists only recently. (I return to Piaget below.)

One of the earliest discussions of learning within the cognitive tradition is an essay by D. Rumelhart and D. Norman published in 1978. Since this is one of the few comprehensive discussions of the topic it is useful to summarize it. Rumelhart and Norman's main contention is that learning is not a unitary process and their main contribution is an attempt to distinguish three types of learning labeled accretion, restructuring and tuning (p. 38). Accretion involves adding new data to the existing data base of knowledge. When existing memory structures or "schemata" are not adequate to account for new knowledge, either old structures must be modified—"tuning"—or new structures have to be generated—"restructuring". Though accretion is the most common kind of learning and the most studied, the other two are more significant (p. 39).

Rumelhart and Norman tell us that restructuring is the most significant, and often "takes place only after considerable time and effort" (ibid., p. 39). They link such restructuring with the subjective experience of "understanding." Although the authors have little to say about the processes which result in the different forms of learning, what they do say is revealing for our purposes. They distinguish two ways in which a schema can be restructured ("pattern generation" and "schema induction"), and four ways in which a basic structure or schema can be "tuned" (ibid., p. 47): 1   improving the accuracy, 2   generalizing the applicability, 3   specializing the applicability, 4   determining the default values. I shall not discuss each of these rather formidable terms, but a brief discussion of one or two of them will capture an important point. The authors illustrate 3 with reference to research by Gentner on children's extension of the range of applicability of the word "have" from "Sam has a large kettle" to "Sam has a nice apartment" to "The kettle has an enamel coating" to "Sam has good times."

> Presumably the verb "have" gets a primary meaning of something like "own." By extension, aspects of the owning relationship become inessential to the application of the concept of "having." Originally "have" would seem to require the owner to be one with complete control over the object in question. As the usage gets extended, the requirement of having complete control is loosened until finally by sentence (4), it appears to require only that the object in question be strongly associated, in some way, with the subject (ibid., p. 48).

The fundamental point for our purposes is that, whether such generalization is made consciously or unconsciously, it appears to involve some kind of inferential process, a going beyond the information given, that is thinking. Sometimes, of course, children overgeneralize. They may call all small animals "doggie," for example. In that case, the child must

> specialize its understanding of the schema by either restricting the range of the variable terms or by adding more terms that must be followed before the schema is acceptable. Specializing by the first method fits our notion of tuning. Specialization by the second actually would be a form of patterned generation of schemata: forming a new schema based upon the old but modified by adding a few more terms (ibid., p. 49).

Since what is acquired, presumably, is not just a few isolated bits of information, e.g. *this* is a dog and *that* is not, but a way of differentiating dogs from, say, cats and cows on all kinds of occasions, of being able correctly to say and understand all kinds of things about them, we can again see that these are clearly inferential processes which require people to form and check hypotheses on the basis of limited information. Simon, one of the pioneers in cognitive science, has also formulated a number of plausible learning mechanisms to explain how humans learn to solve problems they have not confronted before (Simon, 1981). To take one example, he and his co-workers have discovered a plausible mechanism to account for how students learn to solve algebra problems from the examples given in their textbooks. The mechanism is essentially one of inductive generalization based on discovering differences between successive lines of the equation in the example. Learning is here clearly itself just one species of problem solving in which a more general problem-solving strategy, means-ends reasoning, is "tuned" to a particular domain (see J. R. Anderson, 1983, for a related account).

Specific theories and hypotheses about learning are not my concern here. What I am interested in is the relation between learning and thinking as encountered in the newer cognitive psychology. Recall that within the behaviorist tradition, complex problem solving, when it was discussed at all, was assumed to be amenable to the same treatment as any other kind of behavior. If it were not the result of random trial-and-error behavior, it would have to be accounted for in terms of learning, that is of the organism's reinforcement history. In the cognitive tradition, we have almost the inverse: learning is ignored for the most part, and where psychologists do try to account for learning they do so in terms of fundamental problem-solving processes which are presumed to operate at both a conscious and an unconscious level. Both the behaviorist and the cognitive approaches to psychology have, then, tended to undermine the common-sense separability of thinking and learning. As Chipman and Segal state in their introduction to a collection of articles on thinking and learning (Segal, Chipman, and Glaser, 1985a):

> The distinction between acquiring knowledge and making flexible use of that knowledge to confront new situations is helpful, but it cannot be sharply drawn. Especially when it comes to taking steps to improve one's state of knowledge, there is a problem solving aspect to learning (p. 7).

4 Children's thinking

I mentioned earlier that the cognitive approach to learning was already taken by Piaget a long time ago. Indeed, Rumelhart and Norman's accretion and restructuring bear a strong similarity to Piaget's assimilation and accommodation, though Piaget is not tioned by them. Mandler, a contemporary American psychologist who is well aware of Piaget's work writes:

> I use the term "schema" to conform with current usage and also to evoke similarities with Bartlett's and Piaget's usage....
> Schemas are built up in the course of interaction with the environment. They are available at increasing levels of generality and abstraction[6] (Mandler, 1985, p. 36).

It is noteworthy that these words were written by one of the American heralds of the cognitive revolution in psychology. No mainstream psychologist could have uttered such words with impunity during the behavioristic hegemony. Since the study of children's thinking ought to have considerable bearing on the design of educational programs to facilitate thinking, we need to take a look at this topic. Neither Rumelhart and Norman's discussion of learning nor Simon's is focussed on children (or adults) in particular but applies to learning at any age. If learning did not vary with age, and if learning were the result of the kinds of problem solving described by those investigators, we would have to infer that children's thinking is not so different from that of adults. This seems contrary to the view of children we have come to associate with Piaget. For if there is one thing he has allegedly taught us ·it is that children's thinking *is different* from that of adults. Which view is correct or are they somehow compatible?

In fact, there is considerable controversy on this question, controversy both about what children can actually do and on how to interpret their performance (see Vuyk, 1981, vol. 2). An entire volume could easily be written about each of these matters, but I restrict myself to some remarks about the second. It need hardly be said that all are agreed that children do not have the same understanding or display the same competence as adults. Consider a couple of examples of children's performance which have been extensively studied by Piaget and other investigators: animistic thinking and inability to seriate (Carey, 1985b; Flavell, 1963; Piaget 1962; Piaget and Inhelder, 1969; Vuyk, 1981; Young, 1978).

Piaget (1962) defines childhood animism in this way:

> Since the child is unaware of the subjectivity of his thought, his intentions, his effort, etc., these internal elements are attributed to any external situation capable of corresponding to his movements and his activity, by an analogy which is immediate and not conceptual (p. 254).

So for example Piaget records a one-year-old saying, "'no, no-o' to her blocks as if to people who were opposing her wishes" (p. 250), and at 2 years old she says, "'You can hear the wind singing. How does it do it?'" At 5 years: "'Why don't stones die like insects when you put them in a box?'" (p. 251). By age 6 there were, according to Piaget, few remnants of such animism. Piaget uses the word "subjective" in the above quote. Another term, frequently used by Piaget and his disciples in this connection is "egocentric." The term denotes an epistemological rather than a moral disability, the child's tendency to perceive and understand the whole world from only one point of view, its own (Flavell, 1963; Piaget and Inhelder, 1969). Evidence of animism is also used by Piagetians to argue that the child, lacking an understanding of mechanical as contrasted with intentional causality, is at what Piaget called a "preoperational" level (see Carey, 1985b, chap. 1).

The "seriation" task provides further evidence as to whether children have reached the operational stage of thinking. Seriation "consists in arranging elements according to increasing or decreasing size" (Piaget and Inhelder, 1969). In a typical seriation task, children are given a number of rods with small differences in length and asked to arrange them in order of increasing or decreasing size. Several stages of development are observed (ibid., pp. 101–2). In the earliest stage, the child will separate the rods into groups of two or three and then order the individual rods correctly within each group but find no way of coordinating the groups into a single series. At a somewhat later stage the child will keep rearranging all the rods by "empirical groping" (ibid., p. 101) until the right one is recognized. In the most mature stage, about age 7, a systematic method is invented, "that consists in seeking first the smallest element, then the smallest of those left over, and so on" (ibid.). This stage signals a significant development in children's thinking: a given rod is understood to be both larger than the succeeding rod and smaller than the subsequent one, "which is a form of reversibility by reciprocity" (ibid., p. 102). At this time the child, upon seeing that rod A is shorter than B, that B is shorter than C, can *deduce* that A is shorter than C. This kind of performance marks the arrival of the stage of operational thought.

S. Carey (1985b) carefully studied the evolution of children's understanding of live and inanimate objects. R. Young (1978) studied children's performance on seriation tasks. Unlike some investigators, both largely agree with Piaget's descriptions of what children can or cannot do at different ages. But each parts company with Piaget on the question of whether the evidence is attributable to a defective mode of thinking compared to that of adults', or simply to a lack of understanding of the concepts employed in a particular domain.

Young's research is more fine-grained than Piaget's. Young observed a number of children of different ages performing the task and recorded the way they went about the task in great detail. He then showed that the diverse approaches of different children can be accounted for in terms of a relatively small "kit" of rules which children employ when attempting the task. Young shows that the success of older compared to younger children can be explained in terms of the addition of one or more new rules to the kit. One of Young's conclusions is this:

> Instead of classifying the children's behavior into "correct solutions" and "errors" as does so much research in experimental and developmental psychology, an information processing approach enables one to understand that there are many different ways of tackling the seriation problem, some of which will be successful (in given circumstances) and others not, but that all are to be understood in terms of the same framework. It was by no means obvious beforehand that this would be the case, for a "stage" analysis of seriation leads one to expect that children who cannot seriate may be doing something quite different from those who can. The analysis here suggests that they are merely, in a certain sense, doing less (1978, p. 385).

An experiment illustrative of Carey's approach to the investigation of children's conceptual development consists of showing children of different ages pictures of animals and inanimate objects and asking them which ones eat, breathe, etc. and why (1985b, chap. 3). The pattern of correct and incorrect answers enabled Carey to construct a model of the mental processes employed by children of various ages. Although Carey's research is in a very different tradition from Young's, her conclusions are not unlike his in blurring the differences between the capacities of older and younger children. Children certainly have different beliefs about living things at different ages. Piaget understood these differences to derive from the limitations in children's thinking that span every domain. Carey proposes another alternative:

> The changes in conceptualization of the human body ... are indeed interrelated, ... but are not constrained by limitations on the child's thinking. The restructuring we have witnessed is within the domain of understanding human activity. The increasing complexity of this understanding typifies all examples of novice-expert shifts, all examples of theory emergence, regardless of the age of the people involved (ibid., p. 71).

Carey claims that the evidence now suggests that even very young children can make deductive inferences, and do have some appreciation of mechanical causality and of the distinction between appearance and reality, two "foundational notions that underlie all theory building" (ibid., p. 194). Children's notions of causality do develop between the ages of 4 and 10 as they begin to develop an intuitive theory of biology. But, argues Carey,

> The development of explanatory frameworks that can be documented are part and parcel of theory changes—they are not domain general (ibid.).

If Rumelhart and Norman's and Simon's proposals about learning are to be useful they ought to apply to the learning of even the youngest children. But these ideas, as we saw, tie learning very closely to problem solving. Can young children solve problems? Can they think? Superficial students of Piaget (which includes most of us) sometimes attribute to him an affirmative answer to this question, sometimes a negative one. Piaget did try to describe and explain the *evolution* of thinking in the individual human, identifying clear differences in the performance of children of different ages. At the same time he clearly recognized that "systematic intelligence," that is the "invention of new means through mental combinations" usually manifests itself sometime between 12 and 18 months (Piaget, 1963, chap. 6). The conclusions of more recent investigators of cognitive development emphasize the continuity rather than the differences between the intellectual processes of older and younger children (Carey, 1985a).[7] I would say that nothing that we presently believe about children's capabilities prevents proposals about learning of the kind we have considered from applying to even the very young.

But if learning (as conceptualized by cognitive psychologists) depends on thinking, the reverse relationship is just as important. That is to say, the refinement of existing cognitive structures or schemata and the development of new ones provide the basis for development of the ability to solve more difficult problems in specific domains. Carey, in the quote above, likened children's cognitive development to the acquisition of expertise. A number of psychologists, some with a particular interest in education, have been studying just this kind of "novice-expert shift" (see e.g. Chi, Feltovich and Glaser, 1981; Glaser, 1984; Johnson, 1984; Larkin, McDermott, D. Simon and H. Simon, 1980). The domains studied have been primarily chess, algebra and physics; novice-expert differences in the solution of ill-structured problems have just begun to be investigated (Verline, 1986; Voss and Post, in press). The principal difference between novice and expert lies in the fact that the expert knows a great deal more about the domain (Larkin et al., 1980). That is hardly surprising, but the investigations do help us to go beyond this rather self-evident conclusion.

Several findings are noteworthy. (1) Experts have, not simply a larger set of factual propositions (declarative knowledge), but a much larger set of procedures along with explicit conditions for their applicability (Chi et al., 1981). (2) The expert is not merely an "unindexed compendium" of information (Larkin et al., 1980, p. 1342). Expert knowledge is indexed by a large number of patterns which guide the expert to relevant pieces of information. This inventory of patterns immediately leads the chess expert, for example, to focus her more analytic investigation on a small set of plausible alternative moves. It leads the physics expert to categorize the indefinitely large number of different problems into a smaller number of physical principles (Chi et al., 1981, pp. 149–51). (3) Novices classify physics problems in terms of the more superficial features present in the description of the problem rather than by the underlying physical laws or principles (ibid.).

In the last chapter, I suggested that there is a kind of tension in education between encouraging problem solving and facilitating the automatization of procedures so that thinking may be concentrated on ever-more difficult problems. Has the discussion of cognitive psychology helped resolve that issue? Perhaps partially. First of all, we must recognize that thinking and the acquisition of knowledge are not easily separable inasmuch as problem-solving processes underlie the most important kinds of knowledge acquisition and knowledge facilitates thinking. Perhaps more important, we see that the mere possession of a large store of information, whether declarative or procedural is not, in itself, valuable. It becomes valuable only if it can be located by an effective "index" which is in turn related to perceptible features of problem situations.

The tension is, nevertheless, not eliminated. Despite the uselessness of a mere "compendium" of information and despite the limited significance of "accretion" as one kind of learning relative to those kinds which involve transformation of cognitive structure, it remains the case that the ability to perform some operations automatically, supports the development of expertise (see Anderson, 1983; Perfetti and Lesgold, 1978). This is as true of driving a car as of reading a book with understanding, or solving a physics problem. Almost a century later, R. Sternberg (1985) only echoes William James (1923) when he writes that "complex tasks can feasibly be executed only because many of the operations involved in their performance have been automatized" (Sternberg, 1985, p. 71). Such automatization requires many hours of practice to be sure. Still, we might suggest that unless an operation is practiced in contexts where its need is apparent and where it can be integrated with other operations in problem-solving situations, the adaptiveness of the routine is put at risk even as its automatization is enhanced. But here we already enter the discussion of the pedagogical fruits of the new psychology, to which we now turn.

5 Pedagogical implications of cognitive psychology

Cognitive psychology may be, as George Mandler (1985) proposes, on its way to becoming *the* paradigm for psychology. In contrast to behaviorism, it does deal with complex thinking and problem solving and with the development of expertise in rich domains such as physics. Since, within its framework, any learning requires problem solving, the general educational implications of cognitive psychology are certain to apply to education for more effective problem solving. So far, as with behaviorism, cognitive psychology's impact on schools has been minimal, but what might it offer in the future? How important is cognitive psychology for the educator?

Before answering these questions I would like to outline the roles scientific knowledge may play in the improvement of practical pursuits. (A somewhat different account is found in Schrag, 1981, 1983). Scientific understanding enhances our practical pursuits in direct and indirect ways. The direct way, in turn, subsumes two different modes. One involves the more efficient design of means which are already in use. The second involves the invention of novel, potent means which replace traditional approaches. The new means usually exploit fundamental scientific discoveries unknown to earlier practitioners. Borrowing from Rumelhart and Norman's typology of learning, I call the first *direct tuning* and the second *direct restructuring*.

Science contributes to our practical pursuits *in*directly by altering our beliefs about the value of alternative means to given ends. It does this by certifying or discrediting specific means. An altered perception of risks and costs need not result in dramatic transformations of practice but may simply lead to the gradual withdrawal of resources in some technologies or the maintenance of others. I call this *indirect tuning*. But scientific inquiry also has the potential to *restructure* practice *indirectly*—not through the invention of powerful new means—but rather through the way its findings cause us to change our beliefs about the direction we ought to go.[8] Information about what is possible (or impossible) or about hidden costs and benefits of various approaches may spur us to reformulate our agenda. Consider an example of each mode.

Direct tuning: the use of citrus fruit to prevent scurvy was a practice that antedated the discovery of vitamins by at least a century (Shryock, 1969). Provisioning sailboats with natural sources of vitamin C was expensive, however, and the prevention of spoilage on long voyages no easy matter. Subsequent to discovery of vitamin C and its role in prevention of scurvy, it became possible to extract and purify it. It could then be easily packaged and stored for long periods without damage. The prevention of scurvy in regions (or circumstances) where natural sources of the vitamin were scarce was thereby made more reliable and less costly.

Direct restructuring: The most dramatic role scientific research can play in the practical sphere is that of providing the basis for entirely new forms of intervention. As L. Nash (1963) has written: "Science breaks for technology trails not merely new but previously inconceivable" (p. 107). The "design" of frost-resistant corn and of laser beam weapons to intercept inter-continental ballistic missiles are just two illustrations from this month's newspaper.

Indirect tuning: Organic farming without the use of chemical fertilizers or pesticides obviously was the only kind of farming available during most of human history. Recent scientific studies showing the cumulative toxicity of certain chemicals regularly ingested in minute amounts provide some scientific certification for what is otherwise often regarded as an archaic, even irrational mode of agriculture. This information has (to the regret of the adherents of organic farming) not resulted in the elimination of chemical fertilizers and pesticides in agriculture, but it certainly has helped maintain some consumer demand for organically grown produce and even caused a few farmers to convert to more "natural" methods.

Indirect restructuring: Smoking has long been implicated as a causative factor in the development of lung cancer and other illnesses. Over the last twenty years medical research has turned the indictment into a conviction. At the same time dramatic advances in the treatment of lung cancer have not been found. These combined developments have led to a realization that the scourge of lung cancer can best be reduced if not eliminated by striving for prevention rather than cure. The effort to eradicate lung cancer by medical means has been discredited. Now many have come to believe that the heaviest investment should go into educational campaigns to urge young people not to smoke. Recently (winter, 1986), the American Medical Association passed a resolution to ban cigarette advertisements.

Does current psychological investigation of problem solving certify or discredit any particular pedagogical approach? I think so. Let us briefly recall the pedagogy associated with Skinner's behaviorism. More than thirty years ago, Skinner (1982) claimed that typical classrooms violated the principles of learning in several respects: most of the conditioning was aversive while positive reinforcement was a rarity; where positive reinforcement did occur too much time elapsed between the response and the reinforcer; and there was a lack of gradual approximation to the desired complex behavior. To overcome this situation, Skinner suggested that complex responses be analyzed into simpler ones which could be shaped by progressive approximation, that reinforcement be prompt and that negative reinforcement and punishment be eliminated to the greatest extent possible. Programmed textbooks or their computer-assisted counterparts represent the purest pedagogical implementation of behavioristic psychology.

I think it is fair to say that pedagogical programs and devices based on the cognitive approach are considerably more varied than those deriving from behaviorism. Indeed, it could be argued that no specific kind of intervention is certified by the cognitive orientation. Still, I believe that within the educational context, two themes are salient. The first and most significant, the importance of facilitating, even provoking students' active encounters with challenging problems, is conveyed in the following quotation by a leading researcher in applied cognitive science:

> The purpose of education must always be twofold: to teach a variety of knowledge and to teach the skills necessary for applying that knowledge to new problems or situations. These twin goals are perhaps achieved most successfully through what is usually called the Socratic method of teaching.... The central notion is to force the student to reason for himself, to derive general principles from specific cases, and to apply the general principles that have been learned to new cases (Collins, 1977, p. 339).

This theme is echoed in recommendations drawn from a very different tradition in cognitive psychology, that of Piaget, by another applied cognitive psychologist, G. Groen (1978). Groen is careful to distinguish pedagogical approaches which are authentically Piagetian in ancestry from others which draw only superficial lessons or distort Piaget's intentions entirely. Groen identifies two fundamental pedagogical techniques which derive from Piaget's teachings.

> The first technique consists of putting a child in what might be called a free problem-solving situation. The child selects a task and is free to do anything he likes in order to accomplish it. The teacher can (and at times must) intervene, but it is absolutely critical that the child's activities remain spontaneous. There are two models for how this intervention should occur. The first is the Socratic dialogue.... The second is that of the child as an experimenter and the teacher as a research director.... There is

a very crucial analogy here between what a child does and what the scientist or mathematician does. . . .

The second technique is what might be called constructive analysis. A class of tasks and activities is selected and their cognitive demands are analyzed. The goals are to provide some kind of natural ordering of their complexity to specify the kinds of structures a child would have to possess in order to benefit from them and to describe how they can facilitate the construction of new structures (1978, pp. 293–4).

The need for active problem solving in the learning process is found in the approaches applied cognitive psychologists take to learning even so "basic" a skill as reading. A training study by A. S. Palincsar and A. L. Brown (1984) with poor seventh grade readers provides a concrete illustration. After the strategies which underlie reading comprehension had been determined, several activities were identified that would assist their development: summarizing, questioning, clarifying, and predicting. The training consisted of a teacher and student or two students taking turns as student and teacher. After each member of the pair had read the same paragraph, the "teacher" asked a question about the main idea, then summarized it, discussed and clarified any difficulties, and made a prediction about future content. These activities were carried on in as natural a dialogue as possible. The partners then changed roles. This "reciprocal teaching" strategy, is based in part on the notion (derived from the Soviet psychologist Vygotsky) that in natural learning settings,

The adult and child come to share the cognitive work, with the child taking initiative and the adult correcting and guiding when she falters. . . . Initially, the supportive other acts as the model, critic, and interrogator, leading the child to use more powerful strategies and to apply them more widely (ibid., p. 123).

Here, as with many other programs, and in contrast to some Piagetian programs, there is less emphasis on the child's unguided exploration by adults. In some cases adult intervention takes the form of simplifying the task in specific ways or in providing prompts which facilitate the student's employing certain cognitive procedures (Case, 1985; Scardamalia and Bereiter, 1985). But even when the teacher carefully designs the tasks, significant contrasts with Skinnerian approaches remain manifest.

Whereas Skinnerians certify pedagogical programs which structure the student's activity according to a very carefully laid-out path in order to *minimize* the student's need to think things out, programs inspired by the cognitive framework, even those which also prescribe a particular sequence of tasks (e.g. Case, 1985), challenge the child's problem-solving capabilities. Whereas Skinnerians do everything possible to eliminate student errors, here feedback from *in*adequate solutions is considered an *essential* element in the child's growing understanding and ability to solve problems (see Champagne, Gunstone, and Klopfer, 1985; Groen, 1978; Papert, 1980; Segal, Chipman and Glaser, 1985a, b).

A second theme in the pedagogical literature inspired by cognitive psychology relates to the issue of the organization of knowledge. Given that knowledge is essential for effective thinking and that knowledge is learnable and useable only when organized, a number of educational psychologists in the cognitive tradition attempt to devise means to help teachers organize the information they present and students to organize the information they acquire (e.g. Dansereau, 1985; Hayes-Roth, 1977; Heller and Reif, 1984; Novak and Gowin, 1984; Thorndyke, 1977). These authors provide teachers and students with techniques for representing the essential structure of what they are trying to teach or learn.

To take just a couple of examples, Novak and Gowin (1984, chap. 2) propose the use of "concept maps" which depict the logical relations among concepts in a domain; students (or teachers) can test their understanding of how the concepts introduced in a course are related to each other or to the concepts they already have by trying to draw a map which represents those relationships. Heller and Reif (1984) have designed a model of problem description in physics. The model is in the form of a detailed procedure which students can follow to "generate an explicit and detailed initial description of any mechanics problem in terms of the special concepts in this scientific domain" (p. 186).

The two themes are not at all incompatible. Champagne (1985) and her co-workers have designed instructional sequences to facilitate students' cognitive restructuring from an Aristotelian to a Galilean perspective. One group of subjects was a small group of academically talented 11-year-olds. The principal pedagogic strategy used was "ideational confrontation." Students were asked individually to explain or make predictions about typical physical situations such as the motion of a balloon as air rushes out of it. As individuals presented their analyses to the group, they began to attempt to convince others of the validity of their ideas, generating controversy. Then the teacher "demonstrated the physical situation and presented a theoretical explanation of the results, using the particular science concepts, principles, and theory which the demonstration illustrates" (Champagne et al., 1985, p. 105). Finally, the students compared their analyses to that of the teacher. Often the students as well as the teacher were involved in "hands-on" experiences. At the end of the initial segment, the teacher wrote a summary on the blackboard displaying student consensus about the relationships between the physical concepts they were working on. After each succeeding session, the students were asked how they wanted to change that summary. The final summary reflected greater precision and a closer approximation to the understanding of the physicist.

I hope the reader has a reasonably clear picture of at least some of the major kinds of pedagogical interventions which the cognitive account of learning and thinking certifies. Does the knowledge which is accruing in cognitive psychology have the potential for supporting the invention of *novel and potent* modes of pedagogic intervention? Has it already done so? This is not entirely clear, given that it would be hard to demarcate the criteria of potency and novelty with any precision. In an article discussing the implications of cognitive theory for instruction in problem solving, N. Frederiksen (1984) claims that "some of the ideas that have been proposed would be new to many educators" (p. 393). Among those he mentions are setting out to teach automatic processing and "how to deal with the limitations of working memory" (ibid.). I think Frederiksen is mistaking the novelty of the terms used by psychologists with novelty of pedagogical procedures. In fact most of elementary school drill in language and arithmetic is dedicated to the development of automatic processing. Some of the computational algorithms we learn in school are designed precisely to counteract the limitations of short-term memory. In the millenia before the development of literacy, almost all educators were concerned with the problem of retrieval from long-term memory (Ong, 1982). An eminent contemporary psychologist, Gordon Bower (1977), has analyzed the workings of a popular mnemonic device which is attributed to the ancient Greeks and was part of training in rhetoric in ancient Rome. Indeed, one of the current leaders in the design and testing of mnemonic devices for use by students, J. Levin, admits that the basic components of the memory systems used by the ancient Greeks and Romans have not changed much over the centuries (1981, p. 66).

Consider one of the specific techniques previously mentioned, Novak and Gowin's concept map. I have not seen anything exactly like it, but I think it is accurate to characterize it, not as a dramatic pedagogical innovation, but as a refinement based on a long tradition of the pedagogical use of visual aids (see Ong, 1982). Diagrams, outlines of lectures and textbooks, taxonomic charts of all kinds have frequently been used to capture conceptual relationships in visually accessible forms. The periodic table in chemistry may be thought of as an early, successful concept map which has become a permanent feature of every chemistry classroom. Indeed, many teachers, when trying to explain complicated ideas, go almost instinctively to a blackboard to try to represent them visually. I am not trying to denigrate the concept map which I find a well-thought out and potentially very useful learning and teaching aid, I am simply arguing that it does not strike one as a bolt out of the blue, nor is there yet clear evidence as to its potency.

When it comes to the teaching of thinking, whether we take Feuerstein's or de Bono's exercises or any of the others found in current programs, it would be hard to identify one that met the following test: it clearly enhances our ability to teach students to solve problems in a variety of domains, and it does so by employing novel pedagogical techniques or programs whose design is scarcely conceivable in the absence of the investigations of cognitive psychologists.

In previously published articles (1981, 1983), I argued that the failure of the human sciences to generate novel, powerful, new modes of intervention is a symptom not of the primitive level of our understanding of human nature, but rather of the *advanced* "technology" which is already native to the human species under normal conditions of enculturation. I do not want to rehearse the general argument here, but I believe that this position finds confirmation within cognitive psychology itself.

Notice how odd it would be in other spheres of intervention, in medicine or transportation say, to try to develop a technological advance by trying to understand and replicate the expertise of a man who lived 2,500 years ago. Yet this is exactly what A. Collins's (1977) project to derive a formal theory of the Socratic dialogue has been trying to achieve. Many teachers since Socrates have used versions of this approach and Collins says there is little need for teachers to verbalize these strategies, "since their application only depends on an *intuitive feel* as to how to use them. If they are taught, they are usually taught by example" (p. 340; italics mine).

Collins and many others in applied cognitive psychology believe that most humans are prodigious learners and that some are prodigious teachers. Some see their task as trying to understand such teachers' expertise in order to embody it in computer programs. This approach to the improvement of teaching would be like trying to improve medicine by carefully studying the practices of Galen or Hippocrates to capture their expertise. Of course, I do not deny that were Collins successful in embodying these strategies in a computer, this might signal a significant pedagogical advance. My point is that the pedagogical strategies derive not from investigations of the psychology of learning and thinking but from observing *natural* experts. Another leading applied cognitive psychologist, J. G. Greeno (1983) is quite explicit about what cognitive psychology might have to offer:

It is reasonable to suppose that many teachers have acquired implicit knowledge of the psychological principles that are applied in effective instruction. The goal of a psychological theory of knowledge and learning is to discover what those principles are and to formulate them explicitly. Perhaps as a result, successful teaching will occur somewhat more frequently than it does at present (p. 78).

In fact, some investigators, like Palincsar and Brown, appear to go further and argue that in "natural" settings *most* adults are prodigious *teachers*. A. Brown, J. Bransford, R. Ferrara and J. Campione, in a major survey of the literature on learning and understanding (1983) discuss a number of studies in which experimenters try to enhance students' abilities to learn. Who were the experimenters' pedagogical models?

These interactive learning experiences are intended to mimic real-life learning. Mothers ..., teachers ..., and mastercraftsmen ... all function as the supportive other, the agent of change responsible for structuring the child's environment in such a way that he will experience a judicious mix of compatible and conflicting experiences. The interrogative, regulatory role becomes internalized during the process, and the child becomes able to fulfill some of these functions for himself via self-regulation and self-interrogation (Brown et al., 1983, p. 124).

Notice again here, the attempt to understand and replicate pedagogical interventions which are believed to be part of the *intuitive* expertise of many non-professionals in everyday settings. My remarks are not intended to impugn the work of applied cognitive psychologists, nor even to deny that there are promising pedagogical approaches deriving from the cognitive perspective. They are intended to disabuse those who look to applied cognitive psychology for the kinds of revolutionary breakthroughs exemplified by the laser, synthetic materials, or *in vitro* fertilization. Behaviorism has (or at least had) a different aspiration, I believe. From its perspective our native equipment may be said to include some grasp of learning principles; nevertheless, the "expertise" of the average untutored adult (and even the non-behaviorist expert teacher), embodying in its very language a reference to antiquated mentalistic entities, is seen as a *barrier* to rather than a model for educational improvement.

But if cognitive science regards the performance of the average human with a certain degree of awe, it at the same time recognizes definite limitations in the psyche that render it unlikely that the rate of individual progress in learning and thinking can be substantially accelerated. At the conclusion of their study of expert problem solvers in physics, Larkin et al. (1980) note that the amount of knowledge experts need in any domain is demonstrably large so that even the most efficient learners can only acquire such learning with long practice extending to many years. We should not, they argue, "expect to produce the miracle of effortless learning" (ibid., p. 1342). We are accustomed to viewing the expansion of knowledge as necessarily carrying with it an expansion of power, but this need not be the case. At times our relative ignorance gives rise to dreams of mammoth power which greater understanding then dispels. The invention of antibiotic medicines elicited notions of a future disease-free environment, but more adequate understanding has revealed the futility of such a vision (see R. Dubos, 1959). Likewise, preventing aging is an ancient dream of mankind, but modern biology suggests that that too is an unrealizable aspiration (Medawar and Medawar, 1977).

No discussion of the potential of cognitive psychology to generate novel pedagogical techniques can overlook the potential of the computer. Not all designers of educational software are influenced by cognitive psychology, but one of the foremost advocates of using computers to foster the ability to think, Seymour Papert (1980), is a disciple of Piaget. Although some skepticism about the potency of Papert's LOGO to live up to its claims is clearly warranted, I don't wish to enter that debate (see Pea, Kurland, and Hawkins 1985). Nor do I wish to deny that Papert's "Mathland" or physics micro-worlds are genuine pedagogical inventions. I do want, however, to challenge the claim that Papert's inventions are dependent on Piaget.

There is a stronger and a weaker sense in which an invention may be dependent on a scientific theory. In the weaker sense, the inventor's acquaintance with the theory provides him or her with the principles on which the invention is based although these same principles could have been derived from other sources. In the stronger sense, the principles on which an invention depends could not be formulated except *via* acquaintance with that theory. I grant that Papert's pedagogy derives from Piaget's ideas about learning in the weaker sense but not in the stronger. Papert is quite explicit about what he takes from Piaget.

> I take from Jean Piaget a model of children as builders of their own intellectual structures. Children seem to be innately gifted learners, acquiring long before they go to school a vast quantity of knowledge by a process I call "Piagetian learning", or "learning without being taught" (Papert, 1980, p. 7).

Papert develops the metaphor of the child as builder, arguing that his or her success depends on the materials available in the culture. The computer can supply materials which are deficient in our culture, especially materials with which to "construct" mathematics. The computer does not present math lessons to the child; in learning how to program the computer to draw a design of his own choosing for example, the child develops an intuitive understanding of some abstract mathematical ideas.

> When a child learns to program, the process of learning is transformed. It becomes more active and self-directed. In particular, the knowledge is acquired for a recognizable personal purpose. The child does something with it. The new knowledge is a source of power and is experienced as such from the moment it begins to form in the child's mind (ibid., p. 21).

The vision of a new kind of education reflected in these and other passages has an honorable history which precedes Piaget. It is a vision central to educational theorists from Rousseau on and including especially Dewey. More than that, these ideas were educationally embodied in the Montessori schools. (Indeed, Papert's educational views are much closer to Montessori's than to Piaget's.) Speaking of the objects in the "prepared environment" of the Montessori schools, Standing (1962) notes:

> These objects are not chosen at random, or because they happen to arouse a passing interest. Each possesses as it were within it an idea to be realized—not an idea to be announced by the teacher and handed over directly from her to the child. Rather the idea is implicit in, or latent in the material itself. As the material is used, this idea becomes presented—if one might say so— materially and spread out in space (p. 238).

In pointing to these antecedents, I am neither trying to belittle Papert nor challenging the source of his views about learning. The only point I'm making is that the psychological principles which form the basis of his inventions in no sense originated with Piaget, although it is accurate to say that he provided them with scientific certification.[9]

I have so far argued that cognitive psychology does "certify" a specific view of the pedagogical task, but that it is not likely to lead to any dramatic enhancement of pedagogical prowess. We still need, therefore, to discuss its potential to "tune" existing techniques and approaches to make them either more reliable, or more efficient. I shall treat the question at a general level initially, but then address specifically some difficulties inherent in "tuning" pedagogical strategies designed to foster effective thinking.

It is certainly possible that cognitive psychology will lead to interventions which are more efficient or more reliable than "intuitive" ones.[10] The ability to generate even a small margin of improvement is not to be disdained. In a recent article, N. L. Gage (1984) showed that medical advances hailed as highly significant are often based on statistical evidence which is no stronger than that which is typically found in educational research. He cites as an example a well-known study of the impact of lowered cholesterol on the incidence of heart attacks. The treatment actually produced only 1.7 per cent difference in the rate of heart attacks (p. 90).

But Gage's analogy is somewhat misleading. To take the incidence of heart attacks in a population as a criterion is to take something that is virtually beyond criticism. Even a small percentage drop in that incidence may mean the saving of thousands of lives a year. Education has no such absolute measures. Even staying in school is no equivalent as there are alternative ways of getting a high school diploma, and we might believe that some young people would be *better* off educationally if they *left* school. The same point may be brought out by asking whether undesirable side-effects are costs worth incurring. When one's life is likely to be at stake, it would be reasonable to forego the pleasure of food high in cholesterol. But suppose for argument's sake, that some rather onerous diet were related to the number of colds a person could be expected to get in a year. A person who stuck to this diet year round would be reasonably likely to contract one less cold that winter. Would the gains be worth the costs? That is far from clear. From the fact that a given educational "treatment" makes a *particular* valued outcome more likely, we cannot conclude that that treatment has thereby been shown to be educationally sound.

An illustration is provided by the work of two cognitive psychologists who are trying to improve the writing of textbooks (Armbruster and Anderson, 1985). In a model chapter on the history of the US Constitution, Armbruster and Anderson "tried to incorporate ... some text characteristics that theory and research in reading comprehension have suggested are important in learning from written materials" (p. 248). There is no need to delve into their strategy or the product. Appended to the sample chapter are the reactions of a number of people, including a thoughtful social studies teacher, B. Walker. She recognizes that the chapter is unusually comprehensible, but argues that this has been achieved at a very high cost.

> The reader is always prepared for what information to expect from the text and how the ideas will flow. However, I do not feel that the strategies used to achieve global coherence make for good

history. Often, the writers' emphasis on structure relegates much of the historical content to the background. That is, the chapter reads like "generic" history (ibid., p. 268).

There is a dilemma in all fields of applied research. Unless the criterion is specified precisely, the relative effectiveness of the "treatment" can't be satisfactorily assessed. Too narrow a criterion of effectiveness, however, is likely to ignore important "externalities." As Dewey reminded us (1963, chap. 7), more than any other professional, the educator needs to take account of all the outcomes and all the costs of an invention, especially the long range ones. When a precisely specified criterion of educational effectiveness has been adopted, it is often easy to point to the authors' failure to demonstrate the educational importance of that criterion or to their failure to discuss how the attempt to achieve that criterion enhances or undermines the achievement of a myriad of other valuable outcomes. Much applied cognitive psychology is vulnerable to legitimate challenge, once these issues are raised. We have here an analogue to the problem of "extremely complex systems" I discussed earlier— only at the applied level.

A second problem, analogous to the problem of the laboratory mentioned earlier, plagues the attempt to "tune" existing pedagogical approaches. To demonstrate effects which are powerful, durable and transferable enough for other researchers or practitioners to take notice, training studies are generally done under conditions which favor the success of the intervention. Student groups are small, teachers are well-trained and enthusiastic about the approach, etc. The studies by Champagne et al. (1985) mentioned earlier are typical in this regard. Even when impressive results are obtained (which is far from clear in this case), one may be properly skeptical of their generalizability to normal children in normal classrooms with normal teachers, etc. Only carefully controlled studies can yield robust generalizations about the relative effectiveness of different treatments. But the conditions needed to achieve such control are usually not representative of conditions "in the wild."

It is possible for applied cognitive psychologists to surmount these problems but it is very difficult. Palincsar and Brown's (1984) study mentioned earlier is exemplary in this regard. The standards of success are clear and stringent, and most important, the "dependent variable," the ability to comprehend material from text, is of almost unassailable educational importance. Although in the first phase of the intervention, there were only six students and the experimenter was also the teacher, in the second phase, the teachers were regular teachers who worked with their normal reading groups. Even in this meticulous study, there are grounds for skepticism regarding generalizability: only four teachers were involved and they were volunteers. Although the experimenters say these teachers were initially skeptical of the approach, it is likely that teachers volunteering to participate in university-based research were somewhat distinctive, or that once having made a commitment, they showed greater than usual dedication to their work with the children.

We should not exaggerate the ease with which unequivocal results can be secured in fields like medicine and nutrition. The continuing debates about the value or danger of certain foods and chemical substances serve to remind us that controversy is no less prevalent in fields which appear superficially so much more objective (see Tracey, 1977). At the same time practicing teachers' disinclination to pick up the latest issue of *Cognition and Instruction* ought not to be attributed to their anti-intellectualism or to a failure in their training. Palincsar and Brown admit that scarcely any studies include multiple, stringent measures of success. Even if they did, teachers would have to be convinced of the educational importance of the outcomes, of the absence of deleterious side-effects, and of the applicability of the particular circumstances to their own classrooms.

I turn finally in a more specific way to the teaching of thinking. I shall not review the various programs here nor attempt to evaluate them as this has been done elsewhere (Segal, Chipman and Glaser, 1985a; Nickerson, Perkins, and Smith, 1985). But several comments are in order. Anyone who has seen the existing programs will immediately sense that they are different from texts and exercise books in other school subjects; yet I maintain there are no general thinking *skills*. What then makes these programs distinctive? I think the answer is very simple. Whether we are dealing with Feuerstein's materials, de Bono's, or any of the others, they share two characteristics: they are intellectually challenging and they depend on everyday rather than academic knowledge. The programs are designed to invite cognitive exploration and, if presented under the proper conditions, may well promote thoughtfulness.

I say "may well" rather than "do" promote thoughtfulness because the assessment of programs designed to improve thinking is extremely problematic. Since none of the programs involve highly novel pedagogical approaches, the measures used to test students need to be sensitive to modest improvements. In reviewing a number of programs to teach problem solving, Polson and Jeffries (1985) underline this need. They argue that some programs are difficult to evaluate because they lack clear statements of cognitive and behavioral objectives. Once the acquisition of "cognitive skills" is better understood, it will be possible, they claim, to "formulate clear instructional objectives and effective worked-out examples" (p. 449). Notice how the image of thinking as a set of skills leads straight down the path to the demand for clear and precise, even behavioral objectives. Here the model of thinking as skill is not only unhelpful but pernicious.

How are we to measure how well students think? Some reflective inquirers (Frederiksen, 1984; Petrie, 1985) have correctly stressed the limitations of the instruments with which we typically attempt to test students. It is not hard to show, for example, that the multiple-choice format so favored for mass testing often constitutes an impediment to serious thinking. My own linking of effective thinking with *thoughtfulness* suggests the difficulty of contriving settings to test how well people think. How thought*ful* people are is presumably independent both of what they know and of how smart they are. If we wanted to investigate how thoughtful people were, we would need some way to discover their approach to the solving of problems of various types, academic and practical, well- and ill-structured, in domains where they were expert and in those where they were not. Since context is an important determiner of the importance of a problem and hence of the kind of care which ought to be taken in solving it, I have my doubts that artificial testing situations would ever provide authentic contexts. Putting that issue aside and omitting any question of cost, it seems to me that any attempt to capture the quality of an individual's thinking would look more like a clinical interview and less like an objective test. But any such device would probably lack the validity and reliability to identify the relative impact of different educational programs.

6 Conclusion

I believe that cognitive psychology not only certifies a pedagogical approach which requires active problem solving, but that it can serve as a catalyst for reevaluating both how time is spent in schools and what functions school can and cannot serve effectively.

(1) One of the important contributions of the somewhat better understanding of cognition which we now enjoy lies, I believe, in the recognition that some of the most important "mental processing" engaged in by experts lies outside conscious awareness. I do not believe there are isolable, general strategies or skills for problem solving, but there may well be strategies for more specific tasks. Consider one which is surely of enormous educational importance, comprehending expository text. Why is this task not the focus of the work of most teachers in most schools? Perhaps for these reasons: since the requisite strategies are not consciously deployed, and seem to develop naturally in some students without explicit instruction, their absence in many children is easy to attribute to defects in the

learners. Moreover, just because of their general usefulness, these strategies do not form part of any particular subject matter and do not receive the attention of teachers except probably some reading teachers in the elementary grades. A gap in teaching the "how" of reading typically exists between about the fourth grade and college. I think we have generally believed that by the end of elementary school, children have acquired the basic tools of learning, so that the middle and secondary schools can be organized around the inculcation of subject-matter competence. If it becomes clear that the presence or absence of some learnable strategies is the key to being able to learn from books, it will be possible for the kind of strategy training explored by A. Brown and associates, by Novak and Gowin and others to move into the foreground, especially beyond the elementary school.

Cognitive psychologists recognize, as I have already mentioned several times, that problem-solving processes of enormously sophisticated kinds are involved in even "simple" things like reading for understanding, taking notes in a lecture, reviewing for a test, or writing an effective essay. Evidence from cognitive psychology can be used to support the notion that training in strategies and techniques to improve skill in reading and note-taking, in reviewing material for examinations and writing expository prose—in other words the strategies underlying effective academic performance across academic domains—needs to move from the periphery, from the remedial-reading or learning-disability classroom or writing laboratory much closer to the center of the school for all except the minority of naturally "gifted" learners.[11]

(2) In our survey of the pedagogical implications of the cognitive approach we saw the importance of intellectual challenge, of actual problem-solving experience not only for the development of problem-solving capabilities but also for the acquisition of expertise in specific domains. There is a rather glaring difference in degree and quality of student mental and physical activity and involvement in the classrooms described or envisioned in the work of Groen, Champagne et al., Palincsar and Brown, Feuerstein, de Bono, and Papert on the one hand—and in the typical classroom on the other. Some read this as a criticism of the "newer" approaches showing their lack of viability in the real world of the school. But one can read the evidence in a different way. One can see in all these works of applied cognitive psychology an *implied critique* of the conventional classroom itself.

This hard-headed empirical tradition in psychology can force us to take another look at the environments we have created for the nurture of thoughtful people. The more philosophical approach of the last chapter also stressed the centrality of the social and physical environment in the nurture of those dispositions we identify with thoughtfulness. Before examining the impact of the environment on the development of this character trait, which will be done in the next chapter, we ought to ask whether there is any empirical evidence concerning the significance of these dispositions themselves.

There is, as I intimated in the last chapter. Psychologists investigate such tendencies under the rubric of cognitive style (see Baron, Badgio and Gaskin, 1986, for one recent review). In a recent article Brodzinsky (1985) defines cognitive styles as "preferential modes or strategies of adapting in a problem-solving situation" (p. 150). According to Brodzinsky, two dimensions of "style" have been the most thoroughly investigated, field dependence-independence and reflection-impulsivity. The second is fairly self-explanatory, but the first is not. Field dependence-independence concerns the "degree to which one is connected to versus independent of referents external to oneself" (p. 151). I think it is not inappropriate to connect de Bono's efforts at loosening up perception with the development of greater field-independence.

Likewise, Feuerstein and many others aim to enhance young people's reflectiveness, "the tendency to pause and reflect upon alternative answers in problems involving moderate to high response uncertainty" (Brodzinsky, 1985, p. 152). Both field-dependence and impulsivity are at least partially independent of ability, and tend to diminish as children grow up, but most interesting and important is the suggestion made by Brodzinsky that cognitive styles are an "influential factor in the *development* of cognitive/affective structures" (ibid., p. 166; emphasis in original). What Brodzinsky is here suggesting and providing some evidence for is that young people who are more reflective and more field-independent are also more likely to develop operational thought, one of the hallmarks of cognitive maturity in the Piagetian framework.

We have, therefore, evidence relating to the developmental importance of these dispositions as well as to their independence of innate mental capacity. Since the entire physical and social environment is implicated in the development of any disposition, it is to the study of environments that we now turn our attention.

CHAPTER 3

Contexts for developing thoughtfulness

In chapter 1 I argued that it was appropriate to identify effective thinking with the virtue or character trait of thoughtfulness. I claimed that character traits are linked to habits or dispositions but that, following Lester Hunt (1978), they contain an ideational element as well, an appreciation for the value or importance of certain things. The thoughtful person avoids both impulsive and stereotyped responses because he or she is wont to do so. Thoughtfulness becomes instinctive, but it is not blind or mechanical since it derives from an appreciation of its own value. One motive for conceptualizing thinking in terms of virtue rather than skill was to focus the attention of educators on the environment within which thinking takes place.

My examination of cognitive psychology led to the same need to consider the learning environment. Contemporary studies of thinking and learning highlight the need for students' active involvement in the solution of challenging problems but, unfortunately, these studies (the majority of which are conducted by psychologists), almost universally ignore the environment in which such problem solving is to take place.[1] Learning to be thought*ful* is *not* learning to perform a particular action nor is it acquiring a method of obtaining a particular result; it is developing a "second nature" which transforms heart and mind. How is this accomplished? Socrates was, perhaps, the first to call attention to the crucial influence of the *milieu* for the development of character. In the *Republic*, Plato has him asking,

Do you really think, as people so often say, that our youth are corrupted by Sophists, or that private teachers of the art corrupt them in any degree worth speaking of? Are not the public who say these things the greatest of all Sophists? And do they not educate to perfection young and old, men and women alike, and fashion them after their own hearts? . . .

When they meet together, and the world sits down at an assembly, or in a court of law, or a theatre or camp, or in any other popular resort, and there is a great uproar, and they praise some things which are said or done, and blame other things, equally exaggerating both, shouting and clapping their hands, . . .

at such a time will not a young man's heart, as they say, leap within him? (Bk VI, 492 (Jowett trans.)).

For those who find these sentiments quaint and unscientific here is how they are expressed in more current jargon by eminent students of children's moral development:

> One would expect societal factors to have especially strong influences on children's prosocial development. First, the traditions of social, political, and religious philosophies ... pertain directly to how altruistic and egoistic social actions are regarded. Second, the way life is lived (the organization of work, community life, family structure, age and sex roles, and so on) in many respects regulates in what activities children participate, the models available to them, their goals and challenges, and the systems of rewards and punishments they experience (Radke-Yarrow, Zahn-Waxler, and Chapman, 1983, pp. 494–5).

One who wishes to understand the influence of the environment on the development of character needs to attend to society beyond the school as well as to the environment provided by the school itself. In this chapter, the primary focus is the school. After identifying the characteristics of settings which develop and reward thoughtfulness in section 1, I return to the educational context to discuss the problem of maintaining order in section 2. In 3, I examine the way in which academic tasks, designed to respond to the threat of disorder, undermine the virtue of thoughtfulness. In section 4, I describe and analyze the quality of thinking which goes on in different kinds of classrooms. In 5, I examine the extent to which the "givens" of schooling are amenable to alteration, and finally in section 6, I discuss the origin of the conventional classroom, and offer a practical proposal to create new educational settings which elicit and reward thoughtfulness.

1 Settings which promote thoughtfulness

People have virtues or character traits but as W. Knitter (1985) insightfully observes these may analogically be attributed to settings. By this he means that "activities and their settings (including communities of like-minded individuals) can be so constituted as to foster and be appropriate to the exercise of some set of virtues" (p. 12). Note here that our interest is not just in whether a setting *permits* the exercise of a virtue but on whether it fosters and is appropriate to its exercise. It is also important to recognize that when settings support particular virtues, such as thoughtfulness, then those who exhibit them often serve as models for each other and reinforce those same virtues. In "vicious" settings (that is, settings which undermine the exercise of particular virtues), it is rare for those virtues to be exercised; hence models of virtue are unavailable for others. Before discussing the ways in which conventional classrooms foster or undermine the virtue of thoughtfulness, it is worthwhile to look at the characteristics of those settings outside the school which are designed to foster or inhibit thoughtfulness.

Imagine a spectrum of settings with those designed for supporting thinking at one end and those designed to inhibit thinking at the other. Let's take an example from each end. One setting expressly designed to foster and reinforce exploration is the scientific laboratory. What are its chief characteristics?

Physically, of course, there is little uniformity in design. We might mention, however, that scientific laboratories usually contain various work stations or benches for the actual experimental work and offices or desk space for data analysis, reading, and writing up the work. There is also likely to be a conference room of some kind and a journal library as well. The number of people in a single laboratory will, of course, vary. Laboratories may have as few as two or three, as many as twenty or thirty. But the average number is probably about six (W. Hagstrom, personal communication, December 1986). The visitor to a laboratory is likely to see people engaged in various individual tasks in different parts of the laboratory. They move freely about different parts of the facility to use one or another piece of equipment, and there is frequent conversation about the work as the expertise of a colleague is called upon.

The visitor observes laboratory members engaged in individual or group experiments of varying degrees of complexity. From time to time small groups will gather to discuss problems of mutual interest, and more formal presentations of work in progress by members or visitors will be a regular part of the week's activities.

> In the laboratory sciences, there is usually a sequence of activities involving some preliminary theoretical work, detailed planning of the experiment, constructing or otherwise obtaining equipment, routine analyses of data, solving unanticipated problems, and analyzing experimental results (Hagstrom, 1965, pp. 124–5).

An experiment may take a few hours or months to plan or set up depending on the field and problem; similarly, results may be immediately detectable or may take weeks to analyze. Competition with other laboratories forces intense time pressure, but the work does not permit schedules for precisely when experiments must begin or end. The scientist often has, of course, a clear idea of the results he is seeking, but every experiment is attended by risk. Months of work may come to nothing. Such investment requires courage and persistence (see e.g. Goodfield, 1982).

We are, of course, interested not so much in the laboratory's physical structure as in its social structure. What social-structural characteristics reinforce thoughtfulness? A closer look at the laboratory would reveal that it is not without its own hierarchy with a team leader at the top, junior scientists and advanced students in the middle, and novices and laboratory technicians at the bottom. The reason this hierarchy is not so obvious is that membership is by mutual agreement rather than coercion, communication may be initiated by a person in any rank, individuals appear to come and go as they see fit, supervision of subordinates' work is barely noticeable, and while the technicians perform the more routine work, even they display high levels of skill and enjoy a modicum of discretion concerning scheduling.

Autonomy is clearly necessary for exploration to flourish and the high value the scientific community places on autonomy is reflected in the setting and the social rules which govern it. Autonomy alone, however, does not foster thoughtfulness though it permits it. To understand how the value of thoughtfulness is fostered within the scientific community, we must take a look at the social norms beyond the laboratory itself.

The deflation of stereotyped thinking is in a sense built into the enterprise itself. One may, indeed claim, with J. Ravetz (1971) that the "achievement of new results is the goal of the task of scientific research" (p. 260). A scientific report which merely repeats what someone else has shown or argued will not be published unless its purpose is the replication of a novel result. The routine application of a well-known method or procedure to a new context is of value only if it yields novel findings. The ambitious young scientist realizes that dramatic breakthroughs depend on the ability to look at phenomena from a novel point of view; the majority of investigators may, of course, resist a proposed change in perspective which threatens the validity of their own work, but ultimately the *greatest* prestige is accorded *successful* innovators (see Goodfield, 1982; Ravetz, 1971, chap. 9).

I underline "successful" to make an equally important point which relates to the reinforcement of reflectivity. Bold conjectures are not necessarily difficult to make. Ingenious ideas may even be found in the work of gifted science-fiction writers. How are these kept out of scientific publications? The system of communication in science *via* journal articles makes it unlikely that novel results will be published unless they have a fair chance of being substantiated. The gatekeeping function is performed through the system of referees. One or more experts in a given field assesses every research report submitted to a journal; if they do not deem it worthy of the journal, the editor will not publish it. In some journals the name of the referee is even attached to the published article. If shoddy work is published the referee and the editor of the journal lose credibility, though of course the author's prestige is primarily at stake. (Recently a friend of mine, an eminent scientist, told me about the difficulty he faced in refereeing an article for a prestigious journal by one of his own mentors whose work showed scant familiarity with the latest developments in the field.) The referee studies not only the author's conclusions, but the adequacy of the argument and evidence on which they are based. Failure to *establish* a conclusion in conformity with the standards of the field may jeopardize publication as much as (or more than) lack of originality (see Ravetz, 1971, chap. 10; Hagstrom, 1965, chap. 1).

This brief description of communication in science contains a feature which is so obvious that it might go unnoticed: the scientific report is the intellectual property of its author(s). (See Ravetz, op. cit., chap. 8.) The work, that is to say, issues in a product, the product is available for an audience, and that audience can identify the "makers" of the work in order to apportion praise or disapprobation. Why does this matter? Scientists' reputations may be as, or more important to them than their salary. Any shoddiness or impropriety connected with their own published results or those of associates in their laboratory will, if detected, result in a perhaps irreparable blemish to their reputations. The temptation to engage in heedless or unscrupulous conduct within a highly competitive enterprise is thus held in check.

A word about the nature of competition in science is relevant here. The often hectic race for results and prizes is by now well publicized. But for our purposes, what is important is that scientific competition is almost always between laboratories, not among the individual scientists in a laboratory where cooperation is the rule. (Of course, personal rivalries may exist within a laboratory.) In fact a prestigious award to an individual scientist will benefit that scientist's immediate associates as well. Their own prestige and access to resources are likely to rise—not fall—when one of their colleagues achieves renown.

If the scientific laboratory lies at one end of a spectrum displaying the relative valuing of thoughtfulness, we find the factory assembly line at the other end.

Assembly-line technology divides the process of production into simple, unskilled elementary tasks, and assembly-line work organization gives each operative the responsibility for one, or at most a very few, of these subdivided tasks (Blauner, 1964, pp. 97–8).

Although the pace of work is controlled by the assembly line itself, the foreman oversees the line to make sure the jobs are being done according to requirements set down by management. In addition, quality-control inspectors may examine each product or random samples of products at different stages of production to make sure that the work is being done properly. But the operative will rarely feel a personal stake in the competition between rival manufacturers for a share of the market. Although the foreman may be able to trace a defective product to a particular operator, the consumer will have no idea who contributed what to the final product.

In industrial settings, workers rarely exercise any control over their time but arrive and depart according to a predetermined schedule for beginning and stopping work, for taking breaks of specified duration at specified times, and so on, all spelled out in precise rules and regulations hammered out in the labor contract and enforced by both management and labor. In the factory setting, noise and physical distance from each other on the line may even make conversation among workers difficult.

That such a factory does not foster the virtue of thoughtfulness was apparent even to Adam Smith, one of the first theorists of the factory, who said in an oft-quoted passage:

> The man whose whole life is spent in performing a few simple operations, of which the effects are perhaps always the same, or very nearly the same, has no occasion to exert his understanding or to exercise his invention in finding out expedients for removing difficulties which never occur. He naturally loses, therefore, the habit of such exertions and generally becomes as stupid and ignorant as it is possible for a human creature to become ((1776) 1863, p. 350).

This brief survey of extreme environments designed to nurture or impede cognitive exploration is intended to highlight the salient features of settings which display the virtue of thoughtfulness: 1 a high degree of autonomy accorded the problem solver, 2 extensive collaboration with other individuals exploring the same terrain (but often fierce competition between teams), 3 norms which reward originality, 4 norms and procedures which insure that the contributors are identified and that not only the results but their derivation are evaluated. None of these is present in the factory setting. (It is interesting to note that the majority of these features or their analogues would be found in expeditions dedicated to territorial exploration (see Manning, 1960).)

Of course, it is no coincidence that the motivation of scientific workers may be characterized as largely inherent in the work itself; that of the assembly-line workers is entirely extrinsic since the work itself affords meager satisfaction. But it is not at all clear whether the production worker's lack of autonomy is inherent in modern production itself or merely in the way it is organized on the assembly line. We take this issue up in the next chapter.

Those features of settings which foster the virtues of thoughtfulness are present to *some* degree, not only in scientific laboratories but in other settings in which extensive problem solving is required for success, whether the task be designing buildings or television commercials, repairing automobiles, caring for the sick, or providing legal advice. I make no claim that scientists are more thoughtful or smarter than other people; only that the settings in which they work and the norms and social structures that regulate their work are designed to foster thoughtfulness. These contrast with settings in which the work is capable of being analyzed into explicit steps or procedures which need only be repeated. Here we find not only many factory settings but also settings where clerical work is performed with the help of modern office technology or services such as fast-food restaurants or copy shops (see Simpson, 1985, p. 429).[2]

Some of the relationships between the nature of the task and organizational structure have been formulated in a more general way by sociologists interested in organizations, such as Dornbusch and Scott (1975), Perrow (1970), Scott (1981) and Galbraith (1977). Examination of the various theories and typologies would be distracting, given our interest in schools, but I should like to introduce some fairly straightforward and useful generalizations offered by C. W. Clegg (1984) in an article which, in fact, draws together much of the previous research.

Clegg borrows Perrow's notion of technology as a "variable incorporating more or less uncertainty" (Clegg, 1984, p. 133). Uncertainty is defined (following Galbraith) as the difference between the information needed and that already at hand (ibid.). Thus high levels of uncertainty require large amounts of information processing (read thinking) while low levels do not (ibid.). The critical relationship is that between the information processing requirements of the task and the mode of social control over the worker. When these requirements are low,

> control can be achieved ... by the specification of various standards, rules and procedures. In effect the tasks can be routinized. Furthermore, under these conditions, means-ends

relationships are likely to be relatively predictable. . . . When information processing requirements are low, local control can be achieved through three complementary strategies: the specification of rules and procedures; target setting; and direct supervision. Operationally, the result is a job tightly controlled and circumscribed by management.

At the other extreme, when information processing requirements are high, jobs cannot effectively be pre-specified and routinized. When means-end relationships are uncertain . . . direct supervision is inappropriate and control can only be achieved through the monitoring and evaluation of outputs. . . . Control here is characterized by the specification of general goals (but not the means) and by the establishment of sets of norms and expectations over appropriate behaviours. In between these two extremes, medium levels of information processing are accompanied by a mode of control which delimits targets and constraints and which specifies a repertoire of available procedures and methods for achieving goals (ibid., p. 134).

It is important to understand that the greater autonomy accorded the problem solver is not the result of any special respect or prestige we accord problem solvers or of a desire to make sure they are happy in their work. It is a rational response to the nature of the tasks which require problem solving in the first place. The job simply cannot be done if the worker is not allowed a measure of flexibility in scheduling and carrying out the work. Consider the auto repair shop. The service manager can order the mechanic to work eight hours or to work on the 1982 Chevy first or to finish the job on the 1979 Ford before going on. But it is irrational to order the mechanic to repair the Ford which has just been towed in by four o'clock. Only the diagnosis will reveal how long the job will take. The process involves not just locating the problem, but seeing whether the resources needed to repair the car are available, including the tools and spare parts.

The collaboration and consultation with peers that is built into the lives of professional problem solvers, whether they wear white or blue collars, also follows from the nature of the tasks themselves. Once problems are varied and complex, it is unreasonable to expect single individuals to be in possession of all the information necessary for their solution. The sharing of knowledge and experience is therefore found in settings which differ notably in other respects: the auto repair shop, the law office, and the hospital to name three. The same complexity which invites collaboration also induces the storing of information in books, journals, manuals, etc. It is no accident that each of the establishments just mentioned usually has its own "library" which practitioners may utilize as the need arises. In most organizations, the mode of control is derived from the nature of the tasks to be performed. We have seen how a relatively loose kind of supervision is associated with tasks whose performance requires complex problem solving. The reciprocal relationship may also be influential, that is the tasks themselves may be designed for purposes of control (see Simpson, 1985). Where control is the aim, as in a prison, we would not expect to find the inmates working at tasks with high information-processing requirements. What light does this analysis throw on schools and on conventional classrooms?

2 The school and the problem of order

I shall argue that the conventional classroom is a setting in which there is an inevitable tension between an official dedication to fostering thoughtfulness on the one hand and pressure to inhibit thoughtfulness on the other. According to my view, the deficiency of the setting derives not so much from an inadequate philosophy of education or from a contempt for thinking or children as from the need to provide tasks which help maintain order. W. Doyle (1983) and I. Westbury (1973, 1978) and others have argued in a somewhat similar vein. The discussion which follows takes for granted a number of background features such as compulsory attendance and individual competition for grades. Later on, I discuss the possibility of altering some of these "givens".

That maintaining order is a problem in schools is clear to anyone who has been to school.[3] The vulnerability of the school and its classrooms to disorder is a function of several basic features of schools: (1) the students vastly outnumber the staff, (2) their attendance is coerced, (3) the physical setting is crowded, and (4) the activities to which the school is dedicated are not those which would be chosen voluntarily by many, perhaps most, of the students. As sociologist M. Metz (1978) notes,

> Classroom order is fragile. One child intent upon his own
> purposes can easily destroy the concentration of thirty-six
> others. . . . Classrooms have the peculiar quality of being intimate
> yet compulsory settings (p. 121).

The power of students to wreak havoc in the classroom should not be underestimated. Classroom ethnographies from both England and the United States have given us some graphic reminders of the fragility to which Metz alludes. Here is an episode reported by a California high school student some years ago:

After class, as soon as the bell rang, everybody jumped up. The teacher said, "Everybody sit back down! You're not leaving right now!" So Alice jumped up. She starts walking out. He say [*sic*], "Alice, go sit down!" Alice say, "Who the hell you talking to! I'm tired of school. I'm going home!" She walked to the door. He grabbed her. She looked at him. "I'm gonna count to three, and if you don't get your hands off me... No, I ain't even gonna count! Take your hands off me!" He took his hands off. He say, "We're going to the office this minute!" She say, "You going to the office by yourself unless you get somebody else to go down there with you!" And so she walked away. So she was down talking to some other girls, and he say, "Alice, would you please come!" She say, "No! And stop bugging me! Now get out of here!" I didn't see all of the argument. I just went off and left. When I passed him I said, "Man, you ain't nothing!" He looked at me. Then he say, "One of these days you gonna get yours."

(C. Werthman, 1984, p. 221)

Such episodes are not restricted to urban schools in the United States. English ethnographers report similar ones. A student reported the following to E. Rosser and R. Harré (1984):

She tried kicking me out of the classroom. I'd been mucking around. And none of my mates liked that. They just started getting mad with her and chucking blackboard rubbers, smashing up the lightbulbs and everything, and in the end she just went in to the store cupboard, crying her eyes out, and we locked her in (p. 206).

Open defiance is not randomly distributed. Incidents like the ones cited are rarely found in elementary schools among children who may not be aware that making trouble is an option, who may be more intimidated by teachers, or who may still hope to achieve rewards by conforming to the teacher's expectations. Most of the discussion which follows, therefore, focusses on middle and high school.

Even among adolescents, probably the majority would not think of treating teachers with the utter contempt displayed in the above vignettes. Perceptive observers of high schools such as Cusick (1973) and Powell, Farrar and Cohen (1985) agree that compliance is the rule rather than the exception. Many among those who find school boring or useless still go through the motions. Some comply for instrumental reasons and some for sheer interest in learning. Moreover, behavior in school will vary according to social background and gender. As Woods has argued, an entire spectrum of student responses to school exists (see Woods, 1983).

The rarity of defiance should not seduce us into believing that students are docile or impotent. Indeed, Cusick as well as Powell, Farrar and Cohen document a kind of negotiated treaty between students and staff in which perfunctory compliance is offered by the students in return for an academically undemanding regime. The principal point is that in school, as in any coercive setting, the *potential* for disorder exists, a potentiality of which teachers and school administrators are well aware. Indeed, the ability to control a class is and has always been viewed as the *sine qua non* of effective teaching as W. Waller (1984) recognized in his classic work on schoolteaching.

> [The teacher] must learn that breaches of order committed in his presence or when he is responsible constitute direct attacks upon his authority.... According to the teacher code there is no worse offence than failure to deport one's self with dignity, and the penalties exacted for the infraction of the code are severe (p. 167).

Although it is not difficult to imagine Waller's shocked reaction to the episodes of student rebelliousness cited earlier, this is not because maintaining order is no longer a primary concern of those who judge the success of teachers. In his more recent account of several high schools Cusick (1983) notes that the maintenance of classroom order is the principal concern (no pun intended) of school administrators.

> The basic requirement for teachers was not that they instruct from some agreed-upon course of study. It was not even that they instruct. It was that they be capable of maintaining some state of moderate order among the students, and the proof that they could do that was that their students were neither running about the halls nor showing up in the office (p. 56).

Granted that teachers often do not have the monopoly of power in the classroom which both reformers and radical critics sometimes seem to assume, what resources do they have at their disposal? It is only when we answer this question that we will begin to appreciate why schoolwork takes the form it typically does. Although not beyond criticism (see, e.g. Scott, 1981), a typology devised by Etzioni (1961) is still useful. Etzioni identifies three means by which superiors in organizations can secure the compliance of subordinates:

Coercive power rests on the application, or the threat of application, of physical sanctions such as infliction of pain, ... generation of frustration through restriction of movement; or controlling through force the satisfaction of needs.

Remunerative power is based on control over material resources and rewards. ...

Normative power rests on the allocation and manipulation of symbolic rewards and deprivations through ... allocation esteem and prestige symbols, administration of ritual and influence over the distribution of "acceptance" and "positive response" (p. 5).

So far as coercive power is concerned, the school staff is in an anomalous position. The law requires the attendance of students up to a minimal age, yet expulsion is the school's ultimate weapon. Detention after school is a common punishment but it cannot be enforced physically, as we saw in the episode above. In very few situations will the use of physical force be tolerated, nor would it be effective if it were tolerated.

The school has few penalties which constitute severe deprivation. A withholding of permission to participate in an extra-curricular activity such as athletics, for example, may be perceived as severe but only by students with at least some loyalty to the institution. Teachers and other staff do have some normative power over many students who can be urged to comply in return for the teacher's approval or acceptance (see Dreeben, 1973, p. 459). But this too depends on at least minimal allegiance to the claims of the institution. It is no news that such minimal allegiance is not always forthcoming. This has been well documented in both the United States and England by such observers as Cusick (1973), Willis (1977), and Werthman (1984) whom we have already cited. The following passage from Willis vividly describes the behavior of the oppositional group whom he calls the lads:

The lads specialize in a caged resentment which always stops just short of outright confrontation. Settled in class, as near a group as they can manage, there is a continuous scraping of chairs, a bad tempered "tut-tutting" at the simplest request, and a continuous fidgeting about which explores every permutation of sitting or lying on a chair. During private study, some openly show disdain by apparently going to sleep with their heads sideways down on the desk, some have their backs to the desk gazing out of the window, or even vacantly on the wall. There is an aimless air of insubordination ready with spurious justification and impossible to nail down (Willis, 1977; cited in Woods, 1983, p. 36).

Werthman documents similar behavior on the part of the California gang members he observed in high school. Here is an example:

> The time and circumstances that surround entering and leaving class also have implications for the implicit acceptance or rejection of authority. If a student consistently comes to class on time, he implicitly gives teachers ground to assume that he accepts both their authority and the legitimacy of school rules. This is why gang members frequently make it a point to arrive five minutes late to class (Werthman, 1984, p. 220).

Probably the most distinctive form of power school teachers wield is that which results from their responsibility for the allocation of report card grades to individual students at least four times a year. It is not clear whether grades are best seen as means of remuneration or as symbols of normative power or as combinations of the two. One might think that grades are like money in that high grades are instrumentally valuable for future employment and earnings. The links are indirect, however, and are by no means perceived by all students. The one reward which is probably *perceived* instrumentally is the high school diploma. It is important to realize, however, that for those students not planning to go on to college, the diploma earned with a cumulative average of D is no less valuable than one earned by virtue of A work.

Grades do have, moreover, a number of characteristics which make them quite unlike money. It is rare for someone to value $5.00 over $50.00 but it is not at all rare for a student to value a D over an A. How is this possible? As a normative symbol, any grade above failing reflects a student's willingness to comply with the demands of the institution. For disaffected students, a low grade may become a badge of honor, a symbol of one's refusal to kowtow to the teacher's demands. This is particularly true if the path to a high grade involves a display of deference to the teacher and an acknowledgment of the legitimacy of his or her authority.

Moreover, unlike wages, the value of a particular grade depends to a very large extent on the distribution of grades to *other* students. An A in a class where everyone gets As is not worth as much as an A where only 10 per cent of the class get As. Setting academic standards for allocating grades is, therefore, problematic. If the standards are too low, the more able students will not need to concentrate very hard. If the students are held to too high a standard, the less able will lose all incentive. From the point of view of maintaining order, the ideal system would be one in which the grade depended on the degree of compliance rather than on academic performance. But such a system would be considered extremely unfair by the students themselves, as we can see in the interview with one of the gang members in the California study cited earlier. The interviewer has just asked why the student doesn't change his attitude once he realizes that it is a factor in his grade.

> I wouldn't go kiss up to them motherfucking teachers for nothing! Shit! They prejudiced or they gonna hit you over the head with that fucking grade so you gonna kiss up to them? Well no! We supposed to be graded on what we know. Right? (Werthman, 1984, p. 219).

3 Schoolwork and social control

Despite the limitations of grades as incentives to compliance, once students lose interest in pleasing the teacher, once the schoolwork itself is perceived as onerous, grades remain the primary and often the only incentive students have for doing schoolwork. Students are graded for various tasks performed both in and outside the school: tests, laboratory work, homework assignments, class participation, worksheets, oral reports, to name the most popular. Given that many students are willing to work either to achieve high grades or at least to avoid failing, we can say something about the characteristics of tasks which will optimize student compliance. Consider the dimensions of frequency, difficulty and open-endedness.

(1)   If a teacher bases her entire grade on a single examination at the end of the course, there is little incentive to attend much less to comply during the bulk of the semester. The pressure will begin to build as the end of the term approaches, but a sense of urgency will probably be absent earlier. For the teacher, therefore, it is more rational to distribute tests and other graded tasks with as much frequency as her ability to evaluate them permits. Graded tasks at frequent, regular intervals insure that a poor performance at one point will not be so weighty as to jeopardize a final grade and by the same token an outstanding performance early on will not preclude the need for continued effort.

(2)   School tasks can be difficult in at least two ways: the content may require the students to go well beyond the information they have or can easily obtain; the procedures to be followed may be complex or unclear to the students (see P. Blumenfeld, J. Mergendoller, and D. Swarthout, 1986). Students and teachers both uphold the norm that it is illegitimate to grade them on what they have not

been explicitly taught. If students peceive an assignment as going beyond what they could be expected to know from the textbook and the teacher's presentation, if the procedures or the format are complex or inexplicit, that would be a legitimate reason for giving up and the teacher will be under pressure not to "count" that performance very heavily in determining the student's grade.

The tasks for which grades are given must, thus, be perceived as capable of being mastered through normal effort and perseverance. Unusual aptitude or tenacity cannot be expected. The faith that "buckling down to work" will yield an acceptable grade cannot be dispelled before the end of the semester. No teacher wants to confront a student who must come to class but is without hope of passing the course. If students feel that a decent grade is dependent primarily on their native aptitudes or intelligence, on extraordinary effort rather than on the modicum of work they are willing to undertake, the less talented and ambitious will lose their incentive to comply.

A corollary here is that it is dangerous to follow a curriculum which is too sequential, that is where success in later work is too dependent on mastery of earlier work. In such a case, a student who was either absent or slow in picking up the earlier work would be lost during the remainder of the semester. In college, such a student can drop the course or simply cut the class. In school, where neither of these options is available, the teacher would almost certainly be faced with a "discipline problem".

(3) Students in a given class, we must never forget, are in competition with each other for grades, although we need not suppose that most students are like the thirteen-year-old who told Peter Woods that, "I would rather get 49% and come top than we all get 90%" (1983, p. 98). Because of the competitive situation, it is important that students perceive the grading system to be fairly based on merit and not on irrelevant or subjective factors. As we saw, even the California gang members were concerned about the objectivity of the grading system. This implies that students be able to understand readily the *basis* of their own and other students' grades. But concern for grades goes beyond the desire to outdo one's peers. Unless students are clear about what work is expected for a passing or excellent grade, they will not know exactly how much effort to expend and how to apportion it. Students need to know when work is good enough for the teacher, not when it satisfies their own standards of excellence. When the tasks provide little intrinsic interest, this consideration is salient.

We can imagine tasks to fall on a spectrum from closed to open-endedness. Some tasks require a single response which is either correct or incorrect. True-false questions are the most obvious examples. At the other end of the spectrum lie creative writing assignments where not only is there no "single" correct answer but consensus on the relative merits of work by different students may be hard to achieve. Tasks which lie in the middle of the spectrum may require a single answer but there might be a number of better or worse ways of reaching it and judgment will need to be based on the means used. Discovery of an unknown in a science class or formulation of a proof in geometry provide examples.

The more open-ended the task, the more difficult will it be for the teacher to establish the fairness of the grade in terms acceptable to students. A recent study of four Wisconsin high schools by L. McNeil (1983) explained why social studies teachers tended to reduce all topics to "disjointed pieces of information—lists" (p. 123). The teachers were, according to McNeil "articulate in explaining their view of their job and their rationale for their instructional techniques" (ibid., p. 124).

When filled with lists, the course content appears to be rigorous and factual. It makes teachers appear knowledgeable and gives students a sense of fairness in the grading: they know they have to memorize the lists. Lists and unelaborated items reduce the uncertainty for both students and teachers. For this reason, it is clearly the dominant mode of conveying information (ibid.).

Tasks which can be graded by counting right and wrong answers are not only less time-consuming to evaluate, no trivial concern when one has perhaps over a hundred students who must be graded, but the basis of evaluation is one almost all students can understand and whose legitimacy they can accept. Not only will open-ended tasks be more difficult to grade, but it will be more difficult to spell out in advance precisely what must be done for an A or for a passing grade. Doyle (1983) recounts a typical illustration of student response in a junior high school to writing assignments.

When the teacher introduced writing tasks, the students often asked numerous questions about requirements and the nature of the final product.... Students' questions often delayed the transition from explanations to actually working on assignments and these questions continued to interrupt seatwork. These delays and interruptions produced a choppy flow of events and, in turn, threatened the management of time and activities for the teacher. To avoid management problems and to sustain working, the teacher often gave explicit prompts.... In other words the teacher reacted to immediate management demands by adjusting the requirements for academic work. This adjusting did not occur for grammar or vocabulary tasks which typically involved memory or routine algorithms. In these cases, nearly all the students could participate readily in the tasks with a minimum of instructions or delay (p. 185).

This kind of bargaining in which the teachers reduce the open-endedness or difficulty of tasks in exchange for compliance is prominent in the accounts of Woods and other observers of British classrooms as well (see Woods, 1983; Hammersley and Woods, 1984).

To review, the following kinds of school tasks undermine the teacher's ability to control the class in a context where order can rarely be taken for granted: infrequently assigned long-term tasks, tasks difficult enough to elicit doubt about students' ability to perform them, sequential tasks in which mastery of prerequisites is presupposed, and open-ended tasks in which personal judgment cannot be eliminated from assessment. *Are these not precisely the kinds of tasks which provoke the most intense thinking, the kinds of tasks one might expect scientists, attorneys, architects, budget planners (to name but a few) to be engaged in?* Is it any wonder that students' *own* perception of schoolwork is actually closer to that found on the *assembly line?* Here is H. Gannaway's (1984) summary of students' perception of schoolwork as compared to work done for wages, "jobwork".

1.   Their parents go to jobwork for a certain number of hours each day and the pupils go to school. In both cases it involves massing people together in specific places to perform common tasks.
2.   The organization of time in schools and factories is similar in some respects: "work" interspersed with shorter periods of "free" time. The "work" is usually less enjoyable than the free time.
3.   The "work" in both schools and factories involves the performance of routine activities which in both cases may be very repetitive and, in so far as it does not engage the individual's own preferred creative or recreative interests, it may be boring, especially in view of the length of time spent on it (pp. 202, 203).

4   Thinking in school

Our discussion of schoolwork (including homework) merges naturally with that of classroom activities, though the two are not synonymous inasmuch as students typically get graded for work done at home as well. Recent descriptions of classroom life, whether from the students or the observers' points of view, do nothing to allay the impression that classroom activities do little to encourage thoughtfulness. A recent visitor to "scores of English, Math, Science and Social Studies classrooms" observes "there is absent lively questioning, a sense of search, a premium on student thought" (Buttenwieser, 1985). Here he echoes J. Holt who twenty years ago saw that,

> Schools give every encouragement to *producers*, the kids whose idea is to get "right answers" by any and all means. In a system that runs on "right answers", they can hardly help it. And these schools are often very discouraging places for *thinkers* (Holt, 1965, p. 125; italics in original).

Studies of classroom activities, in fact, reveal a sriking stability. The systematic observational studies of A. Bellack et al. (1965) yielded generalizations which coincide with both earlier and more contemporary studies to a remarkable degree (see Hoetker and Ahlbrand, 1969; Cuban, 1984).

> What Bellack observed, ... was that his teachers, despite differences in the sizes, ability levels, and backgrounds of their classes, acted very much like one another. They talked between two-thirds and three-quarters of the time and their major activity was asking and reacting to questions that called for factual answers from students (Hoetker and Ahlbrand, 1969, p. 148).

About fifteen years later, researchers associated with J. Goodlad's *A Place Called School* (1983) studied over 1,000 elementary and secondary classrooms. K. Sirotnik (1983), reporting the principal findings, also found that teachers "'out-talk' students by a ratio of nearly three to one" (p. 20). Most teacher talk during the lesson, especially in middle and high school, will be exposition and explanation. Consider, then, whether the lecture fosters or impedes thoughtfulness.

All of us have been intellectually challenged in lectures we've been to, for a lecture may exhibit as well as elicit the most intricate patterns of thought. It is sometimes alleged that lectures render students intellectually passive but that is a half-truth: to grasp the steps in a sophisticated argument which is heard but not seen requires enormous attentional and intellectual resources. Understanding a lecture is a protypical sequential task. Herein lies the problem: a momentary loss of concentration may leave one lost for the remainder of the hour. Few of us have the stamina to maintain that kind of attention for long stretches. Quite aside from its duration, the problem with the lecture as a format for stimulating thinking is that each one in the class is "pulled along" at the same pace, a pace almost invariably too brisk for some and frustratingly slow for others. If a student pauses either because she is "stumbling" or because she can see a problem or objection to the presentation, she loses the train of thought. At this point, she may as well sit in the depot and wait for the next train.

I have no wish to deny the pedagogical legitimacy of the lecture. But the teacher's proclivity for lecturing *even* when he or she knows that many students are bored or lost comes not just from the desire to convey information, but from the advantage it provides from the point of view of control. A few students may close their eyes or whisper softly, but unless the teacher has lost all authority, the classroom will still maintain the *appearance* of orderly learning which is so important.

Although the lecture format is prevalent even at the high school level, most class sessions feature some degree of verbal interaction between teacher and students (see Hargreaves, Hestor, and Mellor, 1984). How can such interactions be characterized?

According to Sirotnik,

> Scanning the array of teacher-to-student interactions we find that barely 5% of the instructional time is spent on direct questioning—questioning which anticipates a specific response like "yes", "no", "Columbus", or "1492". Less than 1 percent of the time is devoted to open questions which call for more complex cognitive or affective responses (1983, p. 20).

British classrooms do not look much different. Here is a typical interchange between teacher (T) and pupil (P) recorded by M. Hammersley (1984).

T: Anybody tell me what a legend is?
P: It's a story
T: Sh; what is a legend?
P: Sir it's a story that's been told thousands and thousands of years ago and people still believe in it
T: A story that's been told thousands and thousands of years and people still believe in it. Can anyone improve on that answer?
P: Sir sir
P: Sir it's a story that's been made about something that's happened and er people—everybody knows about it (nearly everybody) sir
T: Yes. Yes Campbell?
P: Sir it's half true and half not true sir
T: It's?

P: Sir sort of made up sir, half true.
T: It's half true, yes. The actual definition, that means the meaning, of a legend is a story that is probably true but not absolutely true. Can anybody tell me a legend they know?

(p.21)

Note here how playing "Guess What the Teacher is Thinking?" as my colleague H. Kliebard calls it, discourages thoughtfulness: concern is focused on the single, correct answer which is on the teacher's mind but which may not be the most logical or intelligent response to the query. No interest is given to a, perhaps, original formulation, nor is there any interest in understanding *how* a student arrives at a particular response.

Whatever its educational limitations, the recitation does have advantages for maintaining control of the class, as Dreeben (1973) and others have recognized. The teacher's rapid fire questioning "limits pupil engagement largely to occasions created by the teacher" (p. 466). Since the teacher often calls on the student only after a question has been asked, a premium is placed on maintaining attention. But this is no discovery of contemporary sociologists of education. It has been understood by some teachers for centuries. As early as 1658 Comenius in his *Great Didactic* urged that:

> The teacher ... should give his attention first to one scholar, then to another, more particularly with the view of testing the honesty of those whom he distrusts. For example, if the scholars have to say a repetition lesson, he should call first on one pupil, then on another, first one at the top of the class and then one at the bottom, while all the rest attend. He may thus ensure that each one will be in readiness, since none can be certain that he will not be examined (1957, p. 68).

The recitation format can be contrasted with the Socratic which, as I mentioned in the last chapter, is recommended by such leading cognitive psychologists as A. Collins (1977). Here is an illustration which he, himself, provides:

T: Do you know why there is a sparse population in Tibet now?
S: Because it's a desert?
T: No.
S: No? I don't know. Oh you said it was mountainous.
T: Very mountainous.
S: So it isn't good farmland.
T: O.K. It's very tough to farm when you have mountains there. You only have the valleys to farm in, O.K. Now do you think it's very dense in Alaska?

S: No.
T: Why?
S: I would imagine because of the cold.
T: The cold climate. And why does a cold climate ... ?

(p. 349)

This excerpt from a Socratic pattern of questioning is characterized by the effort to encourage the student to draw warranted inferences about conditions needed for population density from the information he already has about where population is and is not sparse. The subject of the lesson is geography but the teacher's interest clearly goes beyond conveying information about population density to helping the student *figure out why* things are the way they are. In contrast to the recitation, the Socratic pattern is fraught with problems from the point of view of social control.

Extended questioning of one student gives the other students more opportunity to carry on their own potentially subversive activities. Additionally, it may be harder for the other students to follow the line of questioning since it goes beyond the information in the overt lesson and it is harder to judge whether answers are "correct" or not because the teacher tries to withhold the normal cues of approbation and disapprobation. Finally, the open-ended nature of some of the questions presents two dangers which the request for factual information does not: the student may just invent something silly which will distract the class from the issue, or may come up with a brilliant answer which the teacher had not, herself, anticipated. Prudence counsels the avoidance of open-ended and difficult tasks and questions. But if these are not the focus of discussion, it is difficult for the teacher to become a model of thoughtfulness which students can try to emulate.

In their recent book based on extensive observations of high schools, Powell, Farrar and Cohen write:

When speaking in class does not require complete sentences, and where the words that students speak are not grounded in a longer conversation permitting follow-up, the uses of speaking to develop, practice, or exhibit thinking are compromised.

The wholesale absence of intensity about thinking is especially noticeable when there is no relation at all between one classroom comment and the comments that follow it. ... In many classes there is a near total randomness in what is said. The mood is one of desperate chaos. Anything goes. Nothing matters, except keeping things going until the end (1985, p. 103).

W. Doyle (1985) an equally experienced classroom observer reaches virtually identical conclusions:

> In many hours of classroom observation, I have seldom seen students accomplish tasks in which they are required to struggle with meaning. Of course, they often struggle with the meaning of work: what they are supposed to do, when they have to finish, what is the answer to the fifth item, etc. But meaning is seldom at the heart of the academic tasks they work on. Grammar usually consists of selecting one of two words in parentheses that seem to sound right rather than an effort to express a thought accurately and clearly. Literature often involves memorizing the facts of a story, expressing an opinion, or learning the standard interpretation of a passage rather than groping to understand what the story or poem means. And writing frequently requires following a format to construct a text that has a specified number of adverbs and transition words rather than an occasion to communicate an idea (p. 20).

Our consideration of schoolwork and classroom activities provides some understanding of why school is the way it is. The teacher's need to maintain order in a group of young people, and the conventional system for awarding grades conspire to produce a setting in which thoughtfulness is rarely elicited or rewarded. The traditional classroom represents, in other words, the intelligent adaptation of rational actors to perceived imperatives.

A Some unconventional classrooms

But schools and classrooms are not monolithic and before exploring the rigidity of some of the background constraints which we have hitherto taken for granted, let's take a look at some school settings which do foster thoughtfulness to see what we can learn from them. Champagne's work with a small number of talented 11-year-olds in physics has already been described. Since this setting is rather atypical, let's consider another science class, a sixth grade class in Massachussetts taught by Tom Smith who describes his work to Ken Macrorie in *Twenty Teachers* (1984). To get a feel for this setting and teacher, I quote directly from his account of one part of a unit on sound and vibrations:

> One of our favorite vibrations is a pendulum. It goes back and forth at a regular pace. The first question we ask the kids is, "How could we change how fast it goes back and forth?" ... We get all kinds of hypotheses. One kid says, "I know, put a heavier weight on it." Another says, "Put a lighter weight on it".

We say, "Well, what would a heavier weight do?" Somebody says, "No, it'll make it slower because heavier weights are harder to move." And both seem reasonable don't they? We run an experiment. We keep everything the same except for altering the weights at the end. Much to everyone's surprise, it makes no difference....

"What else might change how fast it goes back and forth?" we say. "How long the string is." "O.K., we'll make it shorter and longer but leave everything else the same." And that doesn't change the frequency. We take data on that, and make graphs and charts. And we try other things—how far back you can pull it, for example. It turns out that the most interesting one is the changing of the length. Once they do that and start making charts, they make predictions.

The culmination of this sequence was that in a three-floor stairwell we built this giant pendulum seven meters long, which is like twenty-five feet. We just hung the pendulum over the stairwell. It moves incredibly slowly, takes about six or seven seconds to go back and forth once. Kids love it.... A note on the piano is 440 cycles per second, instead of 7, now has a lot more meaning for the kids. (p. 204).

Macrorie also interviewed Stanyan Vukovich, a social studies teacher in a predominantly black ghetto high school in California. In connection with his teaching of the Civil War, Vukovich organized a newspaper project. He divided the class into two newspaper staffs for an abolitionist and a pro-slavery newspaper based on actual papers which flourished prior to the Civil War. The papers are four-page, five-column publications with front-page banner headlines, and illustrations.

Behind the finished newspapers done by these students lay a great effort of discipline and planning. I chose as editors two students who were super achievers, people who were rarely absent from school. I let them know their responsibilities. They were to assign articles, editorials, commentaries, artwork, want ads, and other tasks to the other students....

The student editors had hounded their staff to meet deadlines. They saw that reporters met in editing groups to check the articles for content, shape, correctness. The editors helped me lay out the dummy sheets, write headlines, and make up the final version of the paper.

The reporters read from assigned readings or materials in the library in order to get their "stories". At the bottom of their reports they had to list the sources they had used, although these "footnotes" would not appear in the newspaper.... They agreed to revise all their articles when asked to do so by the editor or teacher. When they were finished with an article, they read it aloud to the class for responses.... They didn't simply hand it to me and get it back with corrections and a grade.

They read primary sources.... Often these documents were written in highly formal style, but I asked them to write their reports in fresh, vivid prose.... For certain articles they had to imagine what Black dialect of the period might have been. They are not experts in language but they took on different voices far in the past, which allowed them to show that most slaves were uneducated and yet not stupid (pp. 125-6).

I limit myself to these two examples but many others could be cited. I urge the reader to take a look at G. Matthews's *Dialogues with Children* (1984) or to look at some of the thought provoking activities engaged in by the children at J. Dewey's school in turn-of-the-century Chicago (K. C. Mayhew and A. C. Edwards, 1966). An initial reading of accounts such as these is likely to provoke one of three reactions: (1) "You have been arguing that school settings do not promote thoughtfulness, but here is proof that the fault does not lie with the school but rather with the teacher. The only thing lacking in most schools is teachers who have the imagination, the natural authority, the mastery of their own subjects exhibited by teachers like Vukovich and Smith." (2)"You have been telling us that teachers are afraid of students running amuck. That may well be true in a few classrooms in every school or maybe in a few entire schools, but it is certainly not the rule. Wherever you have motivated kids, who come to school prepared to learn, then you will find plenty of teachers like Vukovich and Smith ready to elicit inquiry and foster thoughtfulness." (3) "What stands out about the exemplary classrooms is the authenticity of the tasks the students were engaged in, the building of the pendulum and the publication of the newspapers. Once genuine projects as opposed to artifical schoolwork are given center-stage, everything else will look after itself."

None of these responses is unjustified, but they don't go far enough. Suppose the two teachers had unusually motivated children, can we expect all children to be so interested? Why do so many teachers face students who are unmotivated? Might it have something to do with the schools rather than the children? If authentic activities are the answer, why are they so rarely found in classrooms? Surely, the collective wisdom of teachers and curriculum designers already contains abundant ideas and plans for just such projects? Finally, why does the development of thinking depend on teachers of unusual gifts? Barring the anomalous problem or situation, does healing the sick, building homes, drawing up wills and contracts, auditing accounts, mediating management-labor disputes, writing computer programs, depend on practitioners of extraordinary skill? Why not?

B The classroom and the laboratory

Let us look more carefully at the two school settings just described. Observe, first of all, that they mirror most of the features of adult problem-solving settings of which we took the scientific laboratory to be protypical. Both the pendulum and the newspaper project would seem to require considerable autonomy on the part of the students. The projects would even seem to have to permit students to move beyond the classroom for tools, materials equipment or library resources. Since both projects require substantial coordination, we find collaboration among the participants. In the case of the newspaper, the authors and editors are publicly identified.

In projects like these, the teacher, much like the laboratory leader, "loses the position of external boss or dictator but takes on that of leader of group activities" (Dewey, 1963, p. 59). Evaluation of results is part of the process itself, rather than just something externally imposed by the teacher. Both the newspaper and the pendulum project extend over considerable time, later work depends on earlier, and we can imagine that the pace and intensity of involvement are far from constant.

Now notice how most of the features of the conventional classroom and school constitute *obstacles* to undertaking such projects *regardless* of their authenticity or attractiveness to students. The most obvious impediment is the number of students. It would be hard to organize either of these projects with 35 students. I don't know how large Vukovich's class was. Smith's was somewhere around 15. Classes at the Dewey school numbered no more than 15. The physics project described in Champagne's (1985) study enrolled 11 students. Matthews's philosophical dialogues were conducted with groups of children numbering no more than a dozen. Even the physical design of the conventional classroom with 35 individual desks laid out in parallel rows, a design which favors teacher control of the room, would also be an obvious barrier. If the desks were bolted to the floor that barrier would be virtually insuperable. But regardless of the seating arrangement, the mere number of students in the class (to say nothing of the normal teaching load of four or five such classes) is inimical to the conducting of such projects.[4]

The requirement for daily meetings of 40 to 55 minutes would also clearly be an obstacle. At times, if one were in the middle of printing the paper or building the pendulum for example, it would be both practically and psychologically undesirable to have to start and stop at a precise moment. The requirement in most schools that students stay in their classroom, or be allowed beyond its boundaries only at designated moments to travel to designated places with official passes would similarly handicap either of these projects. The requirement that every student be given a grade on his or her report card at the end of a quarter or semester would hardly favor the carrying out of these projects. Since students are working collaboratively, it would not always be clear who should get credit for what. Since they are not all performing the same tasks, it might be difficult to discover a fair and objective basis for the allocation of grades.

The closer one looks at the work of people like Vukovich, Smith, Matthews, or scores of others, the more one appreciates that these teachers succeed either by working in somewhat atypical settings where they *don't* have to cope with all the constraints impinging on the typical teacher in the typical classroom; or that they are unusually gifted individuals who manage to *transcend* the impediments imposed by the conventional setting. I am not arguing that such impediments are insuperable. The point here is that given such impediments, it takes people of *unusual talent* to overcome them. This is not true of other settings which are designed to maximize the effectiveness of able but perhaps not especially talented practitioners.

This tension between educational ideals and school organization is no discovery of mine. Nor can insightful observers, researchers or students of the last two decades receive credit for it. In fact, as on so many educational issues, Dewey saw right to the heart of the matter over eighty years ago:

> It is easy to fall into the habit of regarding the mechanics of
> school organization and administration as something
> comparatively external and indifferent to educational purposes
> and ideals.... We forget that it is precisely such things as these
> that really control the whole system, even on its distinctively
> educational side.... The reality of education is found in the
> personal and face-to-face contact of teacher and child. The
> conditions that underlie and regulate this contact dominate the
> educational situation.... Now the conditions that determine this
> personal relationship, are upon the whole, the survival of the
> period when the domination of the three R's was practically
> unquestioned. Their effectiveness lies in their adaptation to
> realizing the ends and aims of that form of education (Dewey,
> 1901, pp. 237-8).

5 How inflexible are the "givens" of schooling?

If Dewey is right about this, the possibility for promoting thought-fulness does not lie in the importation of new materials or curricula, be they Feuerstein's, de Bono's, Matthew Lipman's "Philosophy for Children" (see Lipman and Sharpe, 1978) or any other, but in the modification of education settings within the school or the develop-ment of new settings outside school. Such options may depend on the possibility of relaxing the background constraints we have so far accepted as "givens": the coerciveness of schooling, the indi-vidualistic competition for grades among groups of 20-35 young people grouped together for instruction, and the conventional tech-nologies of instruction. How fixed are these "givens"?

The relevance of the first constraint is highlighted when we con-sider the fact that exploration *is* a feature of some classrooms in which the teacher does *not* possess extraordinary pedagogical talent: the law school classroom, the high school physics or chemistry laboratory, the advanced art studio or auto shop, the seminar in college or graduate school. Note that these are for the most part voluntary settings in that most students elect to take painting or physics or auto shop, and are not forced to do so. I do not imply that students are there for the disinterested pursuit of learning. But acceptable grades are generally needed in the pursuit of admission to advanced education or desirable employment be it in an auto repair shop or a law firm.

The advanced seminar and law school class are more likely to feature the Socratic pattern of questioning and a more open-ended discussion in which intellectual challenge and response are com-monplace. The law school setting is especially interesting because the number of students is often as large or larger than the typical high school class, and although the competition between individual students may be fierce, it constitutes no barrier to Socratic ques-tioning. Students may be embarrassed or even humiliated by the law professor, but the threat of disorder is rarely present. Why? Of course the students are older, hence more mature, and better able to control their impulses. The formal and informal sanctions for disrupting other students are perceived to be very potent. Here students do—*correctly*—perceive a direct link between school performance and opportunities in the career which they have chosen. A student who disrupted a class might jeopardize not just the respect of peers but the good will of faculty and even admission to the bar. Moreover, in law school students believe that the dialogue they participate in and observe is a model for subsequent interrogations by apellate judges in their professional practice (Philips, 1982).

Advanced seminars in high school or college often feature

significant amounts of desultory discussion, yet disorder is never an issue because here again students are discussing topics in fields that they have chosen and in which they have a good deal invested. Careful observation of these settings would show that attention often wanders, some students may be reading or snoozing while others hold the floor; however, it would be considered extraordinarily bad form to manifest one's own lack of interest in such a way as to disrupt others. Most important, to engage in such tactics would be putting one's future career at risk.

Whereas some would see the compulsoriness of the school setting as the source of the possibility of disorder, others would point to individualistic competition for grades as the school's fatal flaw. Such critics would point out that the threat of disorder is to a large extent an artifact of a grading system in which one student's success can only be purchased by another's failure. If, for whatever reason, some have a much better chance of academic success from the very outset, then a group of students with a continuing history of failure is the inevitable outcome.[5] Obviously the commitment of such students to the official values of the institution will be progressively eroded and the threat of disorder will grow commensurately (see discussion in Woods, 1983, chap. 5).

These two "givens", then, coerciveness and competition for grades work together to create the threat of disorder. It is the student likely to fail *and* forced to attend school whose disaffection is especially likely to lead to trouble. It is not surprising, therefore, to find school reformers reaching the same conclusion from different ideological positions. Rosser and Harré (1984), whom I cited earlier, interpret the rebelliousness of many lower-class students primarily as an attempt to maintain their own dignity in an institution bent on demeaning them.

> Perhaps the "school" could become a community resource, where those who *seek* knowledge and skill could find it, regardless of age and official attainments. And the apprenticeships to violence, which our schools now offer as a major part of the informal curriculum, particularly to those whose physical maturity is denied by the official theory of schooling, could be eliminated from the real curriculum, by letting those who will go free (p. 210; italics in original).

Ironically, a not entirely dissimilar conclusion is reached by educational conservatives whose principal concern is the perceived lowering of standards for the academically able. Here people look to the European countries or to Japan for models. Such reformers favor raising academic standards for satisfactory work to the degree needed to provide intellectual challenge to even the strongest students. If this means that more students will voluntarily leave school or be asked to leave without having earned a diploma, so be it (see e.g. C. E. Finn, Jr., 1984).

Even though Rosser and Harré stop short of calling for the outright elimination of the school as proposed by I. Illich (1970), the likelihood of following such policies, no matter what the motivation is, is infinitesimal. Even if the school leavers were indistinguishable as a group from those who stayed, it would still be difficult to accept discharging a few million teenagers into a society which has neither employment nor alternative settings to engage them. But as a matter of fact such a policy would result in the departure not of an indistinguishable cross-section of the population but of the economically most deprived, the most recent immigrants, and those with the darkest skin. The appearance of inequity would be glaring. Even if the education many of those millions are currently receiving in school is not worth much to anyone including themselves, even if many thousands of them are actually truant every day, at least the appearance of equal opportunity is not shattered.

If compulsory schooling is in no real danger of abrogation, neither is the grading system. Individual grades may be part of the problem, but they are also, as we saw earlier, the only available teacher-controlled resource for gaining compliance. Given that students must be in school and that many, if not most, might prefer to be elsewhere, I can't see how schoolwork without grades would satisfy the teacher or the student or the student's parents. It is, therefore, not easy to see how grades could be eliminated unless the coercive aspect of schooling were eliminated as well.

Of course, it is theoretically possible for grades to be awarded on the basis of group rather than individual performance; but group rewards cannot extend very far since ultimately, at least in our society, neither students nor their parents would tolerate a school where important advantages or disadvantages were allocated to individuals on the basis of the performance of *other* students.

Yet even if compulsory schooling and grading cannot be eliminated, cannot the students' perception of compulsion be mitigated by offering greater curricular choice at the school level or by altering the design and hence the activities of the classroom in such a way as to reduce the perception of teacher domination. The expansion of curricular choice, especially at the secondary level, has probably gone as far as it can go. Almost all the recent reformers (e.g. Adler, 1982; Boyer 1983; Powell, Farrar and Cohen, 1985; Sizer, 1984) advocate a reduction in electives. The opposition to electives has a solid educational rationale, but even if it did not, it would be important to see that as a way of minimizing the perception of compulsion, the expansion of curricular offerings is self-limiting. Long before the choices are sufficiently numerous to cover the interests and predilections of the most disaffected, they will be perceived to include subjects which parents and the general public cannot help but view as frivolous at best and illegitimate at worst. And this feeling of illegitimacy will soon seep back into the classroom itself. Once the pretense of meeting *fundamental* educational needs is abandoned by the school staff, the disaffected student's perception of the school as a pointless if benign prison will only be strengthened.

Although the current mood is one of tightening the fundamental constraints, we must remember that a decade ago substantial creative energy was invested in experiments which modified the physical and social structure of the classroom in part to transform students' perceptions of the coerciveness of the institution. The provision of activity centers and work stations instead of rows of desks facing a teacher, of individual and group activities instead of teacher-centered presentation and recitation, the opening up of the physical space of the classroom, the elimination of an inflexible organization of time, the substitution of detailed feedback and criticism for grades—these were central to the "open education" movement of the 1970s (see e.g. Rathbone, 1972; Myers and Myers, 1973). Indeed, these experiments emerged largely in response to the perceived absence of meaningful learning and sustained inquiry in the conventional classroom (see Silberman, 1970). Somewhat surprisingly, there is a dearth of material relating to the demise of open education although criticisms of its underlying ideology are easy to find (see Myers, 1974).

An evaluation of the "open education" movement is not one of my purposes here, but it is worth saying a word about its deficiencies. It must be recalled that the open classroom was typically implemented for the youngest children, those who are the most distractible and impulsive. Its key defect is no mystery: since children in the open classroom are not all under the teacher's watchful eye, and since the pressure for academic learning is somewhat eased, it is comparatively easy for some children to escape engagement with academic materials, and hence fail to make the adequate gains in "basic skills" which parents and citizens expect. Myers who observed many open classrooms notes,

Every good teacher I have ever seen was working extremely hard—assisting a student with a mathematics problem as two or more other students waited for assistance, while at the same time, one or more other students fooled around in another part of the room (1974, p. 63).

L. Sussman (1984) also notes a considerable degree of malingering in the open classrooms she observed intensively. About one of them, she reports the following:

> However, the system did not work altogether smoothly. One difficulty was that about seven children—nearly a third of the class—were unable to work independently or with other children. A few could work for a while with an adult, but others seemed unable to work at all (p. 191).

Sussman also notes a much less obvious but equally unattractive liability of the fluidity and absence of teacher domination in the open classroom. The cliques and hierarchies, which dominate the playground, now assert themselves in the classroom as well. These groups which are based on non-academic criteria at best and anti-academic criteria at worst, even in the early grades, often have a detrimental influence on the conduct of academic tasks.

Open education enthusiasts were, of course, neither the first nor the only ones to advocate a less centralized, less teacher dominated form of pedagogy, with students working in groups rather than learning on their own. Researchers with no particular interest in open education have recently argued that group learning enhances academic learning while at the same time easing the management problem (e.g. Slavin, 1985; Bossert, 1979). A careful and systematic review of the entire literature on classroom grouping by Bennett (1985), however, reaches the conclusion that "the perceived advantages and the research evidence stand in marked contrast, highlighting the gap between prescription and practice" (p. 116). Why is this the case?

I. Westbury (1973) was perhaps the first to point out the need to consider both the structure of the classroom *and* the technology of teaching if one wished to be serious about transforming traditional education. Simply altering the structure will not do the job. School is after all a place where children are sent at taxpayer and (parent) expense to master certain skills, concepts, and bodies of information and unless an alternative to book, workbook, and teacher talk is available, merely "opening up" or altering the structure will be to no avail.

> If we want to execute a new programme in the schools we must develop an array of new ways and new means that are real alternatives to the tried and true method of the conventional classroom (p. 119).

Since these words were written, some serious people have seen in the microcomputer just such a promise—a technology which is inherently engaging, which elicits and rewards thoughtfulness, and which can facilitate the assimilation of the academic disciplines. The vision of an educational world dominated by computers has aroused enthusiasm, fear, animosity, and skepticism. In the last chapter I argued that Papert's LOGO and his vision of the computer as tutee rather than tutor were not dependent on cognitive psychology. But this does not mean that the vision does not have revolutionary implications for education. It is significant that Papert, perhaps the foremost apostle of the computer's role in education, makes little mention of the role of the teacher in enhancing or monitoring the student's interaction with the computer. Papert has worked to introduce computer projects into school, but his real vision is not of schools full of computers but of computers making schools obsolete.

Although not inclined to the kind of social-structural analysis of schools and classrooms which we have engaged in, Papert seems implicitly to recognize the inhospitability of the classroom setting to the new technology. L. Cuban (1986), refreshingly skeptical about the educational promise of technology, does see the classroom in much the way that I do and for that reason does not discern a glorious future for the computer in that setting. He predicts that at the elementary level, student computer use will not exceed 10 per cent of weekly instructional time, and only half that at the secondary level (p. 99). He concludes this way:

> I predict no great breakthrough in teacher use patterns at either level of schooling. The new technology, like its predecessors, will be tailored to fit the teacher's perspective and the tight contours of school and classroom settings (Cuban, 1986, p. 99).[6]

Cuban may feel that he and Papert are diametrically opposed on the issue of the educational value of computers, but they are not so far apart as he supposes. Both believe that there is an incompatibility between the technology and the setting. Where Cuban takes the setting as a given and hence gives the new technology little chance of having a profound influence, Papert, taking the educational power of the new technology as a given, believes that over the long run it will lead to the collapse of the traditional setting. Cuban (ibid., p. 74) believes that the most fundamental question is whether computers should be used in classrooms. Papert would argue that the most fundamental question is whether education requires classrooms at all.

6 Old and new settings

Papert is neither the first nor the only one who believes that school classrooms are inimical to educational encounters. I have already mentioned Illich. In a recently published book, S. Sarason (1983), a respected scholar and perceptive observer of huge numbers of classrooms, appears to have reinvented Illich's thesis (no mention of Illich appears in his book) when he writes that,

> The problem flows from the hold that custom and tradition have on our thinking, a hold that prevents us from recognizing that the axiom that education best takes place in schools may be invalid (p. 180).

It is easy, however, to fall into the trap which Dewey (1963) labels "either-or" thinking—that is, if schools are not settings which promote thoughtfulness, then let's eliminate schools. The challenge posed by the deschoolers is still useful, however, because it forces upon us one of the most fundamental educational questions: what is the *educational* rationale for the existence of schools? Dewey's answer in *Democracy and Education* (1916) is hard to improve on. The school as a "mode of association" exists for three reasons, according to Dewey. First, it exists because our civilization is too complex to be assimilated in "accidental intercourse with others" (p. 23). Civilization must be "broken up", must be simplified in order to be "assimilated in a gradual and graded way" (ibid.). Second, the environment outside the school has unworthy features, and the school establishes "a purified medium of action. . . . By selecting the best for its exclusive use, it strives to reinforce the power of this best" (p. 24). Finally, the home environment is necessarily one-sided and school provides a more balanced *milieu* which allows an individual "opportunity to escape from the limitations of the social group in which he was born and to come into living contact with a broader environment" (ibid.).

The conventional classroom which we have described in rather unflattering terms, given our concern with settings which foster thoughtfulness, should not be seen as educationally worthless. What we must understand is that the educational purposes to which the conventional classroom is suited are, as Dewey suggested, limited. What are these educational purposes? We can best discover these by trying to identify the activities for which the setting was originally designed. Only then, can we intelligently go on to discuss the creation of settings which promote thoughtfulness.

A The birth of the conventional classroom

We might suppose (I certainly did) that the school and classroom as we know it has existed, if not for ever, at least for a millenium. This is in fact not the case. The classroom that we know did not become dominant until the nineteenth century. Historians of education have, regrettably, not had much to say about the evolution of the classroom. An essay by Brother Azarias (1869) credits its invention to John Baptist de la Salle whose first pedagogical handbook describing the "simultaneous method" dates from the beginning of the eighteenth century. A couple of articles by D. Hamilton (1980, 1981) from Scotland give us a glimpse of the birth of the conventional school and classroom in the English speaking world. The following is a brief account of the evolution of the classroom based entirely on Hamilton's work.

The nineteenth century did not invent the school, we know, but the school which existed during the eighteenth century, at least in England, was different in design and in the activities it sanctioned. In the earlier period, the schoolroom was not a place for instruction at all. Students sat at their desks memorizing assigned passages from texts. Each student held a different rank in the school and was called up in turn to the teacher's desk to recite his passage to the teacher. Some of the schools had anterooms or galleries where instruction was carried on by assistant teachers with individuals or small groups of students. This "individualized instruction" was not well suited to the growing numbers of students or to the learning of writing and arithmetic. Gradually the individual students were organized and assembled into groups of similar age and proficiency and instead of a single schoolroom, a number of smaller, identical classrooms were built.

Instead of hearing students individually, the teacher might have them recite in unison. The term "simultaneous instruction" denoted this form of recital but came gradually to designate something quite different: the teacher's simultaneous command of the attention of the entire group while he or she asked questions. Since the traditional method—asking students to respond in rank order—would not suffice to maintain the attention of the entire class, a new technique evolved: students who believed they could answer would raise their hands, and the teacher would call on individuals. The teacher's job was not limited to interrogating students. He or she also presented material. The formal lecture in Latin was part of university education, but this evolved to an extemporaneous and informal presentation in the vernacular.

Now it is important to understand that these nineteenth century schools evolved as institutions of mass schooling primarily for the working classes. They were, as Dewey noted, intended to transmit the fundamental skills of reading writing and arithmetic, to provide some understanding of the world and the students' place in it, and not to reward thoughtfulness. As Hamilton (1981) notes, one of the strongest motivations underlying the institution of mass schooling was the notion that

> pupils would be more ready to accept the inequalities of society if their schooling had previously demonstrated to them the fact that such social "truths" had a "natural" origin (p. 3).

That the mass of humanity should be equipped cognitively for exploration, inquiry, and invention, was not what the founders intended; it is, therefore, scarcely surprising that the schools which evolved did not promote that goal. But the virtually universal adoption of schools with classrooms just like the ones we're familiar with, and the stability of such classrooms over time (see Cuban, 1984), give us some reason to think that this form of organization is not ill-suited to the first of Dewey's purposes. In a world in which human and financial resources were abundant, conventional schools and classrooms might be rejected even for these purposes. Ideally, perhaps, even rudimentary skill development and initial exposure to the branches of knowledge would take place in settings which put a premium on thoughtfulness, though I am not convinced of this. Both common sense and cognitive psychology suggest that drill, repetition and routinization, have their uses. What I am convinced of is that so far as the cultivation of thinkers is concerned, the conventional classroom does not provide a "purified medium of action" but on the contrary an adulterated one. That is why new settings must be devised.

B Settings for thinking

What I believe to be in the realm of possibility is this: to reduce the time young people spend in conventional classroom settings, to use these settings unashamedly for the systematic presentation of subject matter and the routine practice of particular skills and techniques— activities to which these settings lend themselves—and then to supplement them with settings explicitly designed to foster thoughtfulness. Recall the significant features of such settings: a degree of intrinsic motivation and autonomy; difficult, sequential, and open-ended tasks extending over a significant time period; the need for collaboration; a "product" which has the signature of its "makers".

What exactly do I propose? To create settings which have such features requires first carving out space and time. Long blocks of time are needed; I would suggest that to start with, one afternoon per week be designated. Depending on the project (to reintroduce a notorious educational term), space might be found in the school or in other settings. What do I mean by project? Let me list some illustrations of the kinds of things I have in mind: producing a newspaper or magazine such as Vukovich's students did; building a racing car or airplane; designing an experiment to go on the space shuttle; or writing and producing a play for Black History week; participating in a moot court debate on constitutional law; working with scientists in a research laboratory; organizing a drop-in-center or tutoring program for young children one afternoon a week; planning and carrying out a study dealing with the relative influence of parents and peers on political attitudes; conducting an oral history of the neighbourhood; designing software for simulations in the science classroom; producing a videotape or slide presentation on a local artist for elementary school children; conducting a seminar leading to the publication of a newsletter presenting different responses to a great poem or piece of music.

Most of these are projects which I have read about or come up with based on those I have read about. Some of them are carried on with great difficulty in the conventional school day; others are features of the extra curriculum. Some are bound to a single discipline; others cross disciplines. It does not matter very much if these projects are labeled history or chemistry; what matters is that they afford opportunity and reward for sustained intellectual activity.

Who could be found to lead such projects? Since I assume that the groups would have to be small (12–15), there would not be enough teachers to lead each project. Others would have to be invited to join: professionals, artists, etc. might come into the school for an afternoon and small groups of students would go to other sites to work under a pre-selected leader. The project leaders would, of course, be considered educators, but qualifications would not have to include teaching credentials.

I do not think that leading such projects is easy or that anyone could organize them without training or experience. But such projects have virtues which should not be underestimated. Since the students participate of their own free will and do not receive a grade, since the young people as well as the adult may be presumed to share an interest in the focus of the activity, the basis for what we might call the natural authority of the adult leader is more easily established. Here, unlike the conventional classroom, the setting and the activity it supports are in harmony rather than in tension with each other.

It must be understood that the purpose of such a program is not to give students "practical experience", much less to offer vocational training. It is not even to enlist their cooperation in valuable enterprises designed to foster a sense of responsibility and commitment, although such an enhanced sense of commitment might be one result. The sole purpose of the undertaking is the creation of settings which embody the virtue of thoughtfulness and which, therefore, support the development of that virtue in the young.

A program such as this is no simple undertaking. Nor is it without costs which must be honestly identified: since grades are not given for participation and since strict control of the whereabouts of each student at every moment of the afternoon would compromise the projects, some students would slip away to the pool hall or simply go home. I would hope that enough excitement would be generated in each project that this would become the part of the school week that children would prefer *not* to miss. I would hope that the creation of such settings on even one afternoon a week would create pressure to increase the amount of time given to such pursuits, further limiting the time students are involved in more routine activities. I return to this proposal in the conclusion.

My proposal may, in certain respects, be naive. But it is equally naive to suppose that by adding academic requirements, by lengthening the amount of time young people need to sit in conventional classrooms, we stimulate thoughtfulness or even promote academic achievement. Only those who are rarely in schools and who have repressed their own memories of life in that institution could believe that the virtue of thoughtfulness can be developed within the traditional structures of classrooms and schools.

As we saw, the mismatch between setting and purpose was recognized not long after the beginning of compulsory mass schooling. Although their focus has not been solely on the development of thoughtfulness, educators from Dewey and Kilpatrick down to Gibbons (1984), Newmann and Oliver (1967) and Sizer (1973), have recommended introducing more engaging, more authentic activities into the school or reducing the time spent on more conventional learning in order to free time for the kinds of activities I've just suggested outside the school. If thoughtful people have long recognized that the conventional classroom does not embody the virtue of thoughtfulness (or authenticity, to name another virtue), why have ideas like theirs and mine never really taken hold? Could it be that thoughtfulness is less highly valued than the educational evangelists would have us believe? Could it be that it is not only less valued but that the demand for thoughtful people is not as high as is popularly alleged? These questions require us to view thinking in the context of the society beyond the school. That is the subject of the next chapter.

CHAPTER 4

Thinking in society

Although the school was designed to transmit the rudimentary tools of literacy and numeracy, hardly any American educator in the hundred or so years since the realization of mass public primary and secondary schooling has embraced such limited aspirations. Nurturing the ability to think effectively has certainly been one item on the American educational agenda for some time. Responding to the famous reports of the Committees of Ten and Fifteen which were issued shortly before the turn of the century, a German educator notes

> In the face of the method of instruction in vogue in America it is particularly remarkable that all these committees consider the acquisition of mere knowledge not the aim of education, but the development of the mental powers and comprehension (Schlee, 1974, p. 969).

The dominant pedagogy to which Schlee alludes was the "text-book method" in which students memorized sections of printed texts and recited them to the teacher who corrected the student and explained the text. This method is no longer practiced but as we have documented, its contemporary substitutes are nowhere close to achieving the aims enshrined in official rhetoric concerning the purposes of education.

It has, indeed, become fairly clear to astute observers that the school is not an environment conducive to the cultivation of thoughtfulness; to the extent that teachers are successful in developing students' abilities to think effectively, it is *despite* rather than because of the setting. What accounts for the failure of educational institutions to evolve sufficiently to meet the demands of a more ambitious agenda? Is it merely a failure of imagination as S. Sarason (1983) suggests in his recent book? Does contemporary American society really need good thinkers or are the virtues associated with good thinking merely given lip service on commencement day?

These issues require us to look beyond the school to those settings which support or undermine thoughtfulness, for it is probably safe to say that it is a society's actual demand for "explorers" rather

than its public pronouncements which determine its educational
arrangements. In sections 1 and 2, I focus on the extent to which
thoughtfulness is demanded by the economy; in section 3, I examine
the cognitive requirements of democratic citizenship. Section 4 discusses television's impact on thoughtfulness. In section 5, returning
to the educational domain, I discuss the relationship of the school
to the wider social context.

1 The economy

A The labor process

Among the environments outside the school which have an impact
on the way in which our society does or does not promote thoughtfulness, the workplace is paramount.[1] The impact of the workplace
on the quality and level of intellectual functioning in society is felt
in several ways. Work, itself, may be expected to influence the
character of the workers. Most adults spend a substantial number
of their waking hours at work and R. L. Coser (1975, p. 245),
following E. Hughes, notes that people's occupational identity is
central to their conception of self. But the influence of the workplace
extends beyond the working day. The values and virtues acquired
on the job can be expected to be reflected in the ways people occupy
themselves outside work and also in the virtues they hope to instill
in their children.

In the last chapter, I quoted Adam Smith's observation that
assembly line work has a stultifying effect on the mental powers of the
worker. This is certainly a plausible hypothesis, but is it warranted?
Substantial support is, in fact, found in Melvin Kohn and Carmi
Schooler's (1983) monumental inquiry into the effects of work on
personality. Since it is the only study, so far as I know, that directly
addresses the issue of the impact of work on intellectual functioning,
I shall review some key portions.

For this study, close to 700 men were interviewed extensively, first
in 1964 and then again in 1974, about the nature of their jobs and
an elaborate coding scheme was developed to provide, among other
things, an index of "substantive complexity,"[2]

the degree to which the work, in its very substance, requires
thought and independent judgment. Substantively complex work
by its very nature requires making many decisions that must take
into account ill-defined or apparently conflicting contingencies
(Kohn and Schooler, 1983, p. 106).

Part of the total interview, which took several hours, involved administering various tests and questions to determine an index of what Kohn and Schooler call "ideational flexibility." These included psychological tests of field-dependence/independence as well as simple but challenging problems such as requiring subjects to come up with as many different pro and con arguments for some public policy as they could think of. The resulting analysis shows that, as we would expect, ideational flexibility in 1964 has a significant bearing on the complexity of the job ten years later. Over this period the men moved on to jobs more consonant with their intellectual functioning. But the reciprocal effect, although much smaller, about one fourth the size, is nevertheless, striking.

> This study adds to and helps specify the growing evidence that the structure of the environment has an important effect on cognitive development ... and that cognitive processes do not become impervious to environmental influence after adolescence or early adulthood, but continue to show "plasticity" throughout the life span. ... Our findings reinforce this conclusion by showing that ideational flexibility continues to be responsive to experience well into mid-career and probably beyond (ibid., pp. 122–3).

Moreover, Kohn and Schooler (ibid., chap. 6) show that the conditions of work do, indeed, have a marked effect on people's orientations to self and society. "Occupational self-direction" which is a combination of substantive complexity of the task mentioned previously and the extent to which the work is routinized and closely supervized has pervasive effects on personality:

> Men who are self-directed in their work are consistently more likely to become nonauthoritarian, to develop personally more responsible standards of morality, to become more trustful, more self-confident, less self-deprecatory, less fatalistic, less anxious and less conformist in their ideas (ibid., p. 142).

Kohn and Schooler offer evidence that the degree of autonomy a worker enjoys in the workplace does affect the degree to which he values self-direction in his children (chap. 7). Moreover, they were able to assess the relationship between job conditions and the intellectuality of leisure-time activities. They report a high degree of stability of leisure-time activities over the ten year period of the study.

Nonetheless, several job conditions significantly affect leisure-time intellectuality. The most notable is the substantive complexity of work (ibid., p. 225).

The empirical evidence does support our notions about the centrality of work. To what extent then, we must ask, does the economy demand and provide jobs which elicit and reward thoughtfulness? The workplace can make cognitive demands in two different ways: through the requirements of particular jobs or through the demand for participation in the planning and running of the firm. I shall deal with the first of these here, returning to the second theme only in the concluding chapter.

Students of the evolution of work make rather different assessments of the meaning of past trends for the future. One line of reasoning emphasizes the shift from physical toil to less rebarbative and more cognitive work over time (e.g. Bishop, 1983; Venn, 1964). The earlier industrial revolution is seen as making possible the gradual replacement of arduous and distasteful labor by machine. And in its current phase, computers and robots are seen as assuming the more mindless chores, permitting humans for the first time in history to perform only tasks which require thoughtfulness (see Blauner, 1964; Wirth, 1983). J. O'Toole's (1983) discussion of the evolution of office work provides an illustration of this point of view. He suggests that the introduction of new office technology will eliminate much of the "drudge" and "rote" work of the office. The secretary of the future will make use of "higher-level analytical and reasoning skills to make challenging decisions" (p. 233).

The general outlook is summarized by Bishop in this way:

> In the old days, people were the only resource available to perform the monotonous and mindless repetitive production line work. The significant advances in robotic and other production technologies have eliminated the need for people to function like well-oiled machines. Now most workers are operators, controlling sophisticated systems, using their heads instead of their hands (1983, p. 71).

Wirth (1983) argues in a similar vein that technological development, itself, requires not only a more thoughtful labor force but one that is engaged in more collaborative, open-ended kinds of tasks (see also Carnoy and Levin, 1985). According to this view, the workplace is evolving more of the features which I identified in the last chapter when describing the scientific laboratory. Wirth, following P. G. Herbst (1974; 1976) sees these developments leading to a blurring of traditional lines between management and labor and to a growing need to find alternatives to the hierarchical character of conventional work organizations.

A very different analysis derives from writers within the Marxist tradition, who build on Marx's critique of capitalism. Harry Braverman, author of *Labor and Monopoly Capital* (1974) is perhaps the most powerful contemporary exponent of a position which as its subtitle, *The Degradation of Work in the Twentieth Century* suggests, is almost diametrically opposed to that of Wirth. Braverman does not deny that technological development raises the cognitive demands of some sectors of the labor force or that machines now eliminate much human toil, but these developments, in his view, obscure the principal dynamic associated with capitalism. In the craft system which preceded capitalism, workers had control of both the conception and execution of what was produced. With the advent of capitalism, the owners of capital, needing to assure themselves of a favorable return, sought to extend control over their labor force. This prompted them progressively to remove the planning and design of the production process from the workers themselves, leaving them with the mere execution of the plans devised by others. The principal means of securing that control came from the progressive fragmentation of tasks (legitimized under the rubric of scientific management) to the point that none required more than a bare minimum of either talent or training.

> The novelty of this development during the past century lies not in the separate existence of hand and brain, conception and execution, but the rigor with which they are divided from one another, and then increasingly subdivided, so that conception is concentrated, insofar as possible, in ever more limited groups within management or closely associated with it. Thus, in the setting of antagonistic social relations, of alienated labor, hand and brain become not just separated, but divided and hostile, and the human unity of hand and brain turns into its opposite, something less than human (Braverman, 1974, p. 125).

To take just one illustration, Braverman's analysis of the history of clerical work and his depiction of current trends is significantly at odds with that of O'Toole. He documents the expansion of Tayloristic principles from the factory to the office setting and sees the introduction of office automation as hastening the *de*skilling process of office personnel. Braverman argues that,

> This conversion of the office flow into a high-speed industrial process requires the conversion of the great mass of office workers into more or less helpless attendants of that process. As an

inevitable concomitant of this, the ability of the office worker to cope with deviations from the routine, errors, special cases, etc., all of which require information and training, virtually disappears (pp. 347–8).

Investigators of past trends are not unanimous in their support of Braverman's thesis, but only a few have attempted to assemble all the evidence which bears on the issue. One of the few who has is K. Spenner (1985). Spenner adopts a notion of skill which incorporates two dimensions: "substantive complexity," the same notion which Kohn and Schooler employed, and "autonomy-control" which refers to "discretion available in a job" (p. 135). Spenner's review, which concerns the period from 1900 to the present, takes note of two distinct modes of change: compositional shifts and changes in the actual work content of jobs. The former refers to the creation or elimination of jobs of a given skill and the distribution of persons to those jobs. The direction of change in the two modes need not be consistent. Further deskilling of relatively unskilled jobs can result in the actual raising of the average skill level through a compositional shift. Spenner also assesses two quite different literatures: aggregate studies which try to average skill changes across a wide variety of occupations, and case studies which concentrate on the evolution of jobs in a single firm or industry. What does Spenner's review conclude?

Reviewing the aggregate studies for evidence of compositional shift in substantive complexity, Spenner finds "no appreciable change since 1900" (p. 140), despite the fact that some studies adduce evidence for moderate upgrading. This does not mean that upgrading and downgrading do not exist. There are indeed a few studies which document modest polarization, but there is no evidence for dramatic changes over this period and the net effect of whatever minor changes occur results in the "approximate conservation of total skill" (p. 141). The aggregate data suggests that, "Strong versions of the upgrading and downgrading positions are not consistent with available aggregate evidence" (ibid.).

Evidence from the case studies is too fragmentary to permit strong inferences, but Spenner acknowledges that evidence of downgrading is too pervasive to be merely an artifact. The evidence does not permit an estimate of the magnitude of the effect, however. Spenner hypothesizes that the compositional changes which show modest upgrading are compensated for by the downgrading of particular jobs over time.

Although his explicitly Marxist stance may arouse suspicion in some readers—and although his thesis is not confirmed by Spenner's analysis of past trends—Braverman's view does find support in sophisticated, quantitative projections of the future of the labor market. Levin and Rumberger in one summary (1983) point out that the current decade will create 88,000 jobs for computer operators, while *10 times* that many will be needed as fast-food workers and kitchen helpers. Projections of sizable percentage increases in certain high-technology occupations can be very misleading if those account for only a small per cent of the labor force. According to Levin and Rumberger's analysis, 20 occupations will generate 35 per cent of new jobs during the 1980s and of those 20 only elementary school teaching and accounting require a four-year college education. Of course, credentials required for entry are not an accurate measure of cognitive demand, but they do provide a reasonable indication. In a study of the manpower needs of high-technology manufacturing, Applebaum (1984) maintains that most of the jobs are not only not high-tech but "not even very good jobs" (p. 41). So far as wages are concerned, over 60 per cent of the jobs are in the lowest third of the income distribution, and only 28 per cent in the top third (p. 42). More recently, Bluestone and Harrison (1986) show that although the "high tech" field displays a relatively equitable distribution of wages, since 1979 the "incremental tendency toward low-wage employment is evident even here" (p. 38). Again, we cannot identify wages with cognitive demands, but it is reasonable to suppose that low-paying jobs do not require much problem solving.

Whereas O'Toole forecasts a general upgrading of jobs with a loss of jobs at the bottom of the scale, Applebaum's rigorous analysis projects expansion of *both* the best and the worst jobs at the same time with shrinking opportunity in the middle. She, like Braverman, and Bluestone and Harrison, sees a general decline in the more skilled factory jobs as "the U.S. moves toward an employment structure increasingly dominated by poorly paid jobs that are frequently sex-stereotyped and female" (p. 33). (See also Leontief 1985; 1986.)

Of course, one may recognize that the introduction of new technologies leads to a fragmentation and simplification of the labor process, without maintaining that that introduction was motivated by management's desire to wrest control from the labor force. S. Hill (1981) challenges Braverman's explanation of the motivation for deskilling. He points out that the search for profitability leads quite directly to the introduction of technology which is faster, more reliable, or which simply produces results which are unattainable without it. Yet other writers support Braverman's account of management's motivation. A recent book by H. Shaiken (1984) documents the contention that the introduction of more automatic machinery is motivated by a desire not only to reduce labor costs but to control the labor process. One illustration he cites is an advertisement for robots in *Production* magazine with this caption: "Whenever you have a production machine that is 'operator paced' you have an opportunity for improvement" (p. 172). Hill challenges Braverman on other points as well. He documents workers' sometimes successful resistance to deskilling, and he denies that the introduction of new technologies *must* reduce the complexity of work. But it is noteworthy that despite his substantial disagreement with *Labor and Monopoly Capital,* Hill believes "that Braverman is probably correct about the likely consequences of present trends in productive technique" (p. 116). His overall conclusion, like that of H. A. and T. L. Hunt (1983) in their careful analysis of the human resource implications of robotics, is not inconsistent with that of Braverman:

> Thus the "re-skilling" effect of new technological developments is likely to be very skewed: a few professional engineers and programmers will practise new and arcane skills, while the mass of people who use the artefacts of new technologies will neither need real skill nor have the opportunity to learn those skills involved in the performance of cognitive-planning functions (Hill, 1981, p. 118).

Even if Braverman's deskilling hypothesis cannot be maintained in its strongest form, his extension of the Marxian tradition in the analysis of the labor process is important because it underlines the contention that the evolution of the labor market is dependent not simply on scientific or technological advance *per se,* but on the politico-economic structure or what Marxians call the "social formation" within which it occurs. Braverman is, it should be noted, no apologist for the Soviet Union. In fact, he notes that Tayloristic principles were embraced by Lenin and applied to Soviet industry. We might, in fact, suppose that the divorce of conception from execution in Soviet industry proceeded precisely because of the failure of the proletariat to assume control of the labor process despite their nominal ownership of the means of production after the 1917 Revolution (Braverman, 1974, see pp. 11–24).

Despite the limitations of his analysis, a reading of Braverman forces us to raise a question alternative viewpoints do not: how should a society dedicated to the widest distribution of thoughtfulness in its population organize its economic structure? I return to this issue in the concluding chapter.

Braverman's focus is on the "degradation" of *labor* and his contention is that such degradation has and will continue to occur within a society organized on capitalist lines. But a judgment of the character traits which are nourished or undermined within capitalism as a social formation must consider two additional roles, those of the capitalist and the consumer. Here we see a quite different pattern emerge from the one described by Braverman.

B   Other roles in capitalist society

If the complexity of work is declining, as some authors contend, that is in large measure due to the introduction of machinery which replaces human musclepower and now, increasingly, brainpower. The design and construction of this machinery depends on the ingenuity of an enormous number of inventors. The development of new processes, techniques and materials is reflected in the thousands of new patents taken out every month. But innovation is not limited to the technical side of production. New approaches to recruiting, training and compensating personnel, to accounting, to capitalization, to marketing—all these contribute to the dynamism associated with capitalism. Braverman reminds us of the considerable human costs associated with that dynamic, but he ignores the other side of the ledger completely.

If we strip the word "creative" of any moral connotations, it is not inaccurate to say that the capitalist dynamic is the result of the creative problem solving of large numbers of individuals. Luck may account for the discerning of occasional opportunities which just fall into a person's lap, but most of the innovations I am referring to are the products of months or years of sustained problem solving activity on the part of individuals or groups. And for each successful innovation which finds its way to market there are a dozen others which fall by the wayside. Consider the number of new incorporations in a given year. In 1984 there were 635,000 (Statistical Abstract of the United States–1986, p. 521). Assuming that each one involved several individuals, and assuming that many new businesses are not incorporated, it is fair to say that several million people were involved in the complex problem solving connected with establishing business enterprises.

Two issues of *Newsweek* which happen to lie on my table (March 24 and April 14, 1986) contain accounts of relatively recent successes. The first one describes Wall Street investors who instead of dealing through brokers, use their personal computers and telephone hookups to keep abreast of market activity and execute transactions. This is made possible in part by the development of inexpensive software which allows investors to call up and analyze data pertinent to their investments. The second story describes the way in which the cosmetics industry has succeeded in marketing skin care and other beauty products to men. My point is that these innovations did not magically appear but were the result of substantial problem-solving

activity by small groups of people who were able to discern opportunities to make money where none had previously existed.
These new products would not rank particularly high on most
people's list of contributions to society. Indeed, the second may be
thought to represent precisely the creation of meretricious needs
which Marxian critics find inherent in capitalism. I could just as well
have mentioned the introduction of a host of new devices designed
to improve the quality of life of the physically handicapped described
in another recent article. My point is to call attention to the way in
which what I. Kirzner (1985) calls "entrepreneurial alertness" is
stimulated within a capitalist social formation. The entrepreneur's
discovery and exploration of opportunity for financial gain typically
requires problem solving of the highest order. Socialist countries
under centralist planning do not provide an environment in which
such activity is rewarded. This needs partial qualification for, as
Burawoy and Lukacs (1985) argue, innovation may not be the rule
within the capitalist firm nor is it absent from firms under centralized
planning. But the entrepreneurial alertness they find in the Hungarian
firm they studied is an alertness to the discovery of novel means of
meeting mandated targets for already specified products, not for the
invention of new products to meet existing needs, much less the
design of products to stimulate needs which don't already exist.

Finally, we must consider the stimulus to thoughtfulness derived
from the consumer role in an advanced capitalist society. Markets
exist in even the simplest societies and a certain amount of planning
and calculation are required in order to feed and clothe a family.
Primitive food storage methods are likely to preclude the need to
make many trade-offs between present and future needs, however,
and many staples will have to be purchased daily or weekly. In a less
developed society, a careful purchaser will no doubt inspect the
provisions before buying and may bargain with the vendor, but no
very complex problems are presented. To the extent that competing
products are not available under state socialism, there will also be
limited stimulus to comparison shopping with its attendant cognitive
demands.

A flourishing capitalist economy may be said to provide the same
complexity and conflicting demands which support thoughtfulness
in other areas of life. Most consumers have access to competing
brands and competing stores for most of the products they buy. A
plethora of products of all kinds in all price ranges forces the consumer to think in terms of trade-offs between present and future
satisfaction. In a fascinating article comparing the cognitive character of market and political participation, R. Lane (1983) cites studies
showing that major purchases of cars, appliances or homes may be
totally absorbing for days and months, and that conversation about

purchases occupies substantial amounts of time. As many have remarked, what used to be relatively simple tasks like selecting a telephone service or health insurer or financing a major purchase, if done conscientiously, now demand a level of sophistication and expertise that can overwhelm highly educated people.

Although advertisements in the media may appeal to motives which have nothing to do with the actual merits of the product, in most cases competing products make similar appeals. The net effect may well be to stimulate the consumer to discriminate between relevant and irrelevant claims. Again my point is not to extol the virtues of a consumer oriented capitalist society. I mean to point out only that the way in which manufacturers compete for market shares impels them to expose, some would say bombard, consumers with the kinds of conflicting signals which stimulate cognition. Where choices are few or clearcut, problems are much simpler to solve. Critics of capitalism may denounce the cognitive paths down which consumers are dragged, but they cannot deny that capital's need to insure high consumer demand poses problems which every consumer must solve for him or herself.

While the consumer role is not an optional one, the amount of money one has to spend certainly influences the degree of participation. Many poor people never have to face the problem of what kind of life insurance to buy. Still, we must acknowledge the fact that even the welfare recipient must make decisions about how to spend his or her monthly check and this necessarily involves consideration of trade-offs between personal and family needs, and between immediate and future satisfactions.

In attempting to present a more balanced picture of the impact of economic participation in capitalist society on thoughtfulness than the one found in Braverman and other Marxians, we must, of course, not forget the general point nicely phrased by Hill (1981) that except for workers in skilled trades, the great majority of manual workers "use less manual and intellectual skill in their jobs than they do in driving their cars to work" (p. 119).[3]

2 The polity

The nature of the polity also sets cognitive demands upon its citizens. A democratic citizenry is expected to participate at least to the extent of going to the polls to select its representatives to the governing bodies at national, state and local levels. But higher levels of participation are often considered desirable: working for the nomination of candidates, writing letters in support or opposition to particular measures before the legislature, and so forth (see Schrag, 1975).

Opportunities for political participation exist throughout society of course, at the workplace, the church, the business club or charitable organization, but I limit myself here to the activities connected to membership in the polity. To get a feel for the cognitive demands of taking positions on controversial policies, let us take a brief look at a recent dispute in the Wisconsin state legislature, a measure to raise the drinking age from 19 to 21.

In the wake of an enormous toll of highway deaths among teenagers, deaths in which alcohol is almost always a factor, it might seem that aside from the interests of tavern owners and beer manufacturers—strong lobbies in Wisconsin—the decision is reasonably clearcut. This is not the case at all. Among the main arguments made for retaining the lower age are these: (1) that since the state lowered the age of majority and permits 19-year-olds to marry and raise families, to join the military with all its attendant risks, it is inconsistent to withhold from them the right to purchase and consume alcohol; (2) that teenagers will drink regardless of the law, and that since enforcement of the higher age is impossible, this will lead to reducing respect for law itself; (3) that alcoholism is a serious problem in our society and altering the legal drinking age is not an effective way to deal with it, but simply scapegoats younger drinkers; (4) that raising the age will not reduce drinking or drinking and driving and hence will not reduce the number of highway deaths and injuries due to alcohol intoxication.

To reach a rationally satisfying position on such an issue invites some subtle reasoning concerning the function of law, the meaning of majority status, the conflict between justice and utility, to name a few. A serious effort to reach a conclusion would have to involve weighing the likely effect of raising the age upon accident rates. On this issue, as on so many others, experts divide. The choice of relevant data, their interpretation, and the ability to project that interpretation into the future are all problematic. The point I'm trying to make here is that for a disinterested (not *un*interested) citizen of good will to come to a decision over what appears to be a relatively straightforward issue, one in which the choice is neither momentous nor dependent on really arcane, technical information is no easy matter. The cognitive demands are extremely high.

Now it may be thought that the average citizen is not expected to be a legislator but merely to select one among the slate of nominees who will represent his or her interests in the legislature. But what is the candidate to be judged on if not his or her position on various issues before the citizenry? Of course, party affiliation, endorsements, slogans and 30-second "spots" on radio or television tell something about a candidate's general ideology: whether the candidate is "tough on crime," favors spending for social programs, believes religion should be more (or less) central in American life, believes that "big business is being taxed and regulated to death," believes affirmative action programs need to be strengthened, and so on. And one gets a sense of candidates' eloquence, mastery of information and global personal qualities as one watches them debate on television or reads about the campaign in the press.

But are such judgments which may eventuate in pulling this or that lever every two years tantamount to democratic citizenship? Very few would answer affirmatively. B. Barber (1984), a strong advocate of participatory politics goes so far as to claim that representation "is incompatible with freedom because it delegates and thus alienates political will at the cost of genuine self-government and autonomy" (p. 145). Some may find this too strong, but I think most will agree that when citizens fail to have a grasp of the actual consequences of particular measures before the body politic, when they attend only to the general postures or to the symbolic meaning of the utterances and actions of their representatives, then government by the people becomes little more than a sham.[4]

But the cognitive demands of effective democratic participation are not static. In what direction do they evolve? I shall argue that the very scientific advances which account for a stable if not a falling level of cognitive complexity at the workplace augment the cognitive requirements for effective political participation. In a recent article entitled, "Scientific Illiteracy and Democratic Theory," K. Prewitt (1983) asks:

> What is to be the foundation of intelligent citizen participation in a society increasingly directed by scientific and technical processes often beyond the comprehension of any save the experts? (p. 51)

The theme is not a new one. It was eloquently addressed by Dewey over fifty years ago in *The Public and its Problems* (1946). Dewey's formulation of the issue is still illuminating. How does Dewey define the public?

> The public consists of all those who are affected by the indirect consequences of transactions to such an extent that it is deemed necessary to have those consequences systematically cared for (pp. 15–16).

Now the problem arises because what Dewey calls the "machine age"

has so enormously expanded, multiplied, intensified and
complicated the scope of the indirect consequences ... that the
public cannot identify and distinguish itself (ibid., p. 126).

But if this was evident to Dewey in the 1920s, it is evident to anyone
who reads a newspaper today. The possibility of a few people inciting
a conflagration in which we would all perish did not, after all, exist
in the 1920s. But alongside the augmentation of obviously destructive
powers, there are other, more insidious ways in which the transactions of a few can wreak havoc among many. One need only think
of the myriad ways in which resources may be plundered or delicate
ecological balances upset. For example, there is the question of
whether Wisconsin should be considered as a possible dump for
nuclear waste which preserves its pernicious capabilities for 10,000
years. Here the relevant "public" can *never* even identify itself since
it includes generations yet unborn.

Even when the public is beginning to identify itself, as is the case
with those threatened by nuclear obliteration, the means of averting
such an eventuality are not necessarily brought closer to realization.
That this is not simply a matter of expertise can be seen in the fact
that the experts themselves disagree about what steps to take. If the
question of whether to raise the drinking age is not easily resolved,
the question of how to reduce the risk of nuclear war is immeasurably
more complex.

Not long ago, voters in many states (myself included) supported
a referendum calling on the US and the Soviet Union mutually to
cease the testing of nuclear weapons. But I daresay for most of us
on both sides of this issue, it presented itself largely in symbolic
terms. Whether an agreement with the Soviets to end testing would,
in fact, reduce the risk of nuclear war is far from certain. Why? For
one thing there is the question of whether such an agreement is
verifiable. Experts speak on both sides of the question. Given that
verification can never be foolproof, there is the question of whether
the Soviets (or we) could be trusted to live up to a test ban treaty.
Have existing treaties been violated, and if so by whom? Here experts
also disagree. Then there is the issue of whether a halt at this point
would handicap the United States at a moment when the Soviets
have the "lead" in nuclear weaponry. There is no consensus here
either. Would testing permit the development of much more accurate
weapons, weapons which would *not* have to threaten population
centers to be effective deterrents?

Behind these particular questions, lie large, interrelated issues:
what is the nature of the Soviet regime? What larger, foreign policy
objectives should the United States be guided by? What, if anything,
is special about nuclear arms? Is it, for example, moral to deter

attack by threatening to destroy the innocent? What is the role of the military at the end of the twentieth century and how does one assess relative military strength? What is the meaning of morality in the relationships between nations? The test ban issue is not unlike the drinking age issue in hinging on some subtle and abstract moral issues. But it is unlike that issue in two respects: the decision *is* a momentous one, that is the fate of entire nations could rest on it, and its rational resolution is impossible in the absence of substantial technical expertise.

Both the policy issues I've mentioned are clear cases of what in chapter 1 I referred to as ill-structured problems, that is to say problems in which there are no definite criteria for testing the adequacy of a solution. The nuclear issue cannot be adequately decided by someone who does not have a fairly sophisticated grasp of the technical arguments. But I want to insist that such problems are vexing not simply because one may lack the expertise to deal with them, but because there is no single body of information which can be referred to to resolve them. The experts, themselves, disagree both about what may seem to the layman to be fairly straightforward matters of fact, and about the weight to be put on these facts when considering policy. There may even be disagreement on what factors need to be considered in deciding on a nuclear test ban; for example, is the balance of conventional forces in Europe relevant to this particular issue?

It may be that the American electorate is, itself, becoming aware of the growing complexity of the issues. This increasing sophistication might appear to be inconsistent with the low voter turnout characteristic of recent elections, but a more fine-grained analysis of abstention is needed. Voter "apathy" may be a misleading label to characterize this phenomenon. People, even the most thoughtful, may decide not to go to the polls for (among others) the following reasons: (1) they know exactly which party and which candidate ought to be elected but realize that the desired outcome is not going to occur. This is the plight of the minority in a democracy. (Conversely, they know their candidate will prevail whether they go to the polls or not.) Staying home on election day is arguably a rational response in either case. (2) They do not feel that either of the major parties represents their point of view or reflects their concerns. (It is fair to suppose that such concerns are not very widespread or it would be in the interests of one of the parties to address them.) Here refusing to vote may be a way of sending a message to both major parties that one does not number oneself among their constituencies. (3) They don't clearly see where their own or the polity's interests truly lie. Perhaps a growing number of voters face a situation like that vividly described by Barber (1984):

The long-time family man living on Mulberry Street in New York whose grandfather came from Bologna and who is a shop steward in the sheet-metal workers' union is a portrait in pieces.... As a union man he votes Democratic, but as an insecure blue-collar worker he leans toward moral-majority Republicanism. As a city-dweller he understands the problems of teen-age pregnancy, but as a Catholic he abhors abortion. As a wage-earner he shares the goals of the hard-working Hispanics and blacks at his workplace, but as an ethnic white he fears their inroads into his community and their disruptive impact on his neighborhood. As a father and husband he wants *his* women to act like traditional women, but as a shop steward he is sensitive to his female coworkers' complaints about sex discrimination and sexual harassment on the job. As a taxpayer he resents the mammoth social-security deductions taken off his paycheck, but as a twenty-five year man and potential retiree he feels deeply anxious about the possible bankruptcy of the Social Security Administration (p. 208; italics in original).

A recent empirical analysis of comparative political participation is at least consistent with the suggestion that Barber's portrait is not a mere caricature. G. B. Powell, Jr (1986) tried systematically to analyze and explain voter turnout in the United States compared to other industrial democracies. He shows that so far as interest and involvement in politics are concerned, the United States compares favorably with most other nations. For example nearly 90 per cent of the American public reports discussing politics at least some of the time (p. 19). Yet voter turnout hovered around 55 per cent during the 1970s (p. 23). One reason, according to Powell, revolves around the linkages between political parties and social groups.

For example in Sweden in 1964, 84 per cent of those with manual occupations supported the Social Democrats or the Communists, more than twice the percentage of white-collar workers. This suggests that, given the assumption that voters support their own interests, the choice of whom to vote for required very little thinking in Sweden. Presumably, all manual workers have the same interests or at least believe that they do. In the United States by contrast, in the same year, "the manual labor support for the Democrats exceeded white-collar support by only about 17 per cent" (p. 22). On a measure of the strength of the links between social group (occupation, religion) and party affiliation, the United States came out at the bottom of the list. Do these findings reflect indifference or laziness on the part of 45 per cent of the electorate or a growing awareness of the complexity of the issues facing it? We cannot be sure, but we certainly should not blithely assume that a more thoughtful citizenry should necessarily be expected to vote in greater numbers.

A situation may stimulate thought without rewarding it. To complete our assessment of the relative impact of the polity and the economy on our propensity to be thoughtful, we need to say something more about the reward structure of the two settings. One of the useful features of both the consumer's and the entrepreneur's market is that feedback is relatively prompt and unequivocal. People who select a car for foolish reasons, e.g. the advertisements portray owners as successful with the opposite sex, may find themselves with neither the promised romance nor reliable transportation. Inventors with a new idea for a product, or salespersons with ingenious marketing schemes, may find out before too long whether or not their schemes took all the relevant variables into account. Of course, there is always luck, and even when the message is clear, people may be unable or refuse to face it.

But with politics, it is difficult to say that thoughtfulness really pays off. The choices open to thoughtful citizens on election day are the same as those open to the lazy or the capricious. A well-informed citizen who develops positions on a variety of issues, still must choose between two candidates, neither of whom may agree with him on more than a few issues. Most adults now realize that neither the promises of glory nor the prophecies of doom one hears prior to election day bear much relationship to what actually happens after the election is over. The trail of cause and effect is so difficult to follow that even those who seek information on whether their choice of mayor or governor or president was warranted are hard put to connect the current state of affairs to the political decisions of those in office. On the national level, our system of checks and balances makes tracing accountability more difficult than it is in parliamentary democracies where executive and legislative branches must belong to the same party. When, as has happened not infrequently, Republicans and Democrats each control one branch of government, both parties attempt to take credit for successes and each blames the other for failure.

Moreover, the impact of uncontrollable events on the outcomes of an administration's policies far outweigh the role of "luck" in the economic sphere. A local jurisdiction is subject to the powerful impact of decisions emanating from the statehouse and from Washington, decisions over which it has no control. And an election or assassination in another country, a drought, the discovery of new oil or mineral reserves—events over which the national government may have no control—can have a decisive effect on the outcomes of decisions taken at home. In short, feedback from political participation is scantier and harder to evaluate than feedback from market participation. Finally, there is the simple fact of size. As R. Dahl (1982) notes, "so slight is the effect of a single vote among a million or more others that in a large electorate it is questionable whether even the simple act of voting could be justified as a rational action by the individual voter" (pp. 12–13). No wonder a call to duty rather than self-interest is required to bring many of us out to the polls on election day.[5]

Robert Lane concludes his comparison of the cognitive demands of market and political participation by asking whether the skills learned in the marketplace transfer to the political sector and facilitate the acquisition of the skills and habits of democratic citizenship. Or, on the other hand,

> Does the more concrete ordinary learning of the consumer impede the more abstract learning required of the (somewhat idealized) citizen? Viewed globally and historically, perhaps market cognition can be said to do both and, perhaps sequentially. The market helped to make us more intelligent, but not intelligent enough for true democratic politics in a complex age (Lane, 1983, p. 480).

Must we assume that the ground rules of participation are fixed for ever? Might there be some reforms in the polity, itself, which would contribute to nurturing a more thoughtful citizenry? I again defer specific proposals to the concluding chapter.

3 The impact of television

According to Lane about 1 per cent of the citizenry engage in some citizen activity on an average day while about 35 per cent shop (1983, p. 457). The vast majority of adults spend some time during the average day at work. Of the rest of the available waking time, we can be assured that more is taken up with television than any other pastime. According to N. Postman (1985), "sleeping is the only activity that occupies more of an American teenager's time than television viewing" (p. 189). It is accordingly worthwhile to try to say something about the effect of the medium on thoughtfulness. This is a highly controversial topic in which hard evidence is scarce, yet we should not shirk discussing it since a prominent count in the indictment against television is that it subverts thoughtfulness.

Postman, one of the medium's strongest critics, argues that television "sets *its* curriculum in direct opposition to what educators have always construed as *theirs*" (ibid., italics in original). What does he mean by this? Postman identifies four characteristics which distinguish television from the school curriculum, the primary one being the fact that television is based on pictorial rather than linguistic representations. Because it is pictorial it is, according to Postman, mostly nonpropositional—by which he means that television does not make assertions which are true or false, which can be agreed or disagreed with. Third, television watching neither requires nor nurtures any skills.

> For viewers there can be no standard of excellence or competence or even improvement. The consequences of such an education should be clear. It is enough to say that it mocks the ideas of deferred gratification, self-discipline, and intellectual achievement (p. 191).

Fourth, television is primarily entertaining. The content depends totally on its ability to capture the viewer's attention. "What television teaches is not merely that learning is fun, which quite often it is not, but that learning and entertainment are indistinguishable from each other" (p. 192). Finally, television is fragmented and discontinuous. There is no coherence to what is presented. In his summary argument for the prosecution, Postman asserts,

> The teachings of television are hostile to language and language development, to vigorous intellectual activity, to both science and history, to social order, and in a general way to conceptualization. Television is a curriculum that stresses instancy not constancy, discontinuity not coherence, immediate not deferred gratification, emotional not intellectual response. These are values of television, the rules according to which it conducts its conversation (ibid., p. 193).

Anyone who has watched people, especially young people, sitting mesmerized for hours in front of their television set knows that Postman's accusation is not without foundation (see also Winn, 1977). Yet the indictment is, I think, excessive. I suspect that Postman is comparing the worst of television to the best educational settings. Recall the extent to which many critics, to say nothing of the students themselves, perceive the school's academic program to be incoherent. Ironically, the case is sometimes made against television that it is *too* coherent. Its image of the world is alleged to be dominated by liberalism or conservatism, by the bourgeoisie, by white males, etc. (see e.g. Fiske and Hartley, 1978; Gitlin, 1983).

Critics like Postman constantly and justifiably bemoan the passivity of the viewer, but recall that the same count is prominent in the indictment against the public schools. It is true that most television is not intellectually demanding though not quite as true as Postman thinks. Even among programs designed for mass entertainment, there is an occasional *Hill Street Blues* which requires a considerable amount of cognitive activity to understand what is going on and what it means, perhaps as much as reading many newspapers and magazines. Gitlin notes (1983, p. 274) that during its first season, *Hill Street*'s ratings were low in part because viewers had trouble following the story line. According to Fiske and Hartley, in sports programming the viewer typically "is invited to share the high status role of judge, and in this, to involve his real and culturally valued faculties of discrimination and assessment" (1978, p. 146). More to the point, anyone who has watched some of the recent science programming such as the *Nova* series or *The Ascent of Man*, some of the public affairs programming such as a series on the US Constitution in 1986, or some of the fine dramas, all on public television, will realize that the medium *per se* need not subvert educational values and can in fact serve some of them in a distinctive way.

A large part of Postman's indictment properly refers therefore, not to the medium itself, but to its commercial form in our society. In Britain, according to Fiske and Hartley, the medium has not eroded literate forms of perception to the same degree:

> Since most of the people who control television institutions are deeply committed to literate modes of perception, there is a systematic intervention on their part into its performances which exercises a limiting and transforming influence on its potential output (Fiske and Hartley, 1978, p. 125).

Postman asserts that television asserts no propositions. This must also be qualified. Consider news and public affairs programming, for example, which contains not merely imagery but rather speech against a background of images. The participants typically do make assertions, offer explanations, even arguments. It is not unusual for network programming such as *Nightline* or *MacNeil-Lehrer* to include interviews with analysts who hold sharply divergent views.

But in so far as it is visual, Postman would argue, television can tell us nothing. "Pictures do not make assertions about the world, as language does" (1985, p. 190). But don't maps make assertions which can be tested? Postman's claim that television makes no assertions about the world is contradicted on virtually the next page where, as we have already seen, he states that television "teaches ... that learning and entertainment are indistinguishable." Is this not an assertion? In fact what alarms Postman and fascinates every television critic are precisely the assertions which television does make about our world, assertions made in a medium which combines images with music and talk. Here is an example of such an assertion from T. Gitlin:

> The sumptuous and brightly lit settings of most series amount to advertisements for a consumption-centered version of the good life, and this doesn't even take into consideration the incessant commercials, which convey the idea that human aspirations for liberty, pleasure, accomplishment, and status can be fulfilled in the realm of consumption (1983, p. 269).

It is true that this assertion is not made in propositional form, but it invites corroboration or refutation just as surely as if it had been. It is also true that the assertion is not explicit, but that is equally true of the assertions in literary works. The implicit, indeed concealed nature of such assertions is one reason why it is as difficult to "read" television as to read novels.

Postman appears to believe that assertions, by virtue of appearing in print, stimulate thought, but if most people believe the propositions prime-time television makes about American society, I see no reason to think they become inquiring skeptics as soon as they pick up their local paper.

Fiske and Hartley, while recognizing the distinctiveness of the television medium are more judicious in their criticism of its content. In a comparison of television and newspaper reports of a particular story from Northern Ireland, they claim that the television account was fuller than that which appeared in all but one newspaper the following day.

Recall the point which has run through our analyses of the environment beyond the school: the importance of complexity in stimulating thought. The central issue, it seems to me, is whether television "reality" is monolithic, or whether the signals we receive are sufficiently discordant to stimulate thought. It is foolish to exaggerate the frequency with which dissenting views are portrayed, though we must not forget that some radical documentaries, plays and films have appeared, especially on the public channel. Occasionally a network program like *Roots*, *Saturday Night Live* or *Hill Street* which challenges the view of the world favored by most TV entertainment, gains entry into prime-time, even success. One of *Hill Street*'s writers, Steven Bochco told Gitlin,

> I think people sit at home, and they want to be entertained, they want to laugh, and when it's all done they want to feel that all is right with the world. Even though somewhere back there they know that's not really true. That's a very attractive notion that they would like to see reinforced. We don't do that. We don't

solve problems, by and large. We're constantly dramatizing the frustrations and limits of power (Gitlin, 1983, pp. 306–7).

Fiske and Hartley note that as the medium becomes more self-confident it becomes more self-critical. This is seen, for example, in the satirical advertisements on *Saturday Night Live*. Most of the time television does not challenge. It can't be expected to, as Gitlin and so many others have noted, because its main purpose is still to attract the largest number of viewers in order to sell products.

So the networks do just what they set out to do. They are not trying to stimulate us to thought, or inspire us to belief, or remind us of what it is to be human and live on the earth in the twentieth century; what they are trying to do is to "hook" us (Gitlin, 1983, p. 324).

It is important to distinguish between the medium as such and the uses to which it is put by the networks. In attacking television, it is also important not to overlook the occasional dissonances it introduces or to exaggerate the effectiveness of alternative media. Romance novels are after all not noted for *their* capacity to stimulate thought. If I reject the more extreme thesis of Postman, as I did that of Braverman, I do think that a weaker form of his thesis is undoubtedly right. I argued that even if the workplace doesn't positively undermine thoughtfulness it certainly does nothing to elicit it for the vast majority of people. The same may be said for the bulk of television fare beamed into our homes day and night.

Although some of us may look to television as an escape from the high cognitive demands of the workplace, Kohn and Schooler, in the study I have already referred to, found that the general tendency is for the intellectuality of leisure activities to reflect rather than compensate for those at the workplace. It remains true for the majority of us, that the two contexts in which we spend most of our waking hours, the workplace and the television den, do not provide the nutrients which would help make us a more thoughtful people.

The reason is fundamentally the same in both cases: the erosion of human virtues and talents which results from hour upon hour of exposure to dull tasks and dull programs—that loss appears nowhere on the balance sheet upon which decisions are made by the "captains" of industry, including of course the television industry. Indeed, those who allowed such costs to influence their decisions would probably find themselves out of business before too long. These costs are missing not only from the businessperson's balance sheet but from the economist's as well. Critiquing the economist's conception of work, T. Scitovsky argues:

Work can be pleasant or unpleasant, and its pleasures, comforts, and discomforts play an important role in our lives. Those effects of work are completely missing from the economist's numerical index of economic welfare: the net national income or net national product is *not* net of the disutility of the labor that went into producing it.... The reason is simple. Work which produces market goods may be an economic activity, but the satisfaction the worker himself gets out of his work is not an economic good because it does not go through the market and its value is not measurable (1976, p. 90; italics in original).

A related point is made by A. Clayre in his stimulating *Work and Play*:

To increase one's pay, or even marginally to shorten one's hours, may in fact be no compensation for the replacement of a satisfying or absorbing job by a less interesting one; for the leisure in which the new pay is spent, or to which the further minutes are added, may be made difficult to spend enjoyably by the persistence into it of habits, routines and levels of interest set at work by the less absorbing and satisfying job (1974, p. 174).

But do not network television programming and other cultural commodities accurately reflect the preferences and desires of consumers? Scitovsky rejects this mainstream economics dogma for two reasons: first, consumers can only choose from what is available, and the need to reach vast audiences leads to standardization which would not otherwise be necessary. Eccentric preferences are not reflected in what the mass market produces. Second, although economists take tastes as givens, people are not born with their tastes for television programs; rather their tastes are developed through constant exposure to standardized products. Thus people tend to demand what the market tends to produce.

While Scitovsky is not concerned with thoughtfulness *per se*, he is concerned with an overevaluation of comfort and an underappreciation of stimulation and challenge which he finds pervasive in American culture. He notes, for example, the divergent evolution of the automobile in Europe and the United States. Increasingly, our cars have "freed the driver from the need to know, to do, to think, to exert effort" (ibid., p. 274), whereas European cars cater to the driver's "desire for challenge and the opportunity to display and exercise his skill" (ibid.). The example suggests that even within a single social formation (capitalism), people's attitudes and values can shape the nature of the products that will be produced and consumed, a theme to which I will return in the last chapter.

Let me summarize the argument thus far. The workplace within our capitalist economy stimulates and rewards thoughtfulness for some while the majority find that their jobs neither elicit nor reward thought. The marketplace, on the other hand, stimulates the thinking of both consumer and entrepreneur. Television does little to promote thoughtfulness but the problem does not lie in the inherent characteristics of the medium as much as in the economic structure within which it functions. The cognitive demands of democratic citizenship are, by contrast with those made at the workplace and in front of the television set, extremely high, but the reward structure does not support them. The polity's demand for a thoughtful and informed citizenry is usually expressed at the rhetorical level, but the environments which actually shape cognitive style serve to dull rather than sharpen the mind of the majority of citizens.

It is part of my argument that the economy does not have a uniform impact on all participants. Others (see e.g. Kessler-Harris, 1982) have studied the way in which environmental variability may amplify or dull the intellectual virtues of men and women or of different ethnic groups. Limits of space and expertise prevent me from discussing these. We are indebted to Marxian analysts for the insight that the same process may have quite different, indeed *opposite* effects on different sectors of the population. Some evidence, as we mentioned earlier, supports the notion that we are developing a two-tiered economy. Though this position is not without its critics, let us suppose that it is correct. The economy, following Kohn and Schooler, may be said to match people to jobs in two ways, by seeing to it that people move to jobs commensurate with their cognitive capabilities and by adapting their personalities to the demands of the jobs they already have.

The evidence accumulated by Kohn and Schooler permits us to conjecture that the dynamic of capitalist economic growth *expands the cognitive capacities of some while it depresses that of many others.* Given the failure, indeed the inability of the mass media to compensate for that "depression," we may suppose that technological advance fueled by capitalist competition, at the same time that it raises the cognitive requirements for effective political participation, reduces the capacity of many, perhaps of the majority of the electorate to participate effectively. Recall, moreover, that according to Kohn and Schooler, the cognitive character of the workplace has a noticeable effect on the values parents have for their children. The *cumulative* effects of the mechanism just described in generating political *in*equality may therefore be substantial.

4 Society and schooling

In the previous chapter I considered the conventional classroom and here I've considered the impact of environments beyond the school in generating or undermining thoughtfulness. But what is the connection between the two? How is what happens within the walls of the school related to the patterns beyond the school discussed in the present chapter? Before hazarding my own views, it is important to consider some influential formulations.

Consider R. Dreeben's speculation in *On What is Learned in School* (1968). Dreeben takes the structure of the school as a given and speculates about the norms which it, in contradistinction to the family, instills. The argument is that the social structure of the school facilitates the development of four norms which are "relevant and appropriate to the demands" (p. 146) of the workplace and the polity: independence, achievement, universalism, and specificity. What Dreeben means by the claim that schools support the norm of universalism, to take one example, is that "children come to accept being treated by others as members of categories" (p. 76) rather than as unique individuals. This norm is then tied to the needs of non-school institutions by reasoning of the following kind:

> Assuming ... that the effective operation of a democratic political system requires office holders and members of the electorate to align themselves in broad and loosely organized party coalitions representing a range of political persuasions on current issues, and assuming that a modern, industrial occupational system requires job holders to enter employment contracts, both institutional systems will operate more effectively if the population contains a substantial component of persons who accept the norm of universalism and act according to it *in the political and occupational spheres* (ibid., p. 146).

By "effective operation" Dreeben has in mind rather minimal requirements, such as that (in the case of the polity)

> outstanding disputes get settled over the short or moderately long run, that succession in office occurs continuously and without serious disruptions to the regime (ibid.).

There is no need, here, to discuss the validity of Dreeben's conjectures, but I would point out a couple of important respects in which our accounts differ. His is static. Mine is designed to take into account the demands of different settings not so much in the abstract or at a single point in time but as they evolve over time. His account is pitched at such a high level of abstraction that differences between those playing different roles in the economy do not matter. My account stresses the *differential* impact of diverse roles within the economy.

Dreeben contends that schooling, occupation and politics are "reasonably well integrated" (ibid., p. 144). This contention, he tells us, puts no value on that integration. But the validity of the claim is clearly dependent on what is to count as "integration," a term whose positive connotations are difficult to avoid. My own argument is that schooling and occupation are "integrated" with each other but *not* with the polity. I have stipulated an ability to participate in political decision making at a level which goes beyond what is required for the stability of the polity, a level which might, according to some analysts, even threaten that stability. By adopting minimal standards of integration Dreeben's account conceals a disparity mine is keen on exposing.

S. Bowles and H. Gintis's formulation in *Schooling in Capitalist America* (1976) provides another necessary reference point since it is undoubtedly the most frequently discussed.[6] They posit a "correspondence" between the structure of the school and the capitalist workplace, a correspondence which is no coincidence. The structure of the school was deliberately modeled after that of the capitalist workplace in order to "gear development of personal needs to its requirements" (ibid., p. 131). Among the features of the workplace found also in the school are: hierarchical relations, lack of control over one's work, external rewards, and fragmentation among students due to competition over grades (ibid.). Although Bowles and Gintis do not discuss thoughtfulness, they do emphasize the common personality traits which are rewarded both in the workplace and in school. It is not hard to infer from their data—which show, for example, the negative relationship between creativity and independence on the one hand and supervisors' ratings and school grades on the other (ibid., pp. 131–47), that thoughtfulness is not rewarded in either place.

Although Bowles and Gintis set the stage for subsequent discussion of the role the school plays in the larger society, their analysis contains serious flaws. For capitalism, as our discussion of entrepreneurial activity shows, demands *some* people who are not only thoughtful but creative and independent. Bowles and Gintis argue that to "reproduce the social relations of production, the educational system must try to teach people to be properly subordinate" (ibid., p. 130), but if schools were really successful in doing this for *all* people, capitalism would not be well served. In fact, Bowles and Gintis stress that the very structure and organization of the school— its "hidden" curriculum which students have no more control over than workers have over the content of their job—creates alienated "forms of consciousness" in all students.

At the same time, within the Marxian framework they employ, the polarization between labor and capital is central; Bowles and Gintis therefore emphasize, somewhat inconsistently, the fact that schools *vary* according to the social class of the students who attend them. In nations where future owners and managers do not attend the same schools as future laborers, it is easy to see how school structure might be said to mirror the economic structure. In a nation where "common" schooling has been the rule rather than the exception, the Marxian who wishes to "explain" schooling in terms of the needs of the economy is faced with a choice: either to ignore one side of the equation, the need for planners, inventors, and managers, or to exaggerate the differences between the classrooms of the "working" and "capitalist" classes, or both. At the very beginning of *Schooling in Capitalist America*, Bowles and Gintis claim that any attempt to understand the "critical relationship between education and the capitalist economy . . . must begin with the fact that schools produce workers" (ibid, p. 19). True enough, but it is equally true to say that one must begin with the fact that schools produce entrepreneurs. It is, of course, possible to consider entrepreneurs as workers, but then it is surely incorrect to say that all workers must be trained for subordination.

Bowles and Gintis, in fact, do draw caricatures of the differences between schools attended by children of different social classes.

> Thus blacks and other minorities are concentrated in schools whose repressive, arbitrary, generally chaotic internal order, coercive authority structures, and minimal possibilities for advancement mirror the characteristics of inferior job situations. Similarly, predominantly working-class schools tend to emphasize behavioral control and rule-following, while schools in well-to-do suburbs employ relatively open systems that favor greater student participation, less direct supervision, more student electives, and in general, a value system stressing internalized standards of control (ibid., p. 132).

This is surely an exaggeration. Although a substantial minority of schools, a majority in some cities, are racially imbalanced, relatively few are completely segregated. In schools attended by students from different social and racial backgrounds, differences in treatment may well exist, but they are certainly more subtle than the above portrait would suggest. There may be a small number of "open system" schools in affluent, predominantly white suburbs, but there are probably an equal number of private and prep schools for the same population which maintain rigid disciplinary codes and few electives. Finally, the image of lower- or working-class youngsters being socialized to submit to coercive, arbitrary, repressive authorities, is more a projection of the authors' fantasies than a reflection of the real world of schools as the evidence from the last chapter attests. Even within the political left, Bowles and Gintis's work has been subject to substantial criticisms; here, I limit myself to that of M. Carnoy and H. Levin (1985). (See also M. Apple, 1982; I. Katznelson and M. Weir, 1985.)

Carnoy and Levin chide Bowles and Gintis for exaggerating the fit between the structures of schooling and work, an exaggeration which derives from ignoring "contradictory trends toward equality and democracy in education" (1985, p. 24). According to Carnoy and Levin, the growth of the democratic state, overlooked by traditional Marxist writers, facilitates the growth of these countervaling forces. Given such a conceptualization, one would suppose that the structure of the school would be shown to be the resultant of forces pulling in different directions, undermining the degree of "correspondence" between school and work settings.

Oddly enough, their only description of schools at the level of classroom structures and interactions—which shows the way in which middle- and working-class children are differentially social-ized—might have been written by Bowles and Gintis themselves as it is nowhere inconsistent with that earlier theory. Carnoy and Levin claim that the reason for this superficial similarity is that "at any one point in time within schools we observe only the reproductive nature of schooling practices, and possibly resistance to them" (ibid., p. 111). The "democratic dynamic" induces changes in schooling practices over time, they admit, but these cannot be captured by observing the school at a single time. I find this logic confused. If the point is that no study of a single moment in time can reveal a process, that is true of *both* the "reproductive and democratic dynamics." If the point is that only changes brought about by the "reproductive dynamic" make their way into classroom practices, that claim requires justification which is nowhere to be found.

In another part of their book (chaps 7 and 8) Carnoy and Levin analyze and predict possible reforms in the workplace and in the school. Here the discussion bears directly on our topic. The edu-cational reforms discussed include alternative approaches to teach-ing, such as team teaching and open classrooms. The catalog of possible reforms is large but which are likely actually to be adopted? They admit that all "are not equally likely in the attempt to tighten the correspondence between education and work" (ibid., p. 229). Once again the underlying assumption is precisely that of Bowles and Gintis, that the demands of the workplace exert a compelling influence on the school. Hence they argue that

> Under a team approach, individuals will have a much wider range of potential tasks and decisions. For example, each coordinator will have to make decisions. . . . *Accordingly*, it is likely that schools will shift their emphasis to a much greater extent than at present from memorization and routinization of learning to individual decision making and problem solving (ibid., p. 243; emphasis added).

Note, again, the claim that the pedagogical setting, by some unknown mechanism, will be transformed in order to restore correspondence with the workplace. M. Apple is surely right in seeing Carnoy and Levin's work as primarily a restatement of Bowles and Gintis (see Apple, 1986). Yet there are passages in Carnoy and Levin's *Schooling and Work in the Democratic State* which explicitly reject this simple monocausal account of change within the school. Earlier in the chapter from which the above quotation is taken, Carnoy and Levin make a point of saying that interest group politics is essential for understanding how particular reforms are adopted. Among the groups credited with influence are parents, taxpayers, religious groups, and most importantly education professionals. They claim that the struggle between capitalistic and democratic forces only "sets the larger framework within which the conventional politics of education is found" (ibid., p. 230). In describing the various constituencies which play a role in educational decision making, Carnoy and Levin point to the "semiautonomous nature of public education" (ibid., p. 232). But if all this is true, how can they be so sure that changes in the workplace will be converted into changes in the classroom?

In a review of Carnoy and Levin's book, Apple argues that even when they distance themselves from Bowles and Gintis and admit that the shape of the school is no mere mirror of the shape of the workplace, the authors still fail to take account of all the important forces and factors which impinge on the school at any one time.

> First, cultural forms and practices often have their own politics. They may be related to and limited by class relations and the economy, but they also are "relatively autonomous." . . . Second, there are at least *three* elements operating in this situation, class *and* race *and* gender (Apple, 1986, p. 408; italics in original).

I think that Apple, and Carnoy and Levin in their more pluralistic moments are certainly right that the evolution of the school cannot be understood by any simple extrapolation from the evolution of the workplace. Of course, this admission comes at a price. What made Bowles and Gintis's work attractive was what it aspired to: not just a set of conceptual tools for "reading" educational institutions but a *theory* of educational change which had scientific pretensions, one which was even amenable to empirical testing. Once a more complex set of factors is seen to impinge on the real situation, the hope of constructing a theory with an explicit explanatory agenda, capable of being tested against actual data, diminishes.

I, myself, know of no theory capable of explaining or predicting the incorporation or rejection of particular educational reforms. But that, after all, is not our focus here. Let me reformulate the issue. In the preceding chapter I argued that the conventional classroom does not offer a *milieu* congenial to the development of thoughtfulness. And the historical record shows, I believe, that classrooms were not designed for that purpose. At the same time, we know from studies like that of Cuban (1984) that efforts to change the conventional classroom in ways which would support alternative pedagogical regimes have not been very successful. As the recent descriptions of schools by Goodlad (1983), Boyer (1983), Sizer (1984), Powell, Farrar, and Cohen (1985) make clear, the salient fact about schooling and thinking is not the way in which thoughtful environments are differentially allocated—although some differentiation by economic class is evident—*but their general non-existence in all schools*. What accounts for this? Here is *my* "reading."

School classrooms were invented at a time when the demand for schooling was the demand for a setting which would equip large numbers of children with the most basic tools of literacy and numeracy at the same time that it socialized them for work and citizenship. In the United States, by and large *all* sectors of the population supported the institution of primary schools (Katznelson and Weir, 1985). "Thoughtful" educational settings existed outside the school in the workshops where future artisans received their training, in town meetings where local issues were debated, in the home where some of the elite received their education from individual tutors, and in a few institutions of higher learning. It is imaginable that the expansion of schooling could have been accompanied by the nurture of "thoughtful" settings for children outside the school. But the school was such a successful innovation that alternative pedagogical settings were no longer demanded. I don't mean to deny conflict within communities over what should be taught in school, but the parties to such conflict, then as now, treated the conventional classroom as the arena in which solutions would have to be worked out rather than as part of the problem.

Let me make use here of an idea derived from Piore and Sabel's (1984) interpretation of the history of industrial organization, an idea which is itself inspired by Kuhn's well-known work on scientific revolutions. The analogy with the organization of production is not so far-fetched, for we may profitably think of the conventional classroom as one way of organizing *re*production just as the factory assembly line is one way of organizing production. In their discussion of the organization of production, Piore and Sabel argue that the victory of mass production in its competition with earlier craft modes of organization was never inevitable.

> As with a revolutionary scientific theory, a new technological paradigm imposes order on the confusing practical activity of the preceding period; and in the process of distinguishing the relevant from the irrelevant in conflicting tendencies, the paradigm creates the preconditions for a new orthodoxy.... At best half-aware that their imagination has been circumscribed by convention, technologists push down the new path....
>
> The weak—unable to untangle the complex relation between the practices and the theory of the strong—try to survive by slavishly emulating the former and learning the latter by rote. In any case, victor and vanquished soon see the abandoned paradigm not as a viable alternative to the now dominant one, but as a misstep: a flawed or out-of-date theory that could not have succeeded (1984, pp. 44–5).

Now my suggestion is that schools monopolized reproduction in the same way that mass production monopolized production. Whatever defects the setting may have had from the point of view of thoughtfulness were trivial compared to its evident success. The school provided a relatively efficient way of initiating an entire community's youth into the rudiments of academic, vocational, and civic culture while providing relatively safe and agreeable custody of its charges, all at modest cost to the community. Had the institutions outside the school, especially the workplace and the mass media, evolved in such a way as to require an expansion of thoughtfulness commensurate with the expansion of literacy, the limitations of the classroom as a setting for intellectual socialization might have been exposed. Were there a severe enough discrepancy between the intellectual virtues required inside and outside of school, pressures could arise not to abolish conventional classrooms, but to limit the time students spend in them so that "thoughtful" settings could be established. But this has not occurred and is not going to occur in the near future. Parental and public confidence in their schools is threatened only when the school fails to fulfill its original charter: when students graduate without being able to read and write or without developing the attitudes needed to participate in the work force.

But did I not just mention in my criticism of Bowles and Gintis that they neglect society's evident need for thoughtful, indeed creative people? Where *do* such people come from, on my account? What must be remembered is this: even though the survival of a democratic polity may depend on the *thoughtful* participation of a majority of its populace, the dynamic development of a capitalist society does not.[7] Here, a relatively small number is sufficient. Moreover, as the economy evolves, a larger proportion of the most thoughtful need at the same time to be the most learned. If a minority of homes provide settings which nurture thoughtfulness, if a few classrooms in every school or a few schools and colleges provide such settings, if one or two children in every "thoughtless" setting have "natural immunities" which permit them to resist its influence—then the economy's effective as opposed to merely symbolic demand for good thinkers will be met.

What our society requires is *not* a repressive educational system which instills subordination; what it needs are schools which are just demanding enough to transmit minimal adherence to the norms of institutional life, yet not so repressive as to stultify future innovators.

Of course, Bowles and Gintis are right that schools which were not in some sense "functional" for their society would not endure. That is a truism. They are also, therefore, right in thinking that had society evolved in the direction of a democratic economy as well as polity, the public might seek different virtues in its educational settings. But in so far as they imply that the structure and organization of schools were deliberately chosen by the agents of capital in order to forge a suitably subordinate workforce out of a once independent population, their work has more of the character of mythmaking than analysis.

Piore and Sabel claim that there are "industrial divides," "brief moments when the path of technological development itself is at issue" (1984, p. 5). They believe that the first industrial divide came in the nineteenth century and that we are facing the second today. In the area of reproduction, we may also say that the nineteenth century saw the first educational divide. Although some of the neo-Marxists and non-Marxists such as I. Illich see us now facing a second educational divide, when not only access to schooling but the very organization of reproduction is at stake, I think this is wishful thinking. Society is not now organized in a way which would support, much less demand a more thoughtful population. Still, movement in this direction is possible, and here schools have a role to play.

Conclusion

Marx said in a famous statement in the *Poverty of Philosophy* that the hand mill is bound up with feudal society as the steam mill is connected to industrial capitalism (cited in Elster, 1985, p. 270). In the same way, we might say that certain educational patterns, namely the increasing importance of mathematics and science in the curriculum, and the opening of opportunities for higher education to successful students regardless·of social background are associated with the rise of capitalism (see Schrag, 1986). But plainly, these general trends are neither exclusive to capitalism, nor do they determine educational structures and policies in any definite way. Japan, England, and the United States are all capitalist countries but their educational systems exhibit considerable variation. Conversely, despite a rather different kind of economy, the Soviet Union's educational system is not more different from England's than is Japan's. Still, just as Marx argued that slavery was incompatible with a successful capitalist economy, so one could argue that the latter could not survive if its educational system were limited to the humanities and the arts (see Elster, op. cit., chap, 5).

Assuming then, that a modest degree of "fit" needs to be maintained between political, economic and educational institutions, where do the changes originate? Educational scholars frequently argue about whether the schools are themselves engines of change or whether they merely adapt to changes in other sectors. The most recent wave of leftist educational writers has admonished earlier progressives for their naiveté in suggesting that schools could "build a new social order", to quote George Counts. But if schools are simply epiphenomena, simply reactive institutions, why devote immense energies to criticizing them and to proposing educational alternatives? Even Bowles and Gintis (1976) whose work is a repudiation of the notion that one can transform society by transforming schooling, claim that the "drive for an egalitarian and liberating educational system must be an essential element of a socialist movement" (1976, p. 287). Some cultural Marxists, while not rejecting the centrality of the economy, see the school as at least a site of "struggle" and hence one place where the magnitude and rate if not the general direction of change can be affected (see e.g. Apple, 1982).

Here they seem to me to restate the point Dewey made about fifty years ago. As on so many issues, his statement can hardly be improved upon.

> One factor inherent in the situation is that schools do follow and reflect the social "order" that exists. I do not make this statement as a grudging admission, nor yet in order to argue that they should not do so. I make it rather as a statement of a conditioning factor which supports the conclusion that the schools thereby do take part in the determination of a future social order; and that, accordingly, the problem is not whether the schools should participate in the production of a future society (since they do so anyway) but whether they should do so blindly and irresponsibly or with the maximum possible of courageous intelligence and responsibility (1939, p. 692).

There is a tendency among romantic educational writers, especially some who write for the more general public, such as I. Illich (1970) or A. S. Neill (1960), to advocate utopian educational visions. But more scholarly, more "realistic" assessments often assume a determinism which is, itself, unwarranted. A number of sophisticated analysts such as P. Albin (1948), W. R. Scott (1981) and Piore and Sabel (1984), reject even highly plausible versions of determinism: that technology determines organization on the shop floor or organizational structure, or that advanced capitalism implies industrial mass production.

If a society's educational system were to be compared to a garment which fitted or failed to fit that society's needs, it would be an extremely loose-fitting one. It seems to me that neither parents, teachers or employers demand nor does capital, labor, democracy or any other social "force" require that our schools assume the precise shape they in fact have. But to reject the kind of facile functionalism which supposes that every structure performs a necessary function in no way suggests that significant restructuring is in the offing. The burden of the last chapter is that it is not. Our commitment to the basic structure of schooling would be shaken only if schools were perceived to violate what most would consider their basic mandate: the transmission of fundamental academic skills within a safe environment. I discuss some extra-school changes which support a redefinition of that mandate below. Right now my focus is on the school, itself.

Of course, not all parents or young people hold such limited aspirations. Increasing numbers, even among those who fight for the reform of public education, send their own children to private schools or to elite public schools. No doubt most are motivated by the wish to have their children receive the best foundation for academic success that they can afford. But this is not necessarily inconsistent with an appreciation that some of the conditions which make private schooling a prudent investment also make it a more suitable environment for the promotion of thoughtfulness since it involves fewer discipline problems, and smaller classes.

But do even the "best" schools provide education for thoughtfulness? And just what would such an education entail? There are two reasons for sketching out an ideal version of an education for thinking: first, as Dewey recognized (long before the educational Marxists started talking about "contradictions"), schools reflect society in their *in*coherence. This means that the *conflicting* tendencies found in the wider society are found also in the school, and therefore there is more flexibility, more room for maneuver than is normally admitted. Second, only by seeing what an education for thinking would be like, do we fully appreciate the extent to which the schools we have are *second best* institutions so far as that end is concerned.

Such a Utopia would, as I suggested in chapter 3, involve an expansion of educational environments *and* a contraction of schooling.[1] Unlike Illich and Sarason, I do not advocate closing down the schools. I propose only to use school classrooms for what they are best suited: listening, drill, and testing. These are essential educational activities, not to be eliminated. But they must be complemented by other activities which foster thoughtfulness in environments congenial to exploration.

Creating new settings

If they were to be educated as thinkers, students from the ages of about 12 to 18 would spend about half their time in conventional classrooms and half in one or more "thoughtful" settings. These settings would not fulfill their mission if participation were coerced, if they had groups much larger than a dozen, or if they were boxed into periods much less than three hours. Thoughtful environments could not be confined to the school building. Workplaces which were already designed to foster thoughtfulness on the job would have to develop a new self-consciousness and an educational dimension so that they could become education settings for students.

New settings will also have to be invented. Children's museums provide a model for the *kind* of social invention I am referring to. Just as these provide a way for the young to experience art or science in an environment which is neither a school nor an adult museum but which has features of both, so I would envisage the creation of a historical society for the young, a science laboratory for the young, a social policy institute for the young, a magazine publishing house for the young. These institutions would also be hybrids. They would conduct similar activities to those of their adult counterparts but would be responsive to the limited skills and techniques, experiences and attitudes young people have acquired at different levels of schooling. Although such institutions might issue useful or worthwhile products, this would not be their primary goal. That goal would be active involvement of students in long range projects requiring sustained problem solving activity. As already mentioned, such projects would not be directed by students but by individuals who would function as educators but who might not be certified teachers. I do not suppose that this role is one anyone can play, or that settings can be any more "teacher-proof" than textbooks. But I do suppose that many people who are not certified teachers have pedagogical talents which could more easily be expressed in settings which worked with them rather than against them. After all most on-the-job training, whether in auto repair shops or biology laboratories is done by people without pedagogical training or certification.

Let me elaborate on one of these settings, the social policy institute or "junior think tank" as I like to call it. A group of interested students, under adult guidance from either a teacher or a professional policy analyst, would focus on a problem of concern to the adolescent and adult community: teenage pregnancy, drugs, class or racial segregation in the school, the dropout problem, to name a few possibilities. The group would meet once or twice a week, preferably out of the school and for several hours at a time. As in adult policy centers, the goal would be to learn as much about the problem as possible, to lay out policy alternatives assessing their benefits and liabilities, and to make recommendations to the school and community administrations.

The group would develop its own agenda as it went along with only the general mission agreed on at the outset. Students would encounter and need to resolve issues dealing with a range of issues from the ethics of confidentiality, to problems of research design, to the most effective way to present their results. Pilot projects might try out different ways of dealing with some of these problems. Consultants could be called on as the need arose. Although the adult leader would supervise the effort, the adolescents should be allowed to make their own mistakes. Students would be introduced to some techniques and concepts needed to carry out the work, and would take a look at examples produced by adult centers, but there would be no expectation that the group would employ the sophisticated techniques available to adult policy researchers. Whatever skills or ideas had to be mastered would be learned only because of the actual requirements of the project. The project would be expected to issue a report made available to the entire community.

I would like to counter a likely objection to this vision of reduced time in conventional classrooms. The expansion of knowledge in every field, the development of novel fields of inquiry, it might be said, requires, if anything, an expansion of the time allotted to acquiring the fundamentals of the various fields of inquiry. My vision, it will be said, is not only utopian but anachronistic, hearkening back to a time when there was less, not more, to know. I believe that the explosion of knowledge does not undermine my vision, for it is already clear that no matter how much time is allotted to basic schooling, it would not suffice to initiate students into the modes of inquiry that are currently pursued.

Consider the fields brought together under the rubric of social studies: political science, economics, history, geography, sociology, anthropology, psychology. Each of these in turn covers a multiple of subfields. (Branches of psychology are close to biology, others closer to sociology, still others closer to philosophy.) And, finally, there are multiple hybrids among these fields. School curricula have introduced material from these fields, to the point that many feel that the centrality of history has been undermined. Although excellent arguments can be made for the importance of cultivating a sense of history, similar arguments could be made for almost any of the other fields. In the face of this proliferation of possible fields of study, wiser voices are now, as ever, arguing for the importance of depth in a few fields rather than superficial coverage of many (e.g. Sizer, 1984). In 1929 A. N. Whitehead already admonished schools against teaching too many subjects. Education, he maintained, was "the acquisition of the art of the utilisation of knowledge" (1967, p. 4). Long before the age of computers Whitehead was more prescient than he could have realized.

The vision of reduced classroom time and the proliferation of new educational settings may be utopian but that does not mean that an experiment in this direction here or there might not take root and flourish. At a time when the general public is at least superficially concerned about why Johnny and Janie can't think, some communities are ready to back away from the "basics". But for those communities who are not eager for radical reform, it is still possible for thoughtfulness to be promoted to a greater extent than it currently is within the conventional classroom.

Enhancing thinking in conventional classrooms

Others have reviewed and analyzed the programs in critical thinking or problem solving which are currently on the market (e.g. Chance, 1986; Nickerson, Perkins, and Smith, 1985). I have discussed a couple of these in chapter 1, but here let me make a few brief comments about the extent to which these programs support the general spread of thoughtfulness. Because of the very thoughtfulness which went into the design of many of these programs, their implementation tends to *violate* the pedagogic format of the conventional classroom. In cases where the teachers or students are unusually motivated, such violations may succeed. In most cases, the constraints I spoke about in chapter 3 will, I believe, tend to undermine the permanent institutionalization of such programs.

But even if the new thinking curricula are not widespread or if attempts at implementing them are abandoned in frustration, they serve several important goals. Unlike the perennial chorus exhorting teachers to focus on inquiry rather than memorization, on process rather than product, these programs are more than slogans or ideas. They speak teachers' language, meaning that they include activities, materials, texts, teachers' guides, as well as summer institutes and in-service workshops where teachers can, themselvés, *experience* the ideas *in action*. For teachers who themselves have never participated in classrooms where thoughtfulness was valued, such experience is vital. For only here can teachers develop a feel for the frustration and exhilaration which accompanies cognitive exploration. Only here may they get a feel for what a classroom which did not emphasize coverage of conventional subject matter might be like. Even if many of these teachers decide not to import such programs into their classrooms, they can import a few of the techniques or the ideas underlying them into their more conventional pedagogy. And they, themselves, can develop an awareness of the constraints which prevent them from doing some of the things they might like to. Unless teachers, themselves, are conscious of these constraints their help cannot be enlisted in the effort to transform education.

I have, nevertheless, an uneasiness about some of these programs which derives not so much from their overt curriculum as from the latent implications of the way they are packaged. It is dangerous to put the label "thinking" on any pedagogical package not because people will refuse to embrace its contents but because they will come to identify teaching *thinking* with teaching what is in that particular package. I find some of the labeling quite misleading.

Barry Beyer's (1985a,b) widely disseminated approach to teaching "critical thinking skills", for example, is really aimed at inculcating some specific techniques for evaluating written materials in social studies. Ironically, since programs like Beyer's are congenial to standard pedagogy in the conventional classroom, they have the greatest survival value. Some of these skills may be useful, and I have no objection to teaching them directly. But there is no guarantee that following the five instructional steps Beyer identifies (1985 b, p. 298) will promote thoughtfulness in students.

One of the sub-skills Beyer discusses, for example, is "detecting bias" in written materials. Teachers introduce the skill and students practice applying it, combing documents for emotionally charged terms, overgeneralizations, and the like. It is not hard to see how this "skill" could be incorporated into fairly mindless homework assignments and objective tests with correct and incorrect answers. (Identify the emotionally laden terms in the following, Match each of the following sentences with one of the kinds of bias discussed in class, etc). What I am saying is that just because programs like Beyer's are designed for the conventional classroom, they have great potential for undermining thoughtfulness.

Some programs such as Feuerstein's are explicitly subject-matter neutral, and these present a different kind of danger, namely that educators may infer that thinking is one subject among subjects like English, mathematics, etc. This does not bode well for thinking in the other subjects. Similarly, if thinking is identified with a discrete set of skills which are taught in sequence at a certain hour of the day, then this relieves teachers of having to worry about the way children think at other hours of the day. The parallel with writing ought not to go unnoticed. Just now efforts are being made to integrate writing throughout the curriculum, presumably because most subject teachers mistakenly assumed that teaching writing was the task delegated exclusively to the language arts or English teacher.

Within the conventional classroom, there are several things a teacher can do which cumulatively can help to make the classroom more thoughtful. I'll just mention a few, although these are not intended to be either comprehensive or novel. More challenging questions can be posed and students can be required to defend their assertions. When challenging questions are asked, the teacher may face a situation in which a few students may have ready answers while the others may be too frustrated to know how to answer. In such cases, the less able students will be only too happy to let the others do their thinking for them. This tendency can be mitigated by asking all students to take a minute to formulate their answers in writing before calling on students to see what they've come up with. If students need to explain how they've arrived at their answers, so do teachers. Teachers, whether in science or humanities classes, need to do more than judge the adequacy of students' solutions, more even than provide model solutions to problems. They need to reveal the thinking, insofar as they are conscious of it, which led them to those solutions.

Students, especially intelligent ones, have a knack for discerning what teachers want to hear or read. Providing the teacher with answers which are congenial to his or her point of view is often viewed as the way to academic success. And doing this is often much easier than thinking out one's own position or interpretation. The teacher should send confusing signals from time to time to keep students unsure of just where he or she stands on an issue. This forces the student to think through his or her own interpretation or point of view.

True-false and multiple-choice examination formats should be used sparingly. This is not because they do not invite thinking. They do, but they have two weaknesses. First, the teacher cannot discriminate between the student who thought out an answer and the one who merely took a lucky guess. Correct and incorrect answers do not mark this distinction. Second, the thinking which is stimulated is focused on the wrong concern: to find the answer which matches the one on the teacher's scorecard. Good test takers use subtle cues from the "form" of the test questions and alternative answers, cues which are entirely irrelevant to its "content".

Students often become experts in test taking rather than in mathematics or social studies. They come to realize that thoughtful answers will not be rewarded unless they match the official ones. And they come to believe that most problems have solutions which are either correct or incorrect, a dangerous illusion in a world where ill-defined problems far outnumber well-defined ones. Textbooks, themselves, discourage thinking by reinforcing the assumption that quizzes and unit tests or questions at the end of a chapter will deal only with the material which immediately precedes it. If tests and chapter questions included questions which referred to ideas or material learned in earlier lessons, the students would face a much more demanding intellectual challenge.

Do my suggestions for enhancing the thoughtfulness of conventional classrooms have implications for the training of teachers? The main point I would make here is that only people who have been participants in thoughtful settings will be able to approximate such settings in conventional classrooms or will be able, themselves, to model thoughtful behavior. I am not the first to observe that teachers teach according to the way in which they, themselves, have been taught rather than according to the latest educational precepts. Education students, historically not academically strong, are often treated as second class citizens in the university. They have less access to seminars, and fewer serve as assistants in scientific laboratories. Because of their potential role in promoting thoughtfulness in their own classrooms, future teachers *more than any other group*, must have access to those university settings which promote thoughtfulness.

Encouraging thinking outside the school

I intimated in the last chapter that feasible alterations in the polity and in the economy could both elicit and reward a higher quality of thinking. Consider the economy first. From the perspective of encouraging thoughtfulness, a centralized economy is no improvement. Indeed such an economy may exacerbate the problem by further separating the planning and executive functions. "In statist societies, the working class is exploited by a 'politocracy' which controls the means of both production and domination" (Mouzelis, 1986). What is needed is reform which provides expanded incentives to thoughtfulness without destroying those which already exist in the market. Recall that the workplace can be the source of two kinds of cognitive demands, those deriving from the tasks of actual production and those deriving from the firm's management. Most workers in most firms play no role at all in the latter. We need, therefore, to move in the direction of providing for worker participation in the running of the firm, that is of introducing democratic processes of decision making into the economy. This, in turn, rests on the ability of labour to assume partial if not complete ownership of the firm.

Movement in this direction is an essential part of any society-wide attempt to pay more than lip service to the virtue of thoughtfulness. Because the idea is often associated with Marxism, or worse with the economic system of the Soviet Union, it is important to see that its justification does not depend on the labor theory of value, on a Marxian critique of capitalism, or on a fondness for statist regimes. An eminent mainstream political theorist, R. Dahl is, in fact, one of the most lucid advocates of this extension of the democratic franchise. According to Dahl (1985), such an expansion derives solely from a commitment to democracy itself. There are three prongs to the argument. First, Dahl shows that any association which possesses certain characteristics has a right to self government. Second, Dahl argues that such a right does not violate any prior right of private ownership of corporate enterprises. Finally, Dahl shows that a democratic polity designing an economy in order to maximize its democratic commitments would choose to create democratically controlled enterprises owned by the employees. I consider briefly the first and the third, as the second would take us too far afield.

Dahl believes that if a human association meets seven requirements, then its members have an inalienable right to govern themselves through a democratic process. I mention only those requirements which may be thought to be dubious so far as economic enterprises are concerned.

1.   The collection of people in the association has a need to reach at least some collective decisions that will be binding on all the members of the collectivity. . . .
6.   A strong principle of equality: With respect to all matters, all the adult members of the association . . . are roughly equally well qualified to decide which matters do or do not require binding collective decisions (1985, pp. 57-8).

Dahl recognizes that economic enterprises appear not to meet either of these conditions, especially when contrasted with the state. After all, the employer issues no laws binding on employees; the relation between employers and employees is a voluntary, contractual one. A disgruntled employee is under no obligation to remain with the firm. By way of rebuttal to this objection, Dahl tries to blur the line between a firm and a political jurisdiction. The employee is subject to rules promulgated by management, rules which *are* binding so long as he retains employment. Furthermore, exit is not always an option, certainly not an option without serious costs; more important, in a political jurisdiction, a disgruntled citizen still retains the option to leave and move to another jurisdiction. I am not entirely convinced by this line of argument (see also Lane, 1985). In the economic arena, most employees or prospective employees face a real choice of diverse "regimes" to join, and the costs of leaving one to join another firm are often minimal. Today, a prospective employee who found no offer satisfactory could even withhold his or her labor from any employer and survive at the taxpayer's expense, but a citizen cannot opt out of membership in some polity. While it is relatively easy to move from one local jurisdiction or one state to another, at the national level, the costs of abandoning one's native home and culture in order to find a more congenial political regime in another country are enormous. Still, Dahl is right in showing these contrasts to be matters of degree rather than kind.

On the second issue, Dahl makes it clear that the employees of the firm are neither required nor expected to make every decision facing it. As in the polity, they may delegate many technical decisions to experts, but the experts will be under the control of the employees, not the stockholders. Dahl contends that employees are, relative to stockholders, in a much more favorable position to make basic decisions. Moreover, he marshals considerable theoretical and empirical evidence to support the view that employee-governed enterprises might well make economically sounder decisions regarding savings, investment, growth and employment (see ibid. chap. 4; also McPherson, 1983). He points out, for example, that in worker-owned companies, there is an incentive for workers to reduce their own wages in hard times in order to prevent a firm from going under. So far as competence is concerned, it is hard to see why a person who is not trusted to make decisions regarding levels of investment and savings in his or her own firm, is capable of making those decisions for the nation as a whole.

The part of Dahl's argument I want to stress, however, concerns the contribution a democratic economy would make to a democratic polity. There are two principal points. The less important, given our subject, is the contribution a system of self-governing enterprises would make to the reduction of the immense concentration of wealth in the hands of relatively few owners of property, a concentration that threatens the political equality on which democracy depends. Given our concern, the more important argument for extending democracy into the workplace derives from the tradition of J. S. Mill down to Dewey and C. Pateman among others in our own era arguing for the educational value of democratic participation. The central idea, explicitly stated by Pateman is this:

The major function of participation in the theory of participatory democracy is therefore an educative one, educative in the very widest sense, including both the psychological aspect and the gaining of special practice in democratic skills and procedures (Pateman, 1970, p. 42).

In *The Public and Its Problems* Dewey put it like this: "the cure for the ailments of democracy is more democracy" (1946, p. 146). Is there any evidence to support this? Dahl notes a few studies on the effect of democratic participation on the participants of enterprises that have become self-governing. The outcomes are equivocal. It does not seem that any of these studies were focused on the extent to which such arrangements promoted a greater thoughtfulness among employees; rather they measured degree of worker satisfaction, political attitudes, and the like. Given the limited number of firms which are owned by employees in our country and the limited evidence we have from the Yugoslavian experience, which in any case is embedded in a political system totally different from our own, it is prudent not to draw any decisive conclusions. Dahl is certainly right when he notes that

We cannot confidently predict what changes in character or personality might ensue, not in the short space of months or years, but over many generations (1985, p. 98).

I would argue that democratic procedures within the firm, compared with other arenas, would have the greatest likelihood of stimulating thoughtfulness, for two reasons. Whereas citizens often have a very limited personal stake in decisions made at state and national levels, their own interests are very much bound up with the success of the firm. Major decisions may hinge on technical issues, but it will behoove the members of the enterprise to acquaint themselves with those issues as much as they can or else to find experts who can expound them in non-technical terms. Second, whereas in the broader political arena feedback from decisions is hard to discover and assess, here feedback may be quite direct and clearcut, especially in the case of smaller firms. The penalties for impulsive or capricious behavior are very high.

Aside from its moral or political-theoretic justification, there is an additional reason why economic democracy may be thought to contribute to the promotion of thoughtfulness. This relates back to the demands of the workplace, itself. Work which provides not just a living wage but personal fulfillment and the opportunity to exercise one's talents and gifts is close to the center of many conceptions of the good life, including of course both Christian and Marxian (see e.g. Elster, 1985; Schumacher, 1973; Crocker, 1983).

Whether workers themselves in the past or even now demand work that is satisfying is not clear (see e.g. Clayre, 1974; Erikson, 1986; Lane, 1985). Whether technological advance fueled by market competition inexorably leads to an erosion of the cognitive demands of work for the majority of workers, is still an open question. Some reject not only technological determinism but also the thesis that work "degradation" is an inevitable trend within capitalism. An alternative to the mass-production model which features flexible specialization and a craft model of production is still a viable possibility, argue M. Piore and C. Sabel (1984). P. Albin (1984) notes that many of the changes which reduce the levels of skill needed by the workforce are done to foster short-term productivity, but are deleterious in the long run. One reason alternative job designs which enhance job complexity and autonomy are not chosen is that these typically require retraining. There is no incentive for management to provide this training since it cannot be assured that the benefits will be held within the firm. In some Japanese firms by contrast, Albin argues, the employee is typically hired for life, so this problem doesn't arise. Clearly in an employee-owned firm, workers would have a stake in job redesign which would guarantee them the maximum of autonomy and job satisfaction consistent with operating a profitable enterprise. Unlike management, whose views Shaiken (1984) documents, workers would be much less likely to regard their own participation in production as an unavoidable evil. In employee-owned, democratically controlled enterprises, decisions to expand or limit job complexity would be made by those who not only reap the monetary profits (or losses), but pay the psychological costs of alienation.

If a concern for thoughtfulness leads naturally to an expansion of democracy into the workplace, it leads to certain changes within the polity as well. One kind of proposal, advanced by B. Barber (1984, chap. 10) among others involves the use of the new communications technology to permit a more direct participation of the citizenry. The "electronic enhancement of communication offers possible solutions to the dilemmas of scale" (ibid., pp. 273-4). Barber envisages televised "town meetings" in which citizens could participate by telephoning in questions or comments or by appearing before a television camera at a neighborhood center. Expanding use of the referendum and initiative through electronic voting is also part of Barber's proposal for what he calls "strong" democracy. To facilitate informed voting, he envisages a vast information retrieval system which citizens could access to find information germane to issues before the community.

But in view of our focus on promoting a more thoughtful citizenry, by far the most interesting of Barber's proposals is that concerning a multichoice format in voting instead of the simple yea/nay option. (Barber did not invent this: it has existed for centuries, he tells us, in Raetia in Switzerland.)

> The range of options would include: yes in principle—strongly for the proposal; yes in principle—but not a first priority; no in principle—strongly against the proposal; no with respect to this formulation but not against the proposal in principle, suggest reformulation and resubmission; and no for time being—although not necessarily opposed in principle, suggest postponement (ibid., p. 286).

Barber explains that such a format would not only provide better information to the electorate on the reasons for passage or defeat of a measure, but

> would compel citizens to examine their own electoral opinions ... and encourages voters to have public reasons for what are after all public acts (ibid., pp. 287-8).

As I mentioned earlier, American interest in politics is no lower than in other places; almost all of us discuss politics at some time or other. But it is conceivable that the quality of the discussions is related to the form in which the issues are put to the electorate. Referenda do occasionally get on the ballot, but the yes/no format necessitates a collapsing of several issues that a multichoice format would permit voters to separate. Such a format would require voters to think about the *relative* importance of a particular measure, and the extent to which a good idea was or was not reflected in specific legislation. The multichoice format does not, in itself, prevent voters from capricious voting, but it does provide a stimulus to careful judgment which the cruder format undermines.

In our two-party system, the nuances of divergent positions can't be as clearly reflected as they can in polities where a larger number of parties compete. The institution of proportional representation would foster the development of a multi-party system. Under such a system, seats in legislatures would be apportioned according to the vote-getting strength of the competing parties. Third parties which, under the present system, might not have any elected representatives would probably be strong enough to be represented. The debates in the legislatures would be more sharply drawn and voters would have access to a wider spectrum of opinion. At campaign time, there would be less need to hide differences within political parties behind bland rhetoric. Clearly, systems of proportional representation have dangers, instability being the one most often noted, but from the point of view of stimulating thoughtfulness, they would be worth experimenting with (see Lijphart and Grofman, 1984).

In fostering a climate in which structural changes of the kind envisaged can get on to the agenda, schools clearly have a part to play. Teachers in some classes such as social studies or civics can broaden students' sense of possible ways of organizing society. As G. A. Cohen reminds us, from the time of the Stoics the distinction between nature and convention is the fundamental one for any social critic. (Cohen, 1978, p. 107.) Many of the things we accept, such as the format for voting or the need for democracy in the polity but not the firm, we accept as natural because alternatives never come to mind. And this is largely because the alternatives are never presented.

I don't believe that the social studies classroom will become the locale for vigorous debate; I'm not even sure it should. But it is still possible for teachers to inform adolescent students that our ways of doing things, even those which have the weight of tradition behind them, are not the only, perhaps not even the best ways of doing those things. The changes in society which I propose can come about only through a growing realization that the *status quo* can be improved upon. What prevents issues such as economic democracy from getting on the political agenda is in part the notion that the democratic ideal in the polity has no relevance to the workplace (see Lane, 1985). This kind of mental compartmentalization is surely traceable, in part, to the fact that it is never challenged in the classroom or textbook.

The movement to introduce "thinking skills" into the curriculum is a movement primarily of educational psychologists. Because of the narrow way many of them conceptualize their task, they do not see that a serious commitment to the diffusion of thoughtfulness must include a commitment to a modification of the political and economic agenda, a modification in which educators have a role.

Reprise: The value of thoughtfulness

Throughout this work, I have concentrated on analyzing existing educational institutions or proposing alternatives with a view to enhancing the diffusion of a single virtue—thoughtfulness. I hope the reader will have understood from our discussion in chapter 3 that the tasks which stimulate thoughtfulness and the settings I labeled "thoughtful" support other virtues as well: perseverance, responsibility and cooperation, to name the most important. These are the virtues which are nurtured only too rarely in our schools, and often only outside the conventional classroom.

Thoughtfulness is, of course, an intellectual virtue, but that does not mean that it is unconnected to the moral life. On the contrary. People who are weak thinkers are often not able to escape their own limited perspective on an issue; their rigidity limits them to seeing only their own side of the case (see Perkins, 1986b). One of the meanings of "thoughtful" is "considerate, kindly" according to the *Oxford English Dictionary*. Why should a word whose primary meaning is "given or disposed to, or engaged in thinking" also be a synonym for a virtue many of us don't associate with use of the mind at all? Perhaps our language contains the same insight which philosophers like Ryle and Dewey fought to communicate: that the dichotomy between heart and mind enshrined in both academic and popular philosophies is not only a dubious but a dangerous doctrine.

It is, of course, possible to be thoughtful in the service of evil. Iago in Shakespeare's *Othello* offers a powerful illustration. But it may be impossible to be kind or considerate if one is not thoughtful. To be considerate requires one to be able to see the world from the point of view of the recipient of one's action, to put one's own impulses and needs on hold while one determines what would please another. Sometimes a spontaneous impulse to comfort, console or praise must be hearkened to. But at other times, acting on such impulses is more gratifying to the actor than to the recipient. Impetuousness is dangerous even when motivated by altruism.

In a trenchant critique of Dewey's philosophy, H. Broudy (1950) highlights what he takes to be the limitations of the "problem-solving" model in science and ethics. One of the points Broudy makes is that there are aspects of life which must be thought of in terms of fundamental predicaments rather than problems to be solved. Broudy says

> To strive as if our existence were eternal while never forgetting that death might be lurking just outside the door—that is a mode of existence that is quite different from the mode of existence we call problem solving (ibid. p. 21).

I think what Broudy is saying here is that wisdom is incompatible with regarding every predicament as a problem to be solved. In this he is undoubtedly right, as I'm sure Dewey would agree. If we identify effective thinking with the virtue of thoughtfulness—with a "second nature" trained successfully to counteract our native tendencies to impulsiveness and to stereotyped response—there is no reason to believe that the virtue which makes us good at solving those problems which have solutions must be abandoned when more fundamental predicaments are confronted. On the contrary is there not continuity here? Isn't there every reason to expect the impetuous or doctrinaire person to be foolish rather than wise?

John Kekes (1983) contends that wisdom is needed "where a man must make a decision about hard cases ... and it is unclear what ideals should guide one" (p. 283). Here, if anywhere, impulse and dogma guide the fool. Now what is *true* is that twelve or more years of confronting "well-structured" textbook problems, which always have a single correct answer found in the teacher's guide, may not be the best preparation for confronting such fundamental predicaments. Neither, I would argue and Dewey would concur, is it the best preparation for becoming a problem solver of *any* kind. Most problems encountered outside the classroom, whether in professional, intellectual or personal life, are closer to Broudy's predicaments than they are to the questions at the end of the chapter in the text. This is precisely why I have argued that an education for thoughtfulness cannot be limited to the conventional textbook and the conventional classroom.

I conclude with a recapitulation of the argument. In chapter 1 I argued that the identification of thinking as a skill or set of skills was neither intellectually valid nor educationally fruitful. I suggested that the best way to conceptualize the task of teaching thinking was as the nurture of the character trait or virtue of thoughtfulness. From this point of view, I claimed that most of the standard ways of identifying different kinds of thinking are both dubious and dangerous. In chapter 2 I reviewed and assessed the literature on the empirical study of thinking and tried to draw out its educational implications. I argued that although I see little likelihood that psychological research will lead to dramatic breakthroughs in our abilities to teach people how to think, its conclusions can be employed to mobilize support for certain kinds of pedagogical settings—namely those in which student engagement with challenging problems is at the center rather than the periphery of the enterprise.

In chapter 3, I discussed the characteristics of settings designed to enhance thoughtfulness. I argued that the conventional classroom with its pedagogical diet of lecture and recitation was not well-suited to the nurture of thoughtfulness. At the same time, I tried to show that such classrooms were rational responses to certain basic features of the educational situation. An education for thoughtfulness, would, I contended, have to limit but not eliminate the time students spent in traditional classroom settings. In chapter 4, I argued that failure to incorporate "thoughtful" settings within or beyond the school must be seen in the light of the failure of other institutions to increase the demand for thoughtful people. Finally, I sketched out some directions educators could move in if they were committed to fostering thoughtfulness, and I proposed some changes in the organization of our economic and political life, changes which would support the development of thoughtfulness.

My focus on character and hence on the entire environment within which the young come to adulthood, is consonant with a long tradition in education which includes Plato, Rousseau and Dewey among its forbears. Such a focus is not linked to a particular political ideology. For example, both the late P. Goodman (1960), identified with the left, and the neo-conservative J. Q. Wilson (1985) share this focus.

I began this inquiry with an image of the thinker as explorer. Explorers, whether territorial or cognitive, need specific skills, skills which will vary with the terrain they seek to explore. But no amount of skill training under artificial conditions, no amount of edifying or terrifying discourse, will instill those character traits which the expedition will require: courage, tenacity, inventiveness, and practical wisdom. These are acquired, if at all, only by participating in actual expeditions. Only by watching those one admires facing challenges and facing them oneself, does one gradually develop these attributes.

Not everyone can or need be an explorer whose discoveries are recorded for posterity. But even a conservative social thinker, perhaps especially a conservative, would recognize that to navigate safely through the dangers and temptations of contemporary society requires the virtues of an explorer: so few situations today lend themselves to ready-made solutions, that the capacity for cognitive exploration is needed by everyone who aspires to a satisfying life.

Notes

Chapter 1 What is thinking?
1. I suggest that "information" be interpreted as broadly as possible to include not only linguistic representations but tones, colors, sounds, anything which may serve as a meaning or indicator of something else.
2. It may seem odd to speak of virtues as needed to overcome "impediments" since it is possible to consider the virtues themselves rather than their absence as barriers to the fulfillment of desires. I am borrowing Wallace's somewhat technical notion, itself derived from Aristotle, that virtues are learned acquisitions (analogous to unlearned instinct in animals) which enable humans to function successfully in society. The assumption is that a person without courage or wisdom or temperance is handicapped for life in society. His or her "instincts" are not sufficient for social life.
3. There is, to be sure, an enormous literature on the nature of inference in theoretical and practical reasoning. My blanket assertion is, of course, no argument. See e.g. Raz (1978).

Chapter 2 The educational significance of cognitive psychology
1. I shall not deal with the educational significance of brain research. In my view the *pedagogical* importance of that research is typically exaggerated (see e.g. Grady, 1984). Of course, I do not deny that research on the brain may lead to important new ways of enhancing learning. But these new modes will probably involve more *direct*, possibly chemical, means of influencing human thinking and learning abilities.
2. Ironically, contemporary neuro-psychologists like S. Grossberg (1982) argue that even the behaviorist's atoms of learning cannot be understood without reference to mentalistic concepts such as expectancy.
3. The notion that unconscious inferences underlie our everyday perceptual performance is generally credited to the nineteenth century German scientist Herman von Helmholtz (see Gardner, 1985, chap. 5).

4. A comprehensive yet accessible discussion of this much debated issue can be found in Gardner (1985, chap 11).
5. Curiously, two eminent professors of psychology who reviewed this chapter had opposite reactions to this point. One pointed out that behaviorism is still flourishing in many university departments and there are several journals devoted to work in that tradition. The other claimed that behaviorism is not moribund but already dead.
6. Of course, the term "schema" has a long history, going back at least to Kant.
7. In this article, Carey considers and rejects four possible interpretations of the claim that children think differently from adults: that they employ a different representational format, have different metacognitive knowledge, different foundational concepts, and lack tools of wide application.
8. Of course, the direct modes would not be employed unless we believed them to be superior.
9. Although I put Papert, Piaget, Montessori, and Dewey in the broad tradition which stems from Rousseau, this is not to deny that there are significant differences among them.
10. Some promising efforts at tuning occur with fairly well-structured problems in specific domains. I mention only a few: Fisk and Schneider's (1981) investigations of automatic and control processing appear to have significant implications for the training of air traffic controllers; Case's (1985) information-processing approaches to teaching problem-solving in specific domains significantly enhance students' abilities to solve certain kinds of problems.
11. Scardamalia and Bereiter's (1984) efforts to provide students with tools to improve their own composition processes is one example of applied cognitive psychology at its best.

Chapter 3 Contexts for developing thoughtfulness

1. For example, consider D. Perkins's *Knowledge as Design* (1986a). This insightful and comprehensive guide to nurturing student thinking in school never effectively deals with the school as a social setting.
2. Of course, academics in the humanities and social sciences are effective thinkers in settings which have few of the features of the science laboratory. But the relative solitariness of the work makes such professional thinkers anomalous rather than typical. Most professional problem solvers, I would argue, operate in settings which, from the social-structural point of view, resemble the laboratory.
3. The kind of disorder which may arise in the early grades is, of

course, very different. Although individual unruliness may lead to chaos, there is not the possibility of a collective challenge to the legitimacy of the teacher or the institution.

4. Sandor Brent (1984), in a stimulating analysis of the relationship between the size of social structures and the activities they permit, takes classrooms of different sizes as one illustration of his more general theory. He shows how patterns of interaction in classrooms shift as the number of students increases. Certain patterns are stable within certain ranges of number of students. If 10 students were to be added to a seminar of 12, the alteration would be much more dramatic than if even 20 students were to be added to a class of 50.

5. In most graduate schools, so far as I know, with law school being something of an exception, competition between individual students in a department is downplayed. Even in law school, where the students may be individually ranked, there are strong incentives to form collaborative study groups. In most graduate programs, however, students are not ranked, nor is it usually the case that only a few can earn top grades or recommendations. Almost all students receive a grade B or better, and very few are prevented from continuing once they have been admitted to a graduate program.

6. Cuban mentions a variable here, the teacher's perspective, which I have not so far mentioned and do not wish to discuss. I maintain that the perspective is less important than the setting in this sense, that the perspective is developed by relentless exposure to a single setting. Of course, some teachers are fortunate enough (or perhaps unfortunate enough) to develop pedagogical orientations or "teacher epistemologies" which are at variance with the constraints of the conventional setting.

Chapter 4 Thinking in society

1. In a number of provocative essays, Offe (1985) suggests that in the mature economies of Western Europe and the United States, work no longer is the dominant category. Kohn and Schooler's studies (1983) done during the 1960s and 1970s do not support this, but more recent studies might.

2. Kohn and Schooler's primary sample did not include women. But a parallel study on employed women (1983, chap. 8) showed the same general patterns. Another chapter investigated the nature and effects of household work on psychological functioning (chap. 10). Both men and women were studied. In the case of women (but not men) the effects of complexity of household tasks on ideational flexibility followed the same pattern as that of men and women in paid employment.

3. The preceding analysis refers to work directly required by the job. Opportunities abound for using one's mind on the job in ways not required, and often not even sanctioned by employers.

4. Politicians and the press sometimes criticize the tendency of recent political campaigns to focus more on personalities than on issues, but this may be a rational response to such a growing awareness of the intricacy of the issues.

5. These are not, of course, the only options. One may identify with larger collective interests without being motivated by duty.

6. Bowles and Gintis (1976) are by no means the only or the best to discuss the behavior of the educational system as a function of larger social forces. See e.g. Collins (1979) for a stimulating analysis from a Weberian point of view. But Bowles and Gintis and the Marxists are centrally concerned, as most sociologists of schooling are not, to attempt to relate specific features of the wider society to specific features of classroom and school structure.

7. Not all would, presumably, contend that widespread participation in the polity would be a good thing. Some might argue that the stability of the system would be jeopardized if there were too much or too intensive participation.

Conclusion

1. In a volume entitled *Must We Educate?* (1973) Carl Bereiter reached a rather similar conclusion, but his reasoning was almost the inverse of mine. I claim that society ought to be concerned with character but that schools are not well suited to the task. Bereiter condemned schools because they were molding character when he thought they had no business to do so and ought to stick to imparting skills.

Bibliography

Aanstoos, C. M. (1985), "The structure of thinking in chess." In A. Giorgi (ed.), *Phenomenology and Psychological Research*. Pittsburgh: Duquesne University Press.

Adler, M. (1982), *The Paideia Proposal: An Educational Manifesto*. New York: Macmillan.

Adler, M. (1986), "The latest educational mania—critical thinking." *Paideia Bulletin*, 2(4), 2, 6.

Albin, P. (1984), "Job design within changing patterns of technical development." In E. L. Collins & L. D. Tanner (eds.), *American Jobs and the Changing Industrial Base*. Cambridge, MA: Ballinger.

Anderson, J. R. (1983), *The Architecture of Cognition*. Cambridge, MA: Harvard University Press.

Apple, M. (1982), *Cultural and Economic Reproduction in Education: Essays on Class, Ideology, and the State*. Boston: Routledge & Kegan Paul.

Apple, M. (1986), "Bringing the economy back into educational theory." *Educational Theory*, 36, 403–16.

Applebaum, E. (1984), "High tech and the structural employment problems of the 1980's." In E. L. Collins and L. D. Tanner (eds), *American Jobs and the Changing Industrial Base*. Cambridge, MA: Ballinger.

Arendt, H. (1958), *The Human Condition*. Chicago: University of Chicago Press.

Armbruster, B. B., and Anderson, T. H. (1985), "Producing 'considerate' expository text: Or easy reading is damned hard writing." *Journal of Curriculum Studies*, 17, 247–74.

Azarias, B. (1869), "The simultaneous method in teaching." In B. Azarias (ed.), *Essays Educational*. Chicago: D. H. McBride.

Barber, B. (1984), *Strong Democracy: Participatory Politics for a New Age*. Berkeley, CA: University of California Press.

Baron, J. (1981), "Reflective thinking as a goal of education." *Intelligence*, 5, 291–309.

Baron, J. (1985a), *Rationality and Intelligence*. Cambridge University Press.

Baron, J. (1985b), "What kinds of intelligence components are fundamental?" In S. Chipman, J. Segal, and R. Glaser (eds), *Thinking and Learning Skills*. vol 2. *Research and Open Questions*. Hillsdale, NJ: Lawrence Erlbaum.

Baron, J., Badgio, P., and Gaskins, I. (1986), "Cognitive style and its improvement: A normative approach." In R. J. Sternberg (ed.), *Advances in the Psychology of Human Intelligence* (vol. 3). Hillsdale, NJ: Lawrence Erlbaum.

Bartlett, F. (1958), *Thinking: An Experimental and Social Study.* London: George Allen & Unwin.

Bastick, T. (1982), *Intuition: How we Think and Act.* Chichester, England: John Wiley.

Bellack, A. et al. (1965), *The Language of the Classroom.* New York: Teachers College Press.

Bennett, N. (1985), "Interaction and achievement in classroom groups." In N. Bennett and C. Desforges (eds), *Recent Advances in Classroom Research.* Edinburgh: Scottish Academic Press.

Bereiter, C. (1973), *Must We Educate?* Englewood Cliffs, NJ: Prentice-Hall.

Berliner, D. (1986), "In pursuit of the expert pedagogue." *Educational Researcher, 15*(7), 5–13.

Beyer, B. (1985a), "Critical thinking: What is it?" *Social Education, 49*(4), 270–6.

Beyer, B. (1985b), "Teaching critical thinking: A direct approach." *Social Education, 49*(4), 297–303.

Bhaskar, R. and Simon, H. A. (1977), "Problem solving in semantically rich domains: An example from engineering thermodynamics." *Cognitive Science, 1*, 193–215.

Bishop, R. (183), "Computer integrated manufacturing: The human factors." In H. F. Didsbury, Jr (ed.), *The World of Work: Careers and the Future.* Bethesda, MD: World Future Society.

Blauner, R. (1964), *Alienation and Freedom: The Factory Worker and his Industry.* Chicago: Phoenix Books.

Bluestone, B., and Harrison, B. (1986), *The Great American Job Machine: The Proliferation of Low Wage Employment in the U.S. Economy.* Washington, D.C: The Joint Economic Committee.

Blumenfeld, P. C., Mergendoller, J. R., and Swarthout, D. W. (1986), *Tasks as Heuristics for Understanding Student Learning and Motivation* Unpublished manuscript. Ann Arbor, MI.

Bobbio, N. (1984), "The future of democracy." *Telos, 61*, 3-16.

Bossert, S. (1979), *Tasks and Social Relationships in Classrooms.* Cambridge University Press.

Bower, G. (1977), "Analysis of a mnemonic device." In I. Janis (ed.), *Current Trends in Psychology.* Los Altos, CA: William Kaufmann.

Bowles, S., and Gintis, H. (1976), *Schooling in Capitalist America.* New York: Basic Books.

Boyer, E. L. (1983), *High School: A Report on Secondary Education in America.* New York: Harper & Row.

Bransford, J. D., and McCarrell, N. (1977), "A sketch of a cognitive approach to comprehension: Some thoughts about understanding what it means to comprehend." In P. N. Johnson-Laird and P. C. Wason (eds),

Thinking:Readings in Cognitive Science. Cambridge University Press. (Original work published 1975.)

Bransford, J., and Stein, B. (1984), *The Ideal Problem Solver.* New York: W. H. Freeman.

Braverman, J. (1974), *Labor and Monopoly Capital.* New York: Monthly Review Press.

Brent, S. (1984), *Psychological and Social Structures.* Hillsdale, N.J: Lawrence Erlbaum.

Brodzinsky, D. M. (1985), "On the relationship between cognitive styles and cognitive structures." In E. D. Neimark, R. De Lisi, and J. Newman (eds), *Moderators of Competence.* Hillsdale, NJ: Lawrence Erlbaum.

Broudy, H.S. (1950), "Dewey's analysis of the act of thought: A critical appraisal of the pragmatic theory of problem solving." In A. S. Clayton (ed.), *Three Papers in Honor of John Dewey.* Bloomington, IN: Division of Research and Field Services.

Brown, A., Bransford, J., Ferrara, R., and Campione, J. (1983), "Learning, remembering, and understanding." In P. Mussen (ed.), *Handbook of Child Psychology: vol. 3 Cognitive Development.* New York: John Wiley.

Burawoy, M., and Lukacs, J. (1985), "Mythologies of work: A comparison of firms in state socialism and advanced capitalism." *American Sociological Review, 50,* 723–37.

Buttenwieser, P. (1985), *Coming from the Field: Observations on School Improvement across the Country.* Unpublished manuscript: New York City.

Carey, S. (1985a), "Are children fundamentally different kinds of thinkers and learners than adults?" In S. Chipman, J. Segal, and R. Glaser (eds), *Thinking and Learning Skills: vol. 2 Research and Open Questions.* Hillsdale, NJ: Lawrence Erlbaum.

Carey, S. (1985b), *Conceptual Change in Childhood.* Cambridge, MA: MIT Press.

Carnoy, M., and Levin, H. (1985), *Schooling and Work in the Democratic State.* Stanford University Press.

Carpenter, P. A., and Just, M. A. (1986), "Spatial ability: An information processing approach to psychometrics." In R. J. Sternberg (ed.), *Advances in the Psychology of Human Intelligence* (vol. 3). Hillsdale, NJ: Lawrence Erlbaum.

Case, R. (1985), "A developmentally based aproach to the problem of instructional design." In S. Chipman, J. Segal, and R. Glaser (eds), *Thinking and Learning Skills: vol. 2 Research and Open Questions.* Hillsdale, NJ: Lawrence Erlbaum.

Champagne, A. B., Gunstone, R. F., and Klopfer, L. E. (1985), "Effecting changes in cognitive structures among physics students." In L. West and A. L. Pines (eds), *Cognitive Structure and Conceptual Change.* New York: Academic Press.

Chance, P. (1986), *Thinking in the Classroom*. New York: Teachers College Press.

Chi, M. T. H., Feltovich, P. J., and Glaser, R. (1981), "Categorization and representation of physics problems by experts and novices." *Cognitive Science*, 5, 121–52.

Clayre, A. (1974), *Work and Play: Ideas and Experience of Work and Leisure*. New York: Harper & Row.

Clegg, C. W. (1984), "The derivation of job designs." *Journal of Occupational Behavior*, 5, 131–46.

Cohen, G. A. (1978), *Karl Marx's Theory of History: A Defence*. Princeton, NJ: Princeton University Press.

Cohen, G. (1983), *The Psychology of Cognition* (2nd edn). London: Academic Press.

Collins, A. (1977), "Processes in acquiring knowledge." In R. C. Anderson, R. J. Spiro, and W. Montague (eds), *Schooling and the Acquisition of Knowledge*. Hillsdale, NJ: Lawrence Erlbaum.

Collins, R. (1979), *The Credential Society: An Historical Sociology of Education and Stratification*. Orlando, FL: Academic Press.

Comenius, J. A. (1957), "The great didactic." In J. Piaget (ed.), *Selections*. Paris: UNESCO. (Original work published 1658.)

Coser, R. L. (1975), "The complexity of roles as a seedbed of individual autonomy." In L. A. Coser (ed.), *The Idea of Social Structure*. New York: Harcourt Brace Jovanovich.

Crocker, D. A. (1983), *Praxis and Democratic Socialism: The Critical Social Theory of Markovic and Stonjanovic*. Atlantic Highlands, NJ: Humanities Press.

Csikszentmihalyi, M. (1975), *Beyond Boredom and Anxiety*. San Francisco: Jossey-Bass.

Cuban, L. (1984), *How Teachers Taught*. New York: Longman.

Cuban, L. (1986), *Teachers and Machines: The Classroom Use of Technology since 1920*. New York: Teachers College Press.

Cusick, P. A. (1973), *Inside High School: The Student's World*. New York: Holt, Rinehart & Winston.

Dahl, R. (1982), *Dilemmas of Pluralist Democracy: Autonomy vs Control*. New Haven: Yale University Press.

Dahl, R. (1985), *A Preface to Economic Democracy*. Berkeley, CA: University of California Press.

Dansereau, D. F. (1985), "Learning strategy research." In J. W. Segal, S. F. Chipman, and R. Glaser (eds), *Thinking and Learning Skills: vol 1 Relating Instruction to Research*. Hillsdale, NJ: Lawrence Erlbaum.

de Bono, E. (1970), *Lateral Thinking: Creativity Step by Step*. New York: Harper & Row.

Dewey, J. (1901), "The situation as regards the course of study." In *The Collected Works: The Middle Works, 1*, 332–48.

Dewey, J. (1916), *Democracy and Education*. New York: Macmillan.

Dewey, J. (1933), *How We Think*. Lexington, MA: D.C. Heath.

Dewey, J. (1938), *Logic: The Theory of Inquiry*. New York: Henry Holt.

Dewey, J. (1939), "Education and social change." In J. Ratner (ed.), *Intelligence in the Modern World: John Dewey's Philosophy*. New York: Modern Library. (Original work published 1937.)

Dewey, J. (1946), *The Public and its Problems*. Chicago: Gateway Books. (Original work published 1927.)

Dewey, J. (1963), *Experience and Education*. New York: Collier. (Original work published 1938.)

Dornbusch, S., and Scott, W. (1975). *Evaluation and the Exercise of Authority*. San Francisco: Jossey-Bass.

Doyle, W. (1983), "Academic work." *Review of Educational Research, 53*, 159–99.

Doyle, W. (1985), *Content Representation in Teachers Definitions of Academic Work*. Austin: Research and Development Center for Teacher Education at The University of Texas at Austin.

Dreeben, R. (1968), *On What is Learned in School*. Reading, MA: Addison-Wesley.

Dreeben, R. (1973), "The school as a workplace." In R. Travers (ed.), *Second Handbook of Research on Teaching*. Chicago: Rand McNally.

Dubos, R. (1959). *Mirage of Health*. New York: Harper & Brothers.

Elliott, J., and Connolly, K. (1974), "Hierarchical structure in skill development." In K. Connolly and J. Bruner (eds), *The Growth of Competence*. London: Academic Press.

Elster, J. (1985), *Making Sense of Marx*. Cambridge University Press.

Ennis, R. (1980), "A conception of rational thinking." In J. R. Coombs (ed.), *Philosophy of Education 1979*. Normal, IL: Philosophy of Education Society.

Ennis, R. (1985), "A logical basis for measuring critical thinking skills." *Educational Leadership, 43*(2), 44–8.

Ennis, R. (1986), "A taxonomy of critical thinking dispositions and abilities." In J. Baron and R. Sternberg (eds), *Teaching for Thinking*. New York: W. H. Freeman.

Erikson, K. (1986), "On work and alienation." *American Sociological Review, 51*, 1–8.

Etzioni, A. (1961), *A Comparative Analysis of Complex Organizations*. New York: The Free Press.

Feuerstein, R., Rand, Y., Hoffman M., and Miller, R., (1980), *Instrumental Enrichment: An intervention Program for Cognitive Modifiability*. Baltimore: University Park Press.

Finn, C. E. Jr. (1984), "'Gee, Officer Krupke' and other barriers to excellence in the schoolroom." *Policy Review, 29*, 72–6.

Fisk, A. D., and Schneider, W. (1981), "Control and automatic processing during tasks requiring sustained attention: A new approach to vigilance." *Human Factors, 23*(6), 737–50.

Fiske, J. and Hartley, J. (1978), *Reading Television*. London: Methuen.

Flavell, J. H. (1963), *The Developmental Psychology of Jean Piaget*. New York: Van Nostrand Reinhold.

Frederiksen, N. (1984), "Implications of cognitive theory for instruction in problem solving." *Review of Educational Research*, 54, 363–407.

Gage, N. L. (1984), "What do we know about teaching effectiveness?" *Phi Delta Kappan*, 66, 87–93.

Galbraith, J. R. (1977), *Organization Design*. Reading, MA: Addison-Wesley.

Gannaway, H. (1984), "Making sense of school." In M. Hammersley and P. Woods (eds), *Life in School: The Sociology of Pupil Culture*. Milton Keynes, England: Open University. (Original work published 1976.)

Gardner, H. (1985), *The Minds' New Science: A History of the Cognitive Revolution*. New York: Basic Books.

Getzels, J. W., and Csikszentmihalyi, M. (1975), "From problem solving to problem finding." In I. A. Taylor and J. W. Getzels (eds), *Perspectives in Creativity*. Chicago, Aldine.

Gibbons, M. (1984), "Walkabout ten years later: Searching for a renewed vision of education." *Phi Delta Kappan*, 65(9), 591–600.

Gitlin, T. (1983), *Inside Prime Time*. New York: Pantheon.

Glaser, R. (1984), "Education and thinking: The role of knowledge." *American Psychologist*, 39, 93–104.

Goodfield, J. (1982), *An Imagined World*. Harmondsworth, Middlesex, England: Penguin.

Goodlad, J. (1983), *A Place Called School*. New York: McGraw-Hill.

Goodman, P. (1960), *Growing up Absurd*. New York: Random House.

Grady, M. P. (1984), *Teaching and Brain Research: Guidelines for the Classroom*. New York: Longman.

Greeno, J. (1983), "Reply to Phillips." *Educational Psychologist*, 18, 75–80.

Greeno, J., and Simon, H. A (in press). "Problem solving and reasoning." In R. C. Atkinson, R. J. Hernstein, G. Lindzey, and R. D. Luce (eds), *Handbook of Experimental Psychology*. New York: John Wiley.

Groen, G. (1978), "The theoretical ideas of Piaget and educational practice." In P. Suppes (ed.), *Impact of Research on Education: Some Case Studies*. Washington, DC: National Academy of Education.

Grossberg, S. (1982), *Studies of Mind and Brain*. Dordrecht, Holland: D. Reidel.

Guyote, M. J. and Sternberg, R. J. (1981), "A transitive-chain theory of syllogistic reasoning." *Cognitive Psychology*, 13, 461–525.

Hagstrom, W. (1965), *The Scientific Community*. New York: Basic Books.

Hamilton, D. (1980), "Adam Smith and the moral economy of the classroom system." *Journal of Curriculum Studies*, 12, 281–98.

Hamilton, D. (1981), *On Simultaneous Instruction and the Early Evolution of Class Teaching*. Unpublished manuscript: Glasgow, Scotland.

Hammersley, M. (1984), "The organization of pupil participation." In A. Hargreaves and P. Woods (eds), *Classrooms and Staffrooms: The Sociology of Teachers and Teaching*. Milton Keynes, England: Open University. (Original work published 1974.)

Hammersley, M., and Woods, P. (eds) (1984). *Life in School: The Sociology of Pupil Culture*. Milton Keynes, England: Open University.

Hargreaves, D. H., Hester, S. K., and Mellor, F. J. (1984), "Rules in play." In A. Hargreaves and P. Woods (eds), *Classrooms and Staffrooms: The Sociology of Teachers and Teaching*. Milton Keynes, England: Open University. (Original work published 1975.)

Harris, W. T. (1898), *Psychological Foundations of Education*. New York: Appleton. (Cited in L. Mann (1979), *On the Trail of Process*. New York: Grune & Stratton.)

Haugeland, J. (1985), *Artificial Intelligence: The Very Idea*. Cambridge, MA: MIT Press.

Hayes, J. R. (1978), *Cognitive Psychology: Thinking and Creating*. Homewood IL: The Dorsey Press.

Hayes-Roth, B. (1977), "Structurally integrated versus structurally segregated memory representations: Implications for the design of instructional materials." In R. C. Anderson, R. J. Spiro, and W. Montague (eds), *Schooling and the Acquisition of Knowledge*. Hillsdale, NJ: Lawrence Erlbaum.

Heller, J. I., and Reif, F. (1984), "Prescribing effective human problem solving processes: Problem description in physics." *Cognition and Instruction*, *1*, 177–216.

Herbst, P. (1974), *Socio-technical Design: Strategies in Multidisciplinary Research*. London: Tavistock.

Herbst, P. G. (1976), *Alternatives to Hierarchies*. Leiden, Holland: Martinius Nijhoff.

Hill, S. (1981), *Competition and Control at Work: The New Industrial Sociology*. Cambridge, MA: MIT Press.

Hoetker, J. E., and Ahlbrand, W.P. Jr (1969), "The persistence of the recitation." *American Education Research Journal*, *6*, 145–67.

Holt, J. (1965), *How Children Fail*. New York: Delta Books.

Hudgins, B. B. (1977), *Learning and Thinking*. Itasca. IL: Peacock.

Hunt, H. A., and Hunt, T. L. (1983), *Human Resource Implications of Robotics*. Kalamazoo, MI: Upjohn Institute for Employment Research.

Hunt, L. (1978), "Character and thought." *American Philosophical Quarterly*, *15*, 177–86.

Illich, I. (1970), *Deschooling Society*. New York: Harper & Row.

James, W. (1923), *The Principles of Psychology* (vol. 1). New York: Henry Holt. (Original work published 1890.)

Johnson, P. J. (1984), "The expert mind: a new challenge for the information scientist." In Th. M. A. Bemelmans (ed.), *Beyond Productivity:*

Information Systems Development for Organizational Effectiveness.
North-Holland: Elsevier Science Publishers.

Johnson-Laird, P. N. (1983), "Thinking as a skill." In J. St. B. T. Evans
(ed.), *Thinking and Reasoning.* London: Routledge & Kegan Paul.

Johnson-Laird, P. N., and Wason, P. C. (eds) (1977), *Thinking: Readings
in Cognitive Science.* Cambridge University Press.

Kahane, H. (1976), *Logic and Contemporary Rhetoric.* Belmont, CA:
Wadsworth.

Katznelson, I., and Weir, M. (1985), *Schooling for All: Class, Race, and the
Decline of the Democratic Ideal.* New York: Basic Books.

Kekes, J. (1983), "Wisdom." *American Philosophical Quarterly, 20,* 277–
86.

Kerber, A. (1968), *Quotable Quotes on Education.* Detroit: Wayne State.

Kessler-Harris, A. (1982), *Out to Work: A History of Wage-earning Women
in the United States.* New York: Oxford University Press.

Kintsch, W., Miller, J. R., and Polson, P. (eds) (1984), *Method and Tactics
in Cognitive Science.* Hillsdale, NJ: Lawrence Erlbaum.

Kirzner, I. M. (1985), *Discovery and the Capitalist Process.* University of
Chicago Press.

Knitter, W. (1985), *The Informing Vision of the Practical: The Concepts of
Character, Virtue, Vice and Privation.* Paper presented at the meeting of
the American Educational Research Association, Chicago.

Kogan, N. (1985), "Cognitive styles as moderators of competence; A
commentary." In E. D. Neimark, R. de Lisi, and J. Newman (eds),
Moderators of Competence, Hillsdale, NJ: Lawrence Erlbaum.

Kohn, M. L., and Schooler, C. (1983), *Work and Personality: An Inquiry
into the Impact of Social Stratification.* Norwood, NJ: Ablex.

Lachman, R., Lachman, J. L., and Butterfield, E. C. (1979), *Cognitive
Psychology and Information Processing.* Hillsdale, NJ: Lawrence Erlbaum.

Lane, R. (1983), "Political observers and market participants: The effects
on cognition." *Political Psychology, 4,* 455–82.

Lane, R. (1985), "From political to industrial democracy?" *Polity, 17,* 623–
48.

Larkin, J., McDermott, J., Simon, D. P., and Simon, H. A. (1980), "Expert
and novice performance in solving physics problems." *Science, 208,*
1335–42.

Lehnert, W. G. (1984), "Paradigmatic issues in cognitive science." In W.
Kintsch, J. R. Miller, and P. Polson (eds), *Method and Tactics in
Cognitive Science.* Hillsdale, NJ: Lawrence Erlbaum.

Leontief, W. (1985), "The choice of technology." *Scientific American, 252,*
37–45.

Leontief, W. (1986), "Technological change, employment, the rate of return
on capital and wages." In D. F. Burton, Jr, J. Filer, D. Fraser, and R.
Marshall (eds), *The Jobs Challenge: Pressures and Possibilities.*
Cambridge, MA: Ballinger.

Levin, J. R. (1981), "The mnemonic 80's: Keywords in the classroom." *Educational Psychologist, 16*, 65–82.

Levin, H., and Rumberger, R. (1983), "The future impact of technology on work skills." In H. F. Didsbury, Jr (ed.), *The World of Work: Careers and the Future.* Bethesda, MD: World Future Society.

Lijphart, A., and Grofman, B. (eds) (1984), *Choosing an Electoral System: Issues and Alternatives.* New York: Praeger.

Lipman, M., and Sharp, A. M. (1978), *Growing up with Philosophy.* Philadelphia: Temple University Press.

Macrorie, K. (1984), *Twenty Teachers.* Oxford University Press.

Maier, N. R. F. (1931), "Reasoning in humans." *Journal of Comparative Psychology, 12*, 181–94.

Mandler, G. (1985), *Cognitive Psychology: An Essay in Cognitive Science.* Hillsdale, NJ: Lawrence Erlbaum.

Mandler, J. M., and Mandler, G. (1964), *Thinking: From Association to Gestalt.* New York: John Wiley.

Mann, L. (1979), *On the Trail of Process.* New York: Grune & Stratton.

Manning, H. (1960), *Mountaineering: The Freedom of the Hills.* Seattle, WA: The Mountaineers.

Mason, J., Burton, L., and Stacey, K. (1985). *Thinking Mathematically.* Wokingham, England: Addison-Wesley.

Matthews, G. (1984), *Dialogues with Children.* Cambridge, MA: Harvard University Press.

Mayer, R. E. (1977), *Thinking and Problem Solving: An Introduction to Human Cognition and Learning.* Glenview, IL: Scott, Foresman.

Mayhew, K. C., and Edwards, A. C. (1965). *The Dewey School: The Laboratory School of the University of Chicago, 1893–1903.* New York: Atherton Press. (Original work published 1936).

McMurray, F. (1981), "Animadversions on the eightieth yearbook of the NSSE." *Educational Theory, 31*(1), 73–90.

McNeil, L. M. (1983), "Defensive teaching and classroom control." In M. Apple and L. Weiss (eds), *Ideology and Practice in Schooling.* Boston: Routledge & Kegan Paul.

McPeck, J. E. (1981), *Critical Thinking and Education.* New York: St Martin's.

McPherson, M. (1983), "Efficiency and liberty in the production enterprise: Recent work in the economics of work organization." *Philosophy and Public Affairs, 12*, 354–68.

Medawar, P. B., and Medawar, J. S. (1977), *The Life Science: Current Ideas of Biology.* New York: Harper & Row.

Metz, M. (1978), *Classrooms and Corridors: The Crisis of Authority in Desegregated Secondary Schools.* Berkeley, CA: University of California Press.

Mouzelis, N. (1986), Review of Branko Horvat, "The political economy of socialism: A Marxist social theory." *Economic and Industrial Democracy*, 7, 119–27.

Myers, D. (1974), "Why open education died." *Journal of Research and Development in Education*, 8, 62–7.

Myers, D., and Myers, L. (1973), *Open Education Re-examined*. Lexington, MA: D.C. Heath.

Nash, L. (1963), *The Nature of Natural Science*. Boston: Little Brown.

Neill, A. S. (1970), *Summerhill: A Radical Approach to Childrearing*. New York: Hart.

Neisser, U. (1967), *Cognitive Psychology*. New York: Appleton-Century-Crofts.

Neisser, U. (1976), *Cognition and Reality: Principles and Implications of Cognitive Psychology*. New York: W. H. Freeman.

Neisser, U. (1983), "Components of intelligence or steps in routine procedures." *Cognition*, 15, 189–97.

Newmann, F., and Oliver, D. (1967), "Education and community." *Harvard Educational Review*, 37, 61–106.

Nickerson, R. S., Perkins, D. N., and Smith, D. E. (1985), *Teaching Thinking*. Hillsdale, NJ: Lawrence Erlbaum.

Noddings, N., and Shore, P. (1984), *Awakening the Inner Eye: Intuition in Education*. New York: Teachers College Press.

Norris, P. (1985), "The choice of standard conditions in defining critical thinking competence." *Educational Theory*, 35, 97–107.

Novak, J. D., and Gowin, D. B. (1984), *Learning How to Learn*, Cambridge University Press.

Oden, G. (1987), "Concept, knowledge and thought." *Annual Review of Psychology*, vol. 38. Palo Alto, CA: Annual Reviews Inc.

Offe, C. (1985), *Disorganized Capitalism*. Cambridge, MA: MIT Press.

Ong, W. (1982), *Orality and Literacy: The Technologizing of the Word*. London: Methuen.

O'Toole, J. (1983), "Getting ready for the next industrial revolution." In H. F. Didsbury, Jr (ed.), *The World of Work: Careers and the Future*. Bethesda, MD: World Future Society.

Palincsar, A. S., and Brown, A. L. (1984), "Reciprocal teaching of comprehension-fostering and comprehension-monitoring activities." *Cognition and Instruction*, 1, 117–75.

Papert, S. (1980), *Mindstorms: Children, Computers, and Powerful Ideas*. New York: Basic Books.

Pateman, C. (1970), *Participation and Democratic Theory*. Cambridge University Press.

Paul, R. (1983), *Background Logic, Critical Thinking, and Irrational Language Games*. Unpublished paper presented at the Second International Symposium on Informal Logic at University of Windsor, Windsor, Ontario.

Pea, R. D., Kurland, D. M. and Hawking, J. (1985), "LOGO and the development of thinking skills." In M. Chen and W. Paisley (eds), *Children and Microcomputers: Research on the Newest Medium*. Beverly Hills, CA: Sage.

Pellegrino, J. (1985), "Anatomy of analogy." *Psychology Today*, October, pp. 49–54.

Perfetti, C., and Lesgold, A. (1978), "Discourse comprehension and sources of individual differences." In M. Just and P. Carpenter (eds), *Cognitive Processes in Comprehension*. Hillsdale, NJ: Lawrence Erlbaum.

Perkins, D. N. (1981), *The Mind's Best Work*. Cambridge, MA: Harvard University Press.

Perkins, D. N. (1985), "General cognitive skills: Why not?" In J. W. Segal, S. F. Chipman, and R. Glaser (eds), *Thinking and Learning Skills: Current Research and Open Questions* (vol. 2). Hillsdale, NJ: Lawrence Erlbaum.

Perkins, D. N. (1986a), *Knowledge as Design*. Hillsdale, NJ: Lawrence Erlbaum.

Perkins, D. N. (1986b), *Reasoning as it is and could be: An empirical perspective*. Paper presented at AERA, San Francisco, April.

Perrow, C. B. (1970), *Organizational Analysis: A Sociological View*. Belmont, CA: Brooks/Cole.

Petrie, H. G. (1985), *Testing for Critical Thinking*. Presidential address to the 41st annual meeting of the Philosophy of Education Society, Montreal.

Philips, S. U. (1982), "The language socialization of lawyers: Acquiring the 'cant'." In G. Spindler (ed.), *Doing the Ethnography of Schooling*. New York: Holt, Rinehart & Winston.

Piaget, J. (1962), *Play, Dreams and Imitation in Childhood*. NewYork: Norton.

Piaget, J. (1963), *The Origins of Intelligence in Children*. New York: Norton.

Piaget, J., and Inhelder, B. (1969), *The Psychology of the Child*. New York: Basic Books.

Piore, M. J., and Sabel, C. F. (1984), *The Industrial Divide: Possibilities for Prosperity*. New York: Basic Books.

Plato, *Republic* (B. Jowett, Trans., 1937), In *Dialogues of Plato* (vol. 1). New York: Random House.

Polson, P. G., and Jeffries, R. (1985), "Instruction in general problem-solving skills: An analysis of four approaches." In J. W. Segal, S. F. Chipman, and R. Glaser (eds), *Thinking and Learning Skills: vol. 1 Relating Instruction to Research*. Hillsdale, NJ: Lawrence Erlbaum.

Postman, N. (1985), "Media and technology as educators." In M. Fantini and R. Sinclair (eds), *Education in School and Nonschool settings: Eighty-fourth Yearbook of the National Society for the Study of Education* (Part 1). University of Chicago Press.

Powell, A. G., Farrar, E., and Cohen, D. K. (1985), *The Shopping Mall High School*. Boston: Houghton Mifflin.

Powell, G. B. (1986), "American voter turnout in comparative perspective." *American Political Science Review, 80,* 17–43.

Prewitt, K. (1983), "Scientific illiteracy and democratic theory." *Daedalus, 112,* 49–64.

Puff, C. R. (ed.) (1979), *Memory Organization and Structure.* New York: Academic Press.

Radke-Yarrow, M., Zahn-Waxler, C., and Chapman, M. (1983), "Children's prosocial dispositions and behavior." In P. Mussen (ed.), *Handbook of Child Psychology, 4,* 469–531.

Rathbone, C. (1972), "Examining the open education classroom." *School Review, 80,* 521–50.

Ravetz, J. (1971), *Scientific Knowledge and its Social Problems.* Oxford University Press.

Rawls, J. (1971), *A Theory of Justice.* Cambridge, MA: Harvard University Press.

Raz, J. (1978), *Practical Reasoning.* Oxford University Press.

Reitman, W. R. (1964), "Heuristic decision procedures, open constraints, and the structure of ill-defined problems." In M. Shelly and G. Bryan (eds), *Human Judgments and Optimality.* New York: John Wiley.

Resnick, L. (in press), *Education and Learning to Think.* Washington, D.C.: National Academy of Sciences.

Rips, L. (1986), "Mental muddles." In M. Brand and R. M. Harnish (eds), *Problems in the Representation of Knowledge and Belief.* Tucson, AZ: Arizona University Press.

Roberts, R. (1984), "Will power and the virtues." *Philosophical Review, 93,* 227–47.

Rosser, E., and Harré, R. (1984), "The meaning of trouble." In M. Hammersley and P. Woods (eds), *Life in School: The Sociology of Pupil Culture.* Milton Keynes, England: Open University. (Original work published 1976.)

Rumelhart, D. E., and Norman, D. A. (1978), "Accretion, tuning, and restructuring: Three modes of learning." In J. W. Cotton and R. L. Klatsky (eds), *Semantic Factors in Cognition.* Hillsdale NJ: Lawrence Erlbaum.

Ryle, G. (1949), *The Concept of Mind.* London: Hutchinson.

Ryle, G. (1979). *On Thinking.* Totowa, NJ: Roman & Littlefield.

Sarason, S. (1983), *Schooling in America.* New York: The Free Press.

Scardamalia, M., and Bereiter, C. (1985), "Fostering the development of self-regulation in children's knowledge processing." In S. Chipman, J. Segal, R. Glaser (eds), *Thinking and Learning Skills: vol 2 Research and Open Questions.* Hillsdale, NJ: Lawrence Erlbaum.

Scardamalia, M., Bereiter, C., and Steinbach, R. (1984), "Teachability of reflective processes in written composition." *Cognitive Science, 8,* 173–90.

Schlee, E. (1974), "A German educator describes the latest education reform movements in the United States." In S. Cohen (ed.), *Education in the United States: A Documentary History: vol 2.* New York: Random House. (Original work published 1898.)

Schoenfeld, A. H. (1983), "Beyond the purely cognitive: Belief systems, social cognitions, and metacognitions as driving forces in intellectual performance." *Cognitive Science, 7,* 329–63.

Schrag, F. (1975), "The child's status in the democratic state." *Political Theory, 34,* 441–57.

Schrag, F. (1981), "Knowing and doing." *American Journal of Education, 89,* 253–82.

Schrag, F. (1983), "Social science and social practice." *Inquiry, 26,* 107–24.

Schrag, F. (1986), "Education and historical materialism." *Interchange, 17*(3), 45–52.

Schumacher, E. F. (1973), *Small is Beautiful: Economics as if People Mattered.* New York: Harper & Row.

Scitovsky, T. (1976), *The Joyless Economy.* New York: Oxford University Press.

Scott, W. R. (1981), *Organizations: Rational, Natural and Open Systems.* Englewood Cliffs, NJ: Prentice-Hall.

Segal, J. W., Chipman, S. F., and Glaser, R. (eds) (1985a), *Thinking and Learning Skills: vol 1 Relating Instruction to Research.* Hillsdale, NJ: Lawrence Erlbaum.

Segal, J. W., Chipman, S. F., and Glaser, R. (eds) (1985b), *Thinking and Learning Skills: vol 2 Research and Open Questions.* Hillsdale, NJ: Lawrence Erlbaum.

Shaiken, H. (1984), *Work Transformed: Automation and Labor in the Computer Age.* New York: Holt, Rinehart & Winston.

Shepard, R. N., and Metzler, J. (1977), "Mental rotation of three-dimensional objects." In P. N. Johnson-Laird and P. C. Wason (eds), *Thinking: Readings in Cognitive Science.* Cambridge University Press. (Original work published 1971.)

Shryock, R. H. (1969), *The Development of Modern Medicine.* New York: Hafner.

Siegel, H. (1985), "Educating reason: Critical thinking, informal logic, and the philosophy of education (Part 1)." *A.P.A. Newsletter on Teaching Philosophy,* Spring/Summer, 10–13.

Silberman, C. (1970), *Crisis in the Classroom: The Remaking of American Education.* New York: Random House.

Simon, D. P., and Simon, H. A. (1979), "A tale of two protocols." In J. Lochhead and J. Clement (eds), *Cognitive Process Instruction.* Philadelphia: Franklin Institute Press.

Simon, H. (1977), "The structure of ill-structured problems." In H. Simon (ed.), *Models of Discovery* (pp. 304–25). Boston, Massachusetts: D. Reidel.

Simon, H. A. (1981), "Studying human intelligence by creating artificial intelligence." *American Scientist, 69*, 300–9.

Simpson, R. (1985), "Social control of occupations and work." *American Review of Sociology, 11*, 415–36.

Sirotnik, K. (1983), "What you see is what you get—consistency, persistency and mediocrity in classrooms." *Harvard Educational Review, 53*, 16–31.

Sizer, T. (1973), *Places for Learning, Places for Joy: Speculations on American School Reform*. Cambridge, MA: Harvard University Press.

Sizer, T. (1984). *Horace's Compromise: The Dilemma of the American High School*. Boston, MA: Houghton Mifflin.

Skinner, B. F. (1982a), "Are theories of learning necessary?" In R. Epstein (ed.), *Skinner for the Classroom: Selected Papers*. Champaign, IL: Research Press. (Original work published 1950.)

Skinner, B. F. (1982b), "Behaviorism at fifty." In R. Epstein (ed.), *Skinner for the Classroom: Selected Papers*. Champaign, IL: Research Press. (Original work published 1963.)

Skinner, B. F. (1982c), "The science of learning and the art of teaching." In R. Epstein (ed.), *Skinner for the Classroom: Selected Papers*. Champaign, IL: Research Press. (Original work published 1954.)

Skinner, B. F. (1982d), "Why I am not a cognitive psychologist." In R. Epstein (ed.), *Skinner for the Classroom: Selected Papers*. Champaign, IL: Research Press. (Original work published 1977.)

Skinner, B. F. (1984), "An operant analysis of problem solving." *Behavioral and Brain Sciences, 7*, 583–613. (Original work published 1966.)

Skyrms, B. (1975), *An Introduction to Inductive Logic* (2nd edn). Encino, CA: Dickenson.

Slavin, R. (ed.) (1985), *Learning to Cooperate, Cooperating to Learn*. New York: Plenum.

Smith, A. (1863), *An Inquiry into the Nature and Causes of the Wealth of Nations*. Edinburgh: Adam & Charles Black. (Original work published 1776.)

Spencer, H. (1885), *Education: Intellectual, Moral and Physical*. New York: D. Appleton.

Spenner, K. (1985), "The upgrading and downgrading of occupations: Issues, evidence, and implications for education." *Review of Educational Research, 55*, 125–54.

Standing, E. M. (1962), *Maria Montessori: Her Life and Work*. New York: Mentor-Omega Books.

Sternberg, R. (1980), "Sketch of a componential subtheory of human intelligence." *Behavioral and Brain Sciences, 3*, 573–614.

Sternberg, R. (1983), "Components of human intelligence" *Cognition, 15*, 1–48.

Sternberg, R. (1985), *Beyond IQ: A Triarchic Theory of Human Intelligence*. Cambridge University Press.

Sussman, L. (1984) "Innovation at Coolidge: Open classrooms." In S. Delamont (ed.), *Readings on Interaction in the Classroom*. London: Methuen. (Original work published 1977.)

Taba, H. (1967), "Implementing thinking as an objective in social studies." In J. Fair and F. Shaftel (eds), *Effective Thinking in the Social Studies: 37th Yearbook*. Washington, DC: National Council for the Social Studies.

Thorndyke, P. W. (1977), "Knowledge transfer in learning from texts." In R. C. Anderson, R. J. Spiro, and W. Montague (eds), *Schooling and the Acquisition of Knowledge*. Hillsdale, NJ; Lawrence Erlbaum.

Tracey, M. V. (1977), "Human nutrition." In R. Duncan and M. Weston-Smith (eds), *The Encyclopaedia of Ignorance*. New York: Wallaby Books.

Tversky, A., and Kahneman, D. (1977), "Judgment under uncertainty: Heuristics and biases." In P. N. Johnson-Laird and P. C. Wason (eds), *Thinking; Readings in Cognitive Science*. Cambridge University Press. (Original work published 1974.)

Vanini, V., and Pogliani, G. (1980), *The Color Atlas of Human Anatomy*. New York: Beekman House.

Venn, G. (1964), *Man, Education, and Work*. Washington, DC: American Council on Education.

Vernon, P. A. (1983), "Recent findings on the nature of g." *Journal of Special Education*, *17*(4), 389–400.

Von Wright, G. H. (1963), *The Varieties of Goodness*. London: Routledge & Kegan Paul.

Voss, J. F., Greene, T. R., Post, T. A., and Penner, B. C. (1983). "Problem solving in the social sciences." In G. H. Bower (ed.) *The psychology of learning and motivation*, (vol. 17). New York: Academic Press.

Vuyk, R. (1981), *Overview and Critique of Piaget's Genetic Epistemology 1965–1980* (vols 1–2). London: Academic Press.

Vygotsky, L. S. (1978), *Mind in Society: The Development of Higher Psychological Processes*. Cambridge: Harvard University Press.

Wallace, J. (1974), "Excellences and merit." *Philosophical Review*, *87*, 182–99.

Waller, W. (1984), "What teaching does to teachers: Determinants of the occupational type." In A. Hargreaves and P. Woods (eds), *Classrooms and Staffrooms: The Sociology of Teachers and Teaching*. Milton Keynes, England: Open University. (Original work published 1963.)

Wertheimer, M. (1959), *Productive Thinking*. New York: Harper & Brothers.

Werthman, C. (1984), "Delinquents in school: A test for the legitimacy of authority." In M. Hammersley and P. Woods (eds), *Life in School: The Sociology of Pupil Culture*. Milton Keynes, England: Open University. (Original work published 1963.)

Westbury, I. (1973), "Conventional classrooms, 'open' classrooms and the technology of teaching." *Journal of Curriculum Studies*, *5*, 99–121.

Westbury, I. (1978), "Research into classroom processes: A review of ten years' work." *Journal of Curriculum Studies, 10,* 283–308.

Whitehead, A. N. (1967), *The Aims of Education.* New York: Free Press. (Original work published 1929.)

Willis, P. (1977), *Learning to Labour.* Westmead: Saxon House.

Willis, P. (1984), "Elements of a culture." In M. Hammersley and P. Woods (eds), *Life in School: The Sociology of Pupil Culture.* Milton Keynes, England: Open University. (Original work published 1977.)

Wilson, J. Q. (1985), "The rediscovery of character: Private virtue and public policy." *Public Interest, 81,* 3–16.

Winn, M. (1977), *The Plug-in Drug.* New York: Viking Press.

Wirth, A. G. (1983), "Productive work and learning—in industry and schools." *Teachers College Record, 85,* 43–56.

Woods, P. (1983), *Sociology and the School: An Interactionist Viewpoint.* London: Routledge & Kegan Paul.

Young, R. M. (1978), "Strategies and the structure of a cognitive skill." In G. Underwood (ed.), *Strategies of Information Processing.* London: Academic Press.

Yussen, S. (1985), "The role of metacognition in contemporary theories of cognitive development." In T. Walker and D. F. Pressley (eds), *Metacognition, Cognition and Human Performance,* vol. 1. New York: Academic Press.

Index

Includes authors who are quoted at least once. All authors, including those just referred to, are cited in bibliography.